CLEOPATRA'S NEEDLE

Since she gave up full-time employment in 1987,
Anne Mustoe has spent every winter abroad.
She is a classical scholar and has run her own travel
business, organising specialist tours to classical sites
in Greece, Italy, Turkey and Tunisia. She is
internationally renowned for her best-selling cycling
adventures: *A Bike Ride*, *Lone Traveller* and *Two Wheels
in the Dust* and she is also the author of *Escaping the
Winter — all you need to know about spending the winter
abroad* [all published by Virgin].

Read more about Anne's cycling adventures on her
website: www.annemustoe.co.uk

Other books by Anne Mustoe

A BIKE RIDE
LONE TRAVELLER
TWO WHEELS IN THE DUST

CLEOPATRA'S NEEDLE

Two Wheels by the Water to Cairo

Anne Mustoe

This edition first published in Great Britain in 2004 by

Virgin Books Ltd
Thames Wharf Studios
Rainville Road
London W6 9HA

First published in 2003 by Virgin Books Ltd

ISBN 0 7535 0813 3

Typeset by TW Typesetting, Plymouth, Devon
Printed and bound in Great Britain by
Clays Ltd, St Ives PLC

CLEOPATRA'S NEEDLE

The *Cleopatra,* with the Alexandrian obelisk on board, was safely moored yesterday afternoon in the East India Docks . . . The form of the floating cylinder with parallel pinched ends need not again be described. She is painted buff down to her water-line, and red beneath, carrying two red flags, of which the upper one bears her name, *Cleopatra*, the lower being a simple British merchant's ensign. There was a great crowd at Blackwall, and much enthusiasm was evinced as the afternoon tide approached high-water point . . . As the two vessels passed up the river from Gravesend, there was frequently a display of the very best feeling towards them on the part of the crowds on either bank, and the enthusiasm of the lads on board the training ships broke forth in lusty hurrahs . . . The Queen sent a message from Osborne that she was 'much gratified at the safe arrival of the Needle.'

> From the account of the arrival in London of the *Anglia*, with the *Cleopatra* in tow, *The Times*, 22 January 1878.

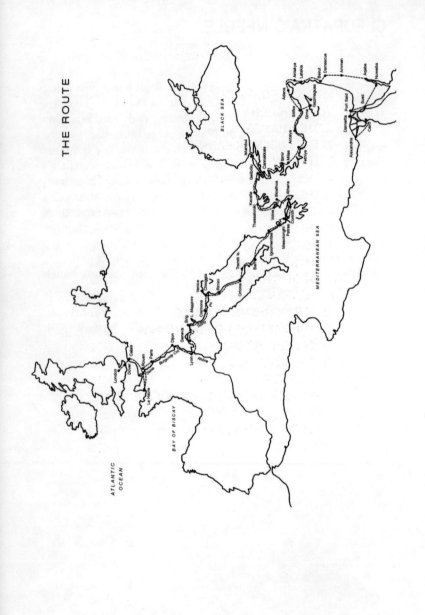

THE ROUTE

ATLANTIC OCEAN

BAY OF BISCAY

London
Dover
Calais
Rouen
Paris
Le Havre
Seine
Dijon
Geneva
Burgundy Canal
Lyon
Rhône
Bray
Mâcon
Cremona
Po
Venice
Chioggia
Rimini
Trieste
Ortona
Bari
Igoumenitsa
Messolonghi
Patras
Vonitsa
Astakos
Athens
Corinth
Missolonghi

MEDITERRANEAN SEA

BLACK SEA

Istanbul
Gallipoli
Çanakkale
Kavalla
Thessaloniki
İzmir
Milas
Antalya
Fethiye
Adana
İskenderun
Antakya
Latakia
Gazimağusa
Girne
Beirut
Damascus
Amman
Alexandria
Damietta
Port Said
Cairo
Suez
Aqaba
Nuweiba

CONTENTS

ACKNOWLEDGEMENTS

My grateful thanks are due to Alan Guest, that encyclopaedia of the Arts, both major and minor, for his invaluable help in researching this book; to the old friends who travelled with me and the new ones I made on the journey; to my agent, John Pawsey, for his constant encouragement; and to my editor, Kerri Sharp, who always supports and never pesters!

A.M.

INTRODUCTION

I do not know much about gods; but I think that the river
  Is a strong brown god.

T.S. Eliot, *The Four Quartets*

In 1819, an Egyptian obelisk named 'Cleopatra's Needle', which had nothing whatsoever to do with Cleopatra, was presented to the British by a non-Egyptian, who had no business at all to be giving away Egyptian treasures. The non-Egyptian was Mohammed Ali, Pasha of Egypt under the Ottoman Sultan. Nelson had just destroyed Napoleon's fleet in the Battle of the Nile and driven the French out of Egypt. The obelisk was presented, according to the inscription on its pedestal, 'as a worthy memorial to our distinguished countrymen Nelson and Abercrombie.'

The Needle, along with its twin, which was later presented to the City of New York, was found in the ruins of Alexandria by Napoleon's expeditionary force. Because Alexandria was once Cleopatra's capital, and because the Needles were a pair, Napoleon's scholars christened them *les aiguilles de Cleopatra*, which probably translates more accurately as 'Cleopatra's knitting needles'. They certainly look more like knitting needles than ordinary sewing needles, being without the customary eyes.

They were not easy gifts to transport. Each obelisk was 68 feet tall (20.7m) and weighed 180 tons. Ours lay in the sands for almost sixty years after its presentation, until 'through the patriotic zeal of Erasmus Wilson FRS [it] was brought from Alexandria encased in an iron cylinder.' But designing a cylinder big enough and buoyant enough to float such a huge slab of granite was not the end of the problem. A terrific storm arose in the Bay of Biscay on the night of 14 October 1877 and the iron cylinder broke loose from the ship which was towing it. In the days before radar, we had to scour the seas for almost three months before we found it bobbing around and were finally able to tow it up the Thames to London. It was erected on the Thames Embankment and unveiled in October 1878. A time capsule was buried under its pedestal. It contained copies of that morning's newspapers, Bibles in four languages, *Bradshaw's Railway Guide*, a set of coins, a razor, a box of pins and photographs of the twelve women considered to be the greatest beauties of the day.

Its sister obelisk, also called Cleopatra's Needle, was presented to the city of New York in 1879 and raised in Central Park just two years later. Either the Americans were vastly more efficient than we were, or they profited from our hard-won obelisk expertise.

Cleopatra's Needles have always lived by the water. Hewn from the red granite quarries of Aswan on the Upper Nile in the reign of Thutmose III (1479–1447 BC), they were floated downstream on special barges to the holy city of On, near modern Cairo. There they stood beside the Nile until they were shipped down to Alexandria by the Roman Emperor Augustus to embellish his temple on the Mediterranean shore. Neglected for centuries after the fall of Rome, they eventually travelled by sea, one to England, the other to America. The American Cleopatra's Needle is now sadly landlocked, but the British half of the pair is more at home, still gazing out across water.

One autumn afternoon, I called in at the Courtauld galleries in Somerset House to see our finest collection of Impressionist paintings in their new, more spacious setting. As I was in the area and had some time to kill before meeting a friend for supper, I decided to stroll along the Thames Embankment in the early evening to see Monet's views of the river, which he painted in the autumn and winter of 1899–1900, in all weathers and all lights. The most prolific of the Impressionists, he was working on an amazing ninety Thames canvasses simultaneously! Half were of the South Bank, viewed from his window in the Savoy Hotel, and half were of the Houses of Parliament from a borrowed room in St Thomas's Hospital.

I was making my way towards his hotel when I passed Cleopatra's Needle. Like most people in London, I had always taken it for granted. There it stood on the Thames Embankment between the Hungerford and Waterloo Bridges, dominating one of Monet's stretches of the river. I must have walked past it hundreds of times, without giving it a second thought. But that afternoon, with an hour or so to spare, I stopped to read the inscriptions on its pedestal. I realised then that I knew nothing about the Needle's history and precious little about Cleopatra.

In that moment, everything came together in a flash of illumination – Cleopatra's Needle, the river and Monet. I had made a potent connection. The Needle travelled from the Nile to the Thames by water. Why not travel on my bicycle from the Thames back to the Nile *beside* water? If I followed water all the way to Egypt, I should be travelling along the shores, rivers and lagoons that so fascinated Monet and other nineteenth- and twentieth-century landscape painters. They had striven to catch the shimmer of light on water, the ghostly ships looming out of the fog, the swirling greys and blacks of the storm, and that evanescent line where sky dissolves into sea. And when I broke free of their Western mists into the radiant blue of Greece, I could turn my attention to Cleopatra, who acted out the drama of her short life in the ports of the eastern Mediterranean. My story would have two heroines, the magnificent queen of a river and seaside empire and my constant companion, water.

I studied my maps and the history of Cleopatra, and found the perfect ride. The southern coast of the Mediterranean was obviously closer to the sea-route of Cleopatra's Needle from Egypt to the Straits of Gibraltar, but it was seriously unattractive. Islamic fundamentalists were rampaging in Algeria, while President Gaddafi continued to posture in Libya. There were hundreds of miles of empty desert along the North African coast, where there would be no hotels and precious little food or water. So I decided on the northern route, through France, Switzerland, Italy, Greece, Turkey and the Middle East to the Suez Canal. It would take me through familiar and much loved country and I should find Cleopatra there – in Actium, Athens, Tarsus and Antioch, before I reached her capital of Alexandria.

As for my second heroine, what could be more important or more fascinating a study than water? As a species we evolved from water. Our bodies are 70 per cent water. The food we eat is 70–90 per cent water. The surface of this planet, which we choose to call Earth, in fact consists of 80 per cent water in liquid, solid or gaseous form. Our civilization developed beside water, along the Awash River in Ethiopia, the Nile, the Tigris and Euphrates, the Indus and the Yangtze. Agriculture developed in the rich deposits of flood plains. We are drawn towards water, to the tranquility of streams and the high drama of torrents and seas. I was born beside water, by 'the smug and silver Trent', and I have lived beside the Cam, the Thames and the North Sea. In my rare bouts of insomnia, I send myself to sleep by imagining that I lie in the shade of a tree beside water. Water, for me, as for most people, is not only essential to life; it symbolises peace, clarity, movement and freedom. There is something healing about water, deep in our genetic memory. Its rivers and seas are alive – mysterious, moody, yet constantly beautiful.

I cycled to the Nile in 2001–02. Floods were sweeping through Europe, China, India, Bangladesh and the USA, as rivers burst their banks and destroyed everything in their path. For too many years, we have tamed them with canals and embankments, checked their flow with dams, changed their courses, then foolishly built houses on their old flood plains. In the course of my ride, rivers reasserted themselves. They showed their latent power and proved that we trifle with them at our peril. Cleopatra might be ancient history, but rivers were suddenly topical.

The names of rivers are still magical. Amazon, Orinoco, Nile, Mississippi – they all breathe romance, but their legends are tinged with nostalgia. Rivers are not what they used to be. Our mania for economically and culturally destructive dams over the last century or so has repressed them and displaced 80 million people, to generate low-priced electricity, much of which is wasted. In the United States, for example, less than 2 per cent of the country's 3,500,000 miles of river and stream is free-flowing. There are 5,500 large and around 80,000 small dams. The Missouri and the Mississippi can no longer spread freely. They have been caged within embankments, straightened and canalised, until they can stand it no longer. When they overflow, they have nowhere to run and recent floods have brought devastation. On my ride, I should see the damage done to the Nile by the 1950s Aswan Dam. Like so many rivers, it was 'mother' to the Egyptians and its floods were 'the tears of Mother Isis'. Those tears no longer flow and Egypt is a sick land.

It was the best and worst of rides. It was the best because it took me through some of the most magnificent scenery in Europe and the Levant, along quiet ancient roads which followed the contours of rivers. I cycled through rural France, the Alps, the great

Renaissance cities of northern Italy, along the dazzling coastline of Greece, Turkey, Syria and Lebanon and up the Valley of the Nile. It was the worst because just about everything that *could* go wrong went wrong. The weather was appalling throughout, roads and bridges were washed away by floods, I had a bad knee, I was robbed in Bari, I fell off my bicycle in Greece and I was in a Muslim country on September 11th when the Twin Towers were destroyed. There were so many misfortunes, both major and minor, that it almost turned into a comedy. It seemed to be an ill-starred ride. But then, just as a glass can be half-empty or half-full, so the same happening can be lucky or unlucky. I am by nature an optimist, a drinker of half-full glasses. I was unlucky to be robbed in Bari but, on the other hand, I was lucky that my passport and credit cards were not in the stolen bag. I was unlucky with my injuries, but lucky to be able to continue my journey. Everything could have been so much worse. It had its wretched moments, but it was still a wonderful ride. I might even make it again one day and hope for better weather!

THE CHALLENGE

I completed my ride from London to On, but all is not *quite* as it seems in the book. Like a writer of detective novels, I am setting a puzzle to exercise 'the little grey cells' and ask the reader to discover why this is so. The answer is on the last page. If you don't enjoy detective fiction, you can always cheat!

1. THE THAMES

When that Aprille with his shoures sote
The droghte of Marche hath perced to the rote . . .
Than longen folk to goon on pilgrimages.

Chaucer, *The Canterbury Tales*

March had not been Chaucer's month of drought. In fact, March and April had been the wettest spring since records began. Every night I lay in bed and listened to the rain drumming on the fire escape; and if by any chance the day started off with a glimmer of sun, the grey clouds soon dampened its enthusiasm. Battling my way through wet and windy London, with my raincoat whipping round my knees, I dreamed of the sunny, easeful South. It was time to escape, 'to goon on pilgrimages'.

Saturday, 28 April 2001. As usual, I started the day by looking out of my window at the Abbey National flag. My luck was in! It was flapping merrily in a blustery north-west wind, the perfect direction for once, and the sun was shining. I put on my smart new scarlet cagoule, locked the front door and raced off down peaceful Saturday morning streets, fizzing with anticipation as I always do when I set off on a long ride. Dorset Square, Montagu Square, Mayfair, Piccadilly, St James's and The Mall were all blissfully traffic-free. Spring leaves were sprouting and London's elegant squares and parks were at their loveliest. I started to have mixed feelings about leaving.

When I reached the Victoria Embankment and the slow, brown-grey Thames, my small send-off party was waiting for me on the steps of Cleopatra's Needle. They took photographs of me posing with my bicycle beside one of the sphinxes – the best they could manage, as the Needle itself was too tall to fit into the viewfinder – then waved me off over Westminster Bridge at the start of my 4,450 mile (7,160 km) ride.

I began my journey where Cleopatra's Needle ended hers, on the Gravesend stretch of the river. A convenient, step-free route round the back of County Hall brought me out on to the Thames Path beside the London Eye. If Monet were to look out today from his window in the Savoy, he would be astonished at the transformation of the South Bank. Once a bleak, windswept wilderness, it is gradually being claimed by Londoners for their amusement. Jogging and skateboarding, they were mingling with strolling tourists, and all were enjoying the market stalls, the buskers and jugglers and the open-air pubs and cafés. The crowds made for slow progress, but I was caught up in the gaiety. As I pushed my bicycle past the Festival Hall, I noticed a fine view of Cleopatra's Needle across the river, so I positioned myself and Condor in front of it and asked a couple of passers-by to take my photograph.

'Where are you off to?' they asked.

'Egypt.'

'On that bike?'

'Yes. All the way.'

They were Australians. 'Did you hear that? This lady's going to Egypt – on her bike!' they yelled to the world at large. Cameras were whipped out and soon I was posing for a large, excited crowd. I escaped into the ancient borough of Southwark.

When London Bridge was the only bridge across the Thames, Southwark was the point at which all the roads from the south of England converged. Travellers and rogues filled its hostelries and its seven prisons. Being outside the City of London proper and free of its censorship laws, it was the racy district where theatres flourished. I cycled past Shakespeare's Globe, now reconstructed, and paused before another reconstruction which was more to the taste of a round-the-world traveller. It was the replica of the *Golden Hinde*, the tiny, fragile wooden ship in which Sir Francis Drake circumnavigated the globe. With its cheerful red and gold paint and its jaunty little golden hind on the prow, it looked no bigger than a fairground ride, or a toy which a child might sail on Hampstead Ponds – a pathetic little vessel for such an epic venture.

In Clink Street, I thought I had had a traffic accident and gone to Heaven. I started to hear angel voices, weaving the magic of Tudor polyphony. All was explained when I turned a corner and had to bulldoze my way through an expectant crowd outside Southwark Cathedral. Nelson Mandela was inside, opening a new annexe, and the service was being relayed on loudspeakers. As he came out of the new north door, everyone cheered and a net of helium balloons was released into the Southwark skies. The cathedral has a long connection with South Africa, as Archbishop Desmond Tutu was once a curate there. It was a piece of sheer serendipity that I happened to be passing by on such a great occasion, and I was silly enough to think that it promised good fortune for my journey.

After Southwark came the workaday Thames, the old docks of Bermondsey and Rotherhithe, with Wapping and the Isle of Dogs across the river. I rattled over cobbles past ghostly warehouses, some in ruins, some dolled up to make riverside lofts for yuppies. The new Tate Modern and galleries of elegant shops added to the gallimaufrey of architectural styles. The best way to see the Thames is from the Thames itself, by river. But the slow-moving bicycle is almost as good. From William the Conqueror's Norman Tower, through Tudor, Classical Revival, Victorian Gothic, South Bank Brutal to the glittering glass towers of Mammon in the Square Mile, I cruised through a breathtaking urban landscape, every building a fragment of London's history.

On the waterfront at Deptford, where Henry VIII built his Royal Docks, I noticed a plaque on the wall and two awestruck Londoners.

''Ere. Just look at this. Queen f****** Elizabeth!'

'Yeah. And Francis f****** Drake!'

'Bloody 'ell! Yer can't believe it, can yer?'

They were middle-aged men with beer bellies and sorely limited vocabularies, but their hearts under their grubby T-shirts swelled with patriotic pride. The plaque which so amazed them marked the spot where Queen Elizabeth boarded the *Golden Hinde* in 1580 to knight Sir Francis Drake at the end of his round-the-world voyage.

I ate my lunchtime sandwiches in Greenwich, where boys were skateboarding in the square beside the *Cutty Sark*, then cycled on to Greenwich Palace, a favourite residence of the Tudors. Neglected under Cromwell, it was a ruin when William and Mary came to the throne. The site was too near the river for King William's asthma, but Queen Mary saw its potential and commissioned one of London's grandest building projects, Wren's Royal Naval Hospital. From the Thames Path I got a generous view of the upward sweep of its classical colonades with their twin domes, and the surprising gap where the architectural climax should come. This was Wren's tribute to his great predecessor, for his own magnificent complex serves as a frame for Inigo Jones's modestly elegant Queen's House which stands behind. At this point, I had to manouevre my bicycle through at least a dozen groups of Germans with their guides. They were obviously much taken with the place. '*Schön! Schön! Wunder-schön!*'

After Greenwich, there was little to see beyond gravel and aggregate yards. The Thames Path was soon obstructed by the forlorn white blob of the Millennium Dome, sticking its quills into the air like a balding porcupine. There was no riverside path and I had to find my way round a huge loop of deserted, unsignposted dual carriageway. Why on earth didn't the planners allow for the Path when they had all those acres of wilderness to play with? I rejoined it for the final stretch to the Thames Barrier. The odd lunchtime shower at Greenwich had turned into a steady downpour and the oily brown river had turned to steel. I sat on a bench in the small garden and pulled on my red waterproof trousers. Little did I know that I was destined to wear them most of the way to Egypt!

At this point, the riverside marshes drove me slightly inland, along featureless highways through Woolwich, Plumstead, the Thamesmead Estate, Erith, Crayford and Swanscombe. London is spreading east along the river, with more new estates for the upwardly mobile than I would ever have thought possible. At Gravesend, where I rejoined the Thames, I looked across the river to Tilbury and tried to imagine the scene in 1588, on the eve of the Armada, when 'Came the Queene on pranceing steede, Atired like an Angell bright' (in the words of a popular ballad), to cheer on her troops. Dressed in a gleaming suit of armour, Queen Elizabeth delivered the immortal words:

> I know I have the body of a weak and feeble woman, but I have the heart and stomach of a king, and of a king of England too, and think foul scorn that Parma or Spain, or any prince of Europe should dare invade the borders of my realm; to which, rather than any Dishonour shall grow by me, I myself will take up Arms, I myself will be your General.

Stirring words, and showmanship at its most dramatic. Queen Elizabeth had no rival in patriotic appeal until Churchill galvanised the nation at the start of World War II. 'Our gracious Majesty hath been here with me to see her camp and people,' wrote the Earl of Shrewsbury in a private letter, 'which so inflamed the hearts of her good subjects, as I think the weakest person amongst them is able to match the proudest Spaniard that dares land in England.' As we know, her good subjects were never put to the test. Despite all the prayers of King Philip in his private chapel, the Spanish fleet was shipwrecked and the land invasion under the Duke of Parma never took place.

Gravesend itself seems to have improved recently. When I worked in Kent in the 1970s, it was a shabby, woebegone town. Even now, it is hard to imagine it as a Victorian honeymoon resort, but its esplanade has been tidied up and Dickens's newlyweds, Mr Prince Turveydrop and his bride Miss Caddy Jellyby, might not look entirely out of place today in its riverside park.

Beyond Gravesend, the south bank of the Thames gets lost in the marshes again. But, thanks to Sustrans, I could cover most of the distance across to the River Medway without losing sight of water. Sustrans has laid a cycle-path along the old Thames and Medway Canal, my first canal of the trip.

It was a spooky ride that lowering evening. The little blue cycle signs led me through derelict wharves and warehouses along the Thames riverfront. Rusty doors rattled in the wind and there were ghostly groans, whistles and creaks. I thought things couldn't get any scarier, until I turned into a narrow dirt path, with a factory wall on one side and a wire fence with overhanging trees on the other. It was deserted – just the place for a mugging, or worse. It was flooded too, and my heavily laden bicycle sank into the mud at the bottom of huge puddles. As I couldn't see the ground, I was expecting a skid or a puncture at any moment, but I couldn't get off and push. The path was too narrow for me and Condor to pass along it side by side and I would have been ankle-deep in water. When I finally got through on to tarmac, I found red and white plastic ribbon sealing off the cycle-path. There was a foot and mouth ban, with a fine of £5,000 or a month in prison! I stood in a downpour and looked at my watch. Five o'clock, the time I had arranged to arrive at Cobham Hall, and I still had miles to go. I decided to risk it. The cycle-path might be sealed off, but an access road along the canal was open, and in any case I knew I was not carrying foot and mouth disease from central London. I sprinted along the canalside road to Lower Higham with the wind behind me, my heart pounding, hoping not to get caught by the police.

At Lower Higham I came to the Higham Tunnel, at 4,012 yards (3,669 m), the second longest canal tunnel ever excavated in

Britain. It was a marvel in its day, with a 200 foot (60 m) hole in the roof at its shallowest point, to enable sailing vessels to pass through. When the railway was constructed in 1847, the canal inside the tunnel was drained and a double rail-track laid, which is still in use today. So my water-route to the Medway was blocked. I cycled up the mighty hill from Lower Higham to Higham, intending to cross the A2 to Cobham by Brewers Bridge. But when I reached Shorne, disaster struck again, on what was turning out to be my unlucky evening. A notice announced that Brewers Bridge was unsafe and was closed to all traffic. In the pouring rain, there were no other cyclists around and no pedestrians to ask, so I had to flag down motorists. They all assured me that the bridge was totally closed, even to walkers and cyclists. I rode wearily along a main road, back towards Gravesend, then up a mountain called Thong Lane to reach the nearest alternative A2 crossing. Of course, I needn't have bothered. We all know that motorists drive with their eyes closed. When I passed the Cobham end of Brewers Bridge, I saw that I could have cycled over it quite easily!

It was a drowned rat who rode up the drive to Cobham Hall, my stately bed and breakfast, nearly three hours late. My headmistress friend, Ros, was peering anxiously out of her window, scanning the rain-swept drive. No waterproofs could withstand the sort of downpours mine had endured since the early afternoon but fortunately Ros had plenty of radiators in her quarters and an airing cupboard to dry off my sodden trainers. I fell straight into a hot bath, then settled down with Ros in front of a log fire to toast my toes and my journey to Egypt with champagne.

Cobham Hall, once the seat of the Earls of Darnley, is a splendid Elizabethan mansion, with state rooms by James Wyatt and a landscaped Repton park. It is an independent girls' school now, and it always feels like home, because I was once deputy headmistress there and later a governor. Yet, even after years of familiarity, I still catch my breath at the stunning beauty of its mellow brick and pepperpot towers. From my bedroom at the top of one of these, I looked out over the park's majestic cedars of Lebanon and knew that I had reached my accommodation peak on my very first night away from home. No hotel, however splendid, would be able to compete with this.

I went to sleep with the rain beating on my leaded Elizabethan panes, and it was still pouring down in torrents when I woke up the next day. As it was Sunday and there was no school, Ros and I spent a companionable morning over coffee and the newspapers, waiting for a break in the clouds. It was noon before I finally risked the run to Rochester, over the Medway bridge where heraldry goes mad. Four great lions couchant, two at each end, guard the approaches with bared teeth. There are lions holding heraldic shields, pillars with rams' heads as bases, and bogus gas lamps with elaborate crowns on top, all tricked out in gold and fairground colours. I rode past Chatham docks, and along the reach of the Medway where the prison ships used to be moored. As this was Dickens's heartland, I thought of the convict Magwich, who escaped from one of those ships and terrified Pip on the marshes.

In the riverside park at Strand, I ate a lunchtime snack, then continued on Cycle Route 1 through Upchurch and Iwade, on country roads as near to the Medway as the marshy land allowed. In the middle of the afternoon, it started to drizzle again. In a grim sort of way, I was amused. When I decided to cycle to Egypt beside water, I was thinking of rivers and seas. I never dreamed of including flooded farms, where ducks and seagulls were enjoying a swim on waterlogged fields. Even less did I think that I should be cycling *through* water. The soil was so sodden that it could take no more and showers ran straight down the grassy verges into the roads. Just my luck to have chosen the wettest year on record for a waterside ride!

Although I had covered only 30 miles (48 km), I had to call it a day in Faversham, as the drizzle had turned to yet another downpour and I was nervous. I had had pneumonia in March and my soaking on the way to Cobham had brought on a cough. It would be stupid to get so wet again. But I had a problem. Faversham was a picturesque town, yet it seemed to have nowhere decent to stay. I rushed around in the pouring rain, searching frantically. There was one very unfanciable pub down by the river and that was it. Then I met Margaret. We often read in travel books about the hospitality of people abroad, how they take in desperate wanderers and treat them with overwhelming kindness – the implication being that our own people are somehow lacking in generosity. Those who underrate the English might change their ideas in Faversham. I stopped Margaret in the street and asked her if she knew of a B & B. She did, but it was some way out of town and the rain was coming down in stair-rods. She hesitated for a moment, then plucked up courage.

'If you're stuck,' she said, 'you could come home with me. I'm just round the corner and I've got a spare room.'

'Well, thank you . . . if you're sure. That would be wonderful. How much do you charge?'

'I don't know. I've never done it before.'

We laughed and walked round the corner together to her flat in a new retirement complex, where my bicycle was safely locked away in the boiler room. Margaret turned out to be a retired nanny, who lived surrounded by photographs of her former charges – naked babies in silver frames, earnest little schoolboys in caps, society weddings, holiday snaps. She gave me tea, then insisted on providing dinner as well. 'I've got to eat something myself, and grilling sausages for two is just as easy as grilling them for one. In any case, you're not going out again in this weather.'

We spent a cheerful evening chatting and watching television together. There was a programme on about the Goons and she knew them all, as she had once worked for a show-business family, so I got plenty of small asides. Her favourite was Michael Bentine. Next morning, we haggled over payment. She was reluctant to take anything and I had to insist.

'I must do this more often,' she said, helping me load my bike. 'I woke up in the night and thought I must be mad, picking up a total stranger in the street. You could have coshed me in my bed and run off with everything I had! But you didn't and I've really enjoyed myself.'

'And you could have coshed *me* and taken all my travel money!'

'Well, you get to know who you can trust, don't you?'

'I suppose it's one of the advantages of being a lone woman. You wouldn't have picked up a man on a bicycle, would you?'

'No. But I know plenty who would! Anyway, it was lovely having company. I think I could take to bed and breakfast!'

Apple and cherry blossom in the Kent orchards, narrow lanes with trees arching overhead, high hedges and birdsong. National Cycle Route 1 was a hilly ride, much harder work than the flat, straight Roman A2, but I breezed down Graveney Hill, across Graveney Marshes, and there at last were the wide skies and the salty tang of the North Sea at Seasalter. The route was worth the extra effort, or so I thought until the wind hit me. True to form, it had swung round in the night to the north east and I had to fight it every inch of the way through Whitstable and Herne Bay. By the time I reached Reculver (Roman Regulbium), it was blowing a gale and I could well understand the attraction of the Wansum Channel.

When the Romans under Claudius invaded Britain in AD 43, they made Richborough (Rutupiae) their main port and first administrative centre. They built a towering four-way arch, faced in Carrara marble, with gleaming bronze statues on top, to be a landmark to shipping; and from that arch they laid the cobbles of Watling Street, that splendid feat of Roman engineering which enabled their legions to march ten abreast all the way from the Kent coast to Wroxeter in Shropshire. The reason the Romans preferred Richborough to the fine natural harbour at Dover was that the Isle of Thanet really was an island in those days, and remained an island until the fourteenth century. Ships could sail up the River Stour, right through to Reculver, and so gain access to the Thames Estuary and London, without having to brave the wild seas around Foreness Point. The Stour is silted up now and the site of Rutupiae is one of those boring heaps of stone that only an archaeologist could find exciting. More dramatic by far are the remains of Roman Regulbium and the monastery built by King Egbert of Kent. On that grey morning, they loomed gaunt and forbidding under the scudding clouds.

My map showed a cycle route which more or less followed the line of the Wansum Channel, but the marshes were too sodden to risk it. Instead, I had a bracing, wind-whipped ride along the sea wall to Westgate and the dizzying chalk cliffs of North Foreland. Their headlong drop was worn by the waves into an arch, the perfect pair to Monet's immortal arch across the Channel at Étretat. When I reached Broadstairs, the rain began again in earnest. I gave up the losing battle and spent what remained of the afternoon in the Dickens' House Museum, where he wrote *David Copperfield*. It appeared in the book as Betsey Trotwood's house. Wandering among the gloomy relics of Dickens's life, I peered through the parlour window at the green where Betsey used to chase the donkeys. It was waterlogged. I found a bed and breakfast, and tried to cheer myself up over a plate of pasta and a half-bottle of Montepulciano. Perhaps tomorrow would be drier.

2. THE ENGLISH CHANNEL

La mer, qu'on voit danser le long des golfes clairs,
A des reflets d'argent, la mer,
Des reflets changeants sous la pluie.

'La Mer', popular song by Charles Trenet

'The loveliest skies in Europe are over the Isle of Thanet,' wrote William Turner, when he moved to Margate. What interested him was not the Heaven of saints, angels and Greek gods, but the Thanet sky of racing clouds and dissolving mists. He broke with tradition, painting the changing colours of the sea at sunrise, the drama of blood-red sunsets and the meeting of sea and sky, where the elements seemed to mingle. He was the first of a new breed of artists, obsessed with the play of light on water. Even when he painted historical scenes, the rain, snow and mist were centre-stage. His characters were powerless against the forces of Nature.

I had just endured a day of rain, wind and menacing storm clouds, ending with a fireball sunset, and the weather was still romantically wild the next morning. Turner would have loved it, but it was not so good for a cyclist. It was raining so hard that I just wanted to get miles under my wheels and reach Dover as soon as possible. I rode through the Gazen Salts Nature Reserve into Sandwich, where I lost my way because it was too wet and windy to stop and consult my map. I missed the cycle-path to Deal and ended up in a downpour on an exposed dual carriageway. The rain was hitting the road like machine-gun fire and bouncing up again vertically. Then it turned to hail. I sheltered under a bridge at the bottom of a hill, but that was a mistake. Streams rushed down at me from both directions and I was soon ankle-deep in water. I spotted a pub, the High and Dry, and no name could have been more cheering. I sprinted across to it and the landlady brought me a heap of towels, while I poured gallons of water out of my shoes and shook a mini-Niagara from my rainproofs. I could feel my shirt clinging icily to my back and pneumonia loomed again. They didn't have rooms at that particular pub, but they phoned the Plough and Harrow, two miles back. I treated myself to a whisky there, while I soaked in a hot bath. Then I spent the afternoon in bed, with my gloves, hat, shoes and all my clothes down to my vest draped over the radiators to dry. I had cycled less than 20 miles (32 km).

As I was on my way to Egypt, I was looking out for Egyptian associations. Apart from one hotel, the Luxor, the only connections I found in Kent were echoes of Lord Nelson and the Battle of the Nile. Nelson Crescents abounded in the Regency bathing resorts. At the Royal Hotel, Deal, he spent weekends with Lady Hamilton, who wrote in a letter to him that if she were King of England, she would make him 'the most noble, puissant Duke Nelson, Marquis Nile, Earl Alexandria, Viscount Pyramid, Baron Crocodile and Prince Victory, that posterity might have you in all forms.' (He in fact took the far more modest title, Baron Nelson of the Nile and Burnham Thorp.) Finally, it was in Margate that his flagship, the *Victory*, bearing his body, anchored in December 1805.

But if I was short on things Egyptian, I was certainly long on my second theme, water. When I woke the next morning, the rain was still pouring down. It cleared up a little after breakfast and was only moderately drizzly for the run to Dover. It had been a diabolical ride all the way from London and my beautiful orange Condor was brown with mud. But it still flew like the wind. As we hurtled down the hill to the Eastern Docks, we broke the 30 mph speed limit and arrived in the passenger terminal with a flourish. 'Nice bike,' said the booking clerk. 'My friend used to have one of those.' Hailstones as big as mint imperials started to rattle against the windows and the sea turned a livid, bruised grey. I sat out the storm on the boat to Calais, where the weather was marginally better. No hail – just raining cats and dogs.

We nosed into the docks, which seem to be more extensive every time I land there. I cowered on the car-deck and looked out across the vast acres of empty tarmac, bracing myself for the dash to the harbour buildings. I whizzed down the ramp, sped across the rainswept yard, accelerated, changed gear – and the chain came off. I ran the swiftest hundred metres of my life to an overhanging eve, crouched down in the semi-dry to fix it and got myself thoroughly messed up with oil. Then came the obstacle race. I had to cycle through a sort of child's paddling pool, blue plastic brimming with disinfectant, and over a series of lumpy mats, to stop me from spreading my British foot and mouth disease over hygenic France. The arrangement was fine for motorists, but no one had spared a thought for poor wobbly cyclists. A couple of flyovers and a few miles of concrete later, I finally reached passport control. By that time, the cars and trucks from the ferry had all driven away and I was alone in the rain.

Two officials jumped out of their kiosk to bar my exit. One looked as if he was approaching retirement age; the other was a lad in his twenties.

'Are you taking a cycling holiday in the area?' asked the older one.

'No. I'm just passing through. I'm on my way to Egypt.'

'On your bike? You're joking! How old are you?' asked the young man.

'You should never ask a lady her age,' said his colleague. 'In any case, I can tell you.'

'Yes. I saw you having a good look at my passport.'

'Of course I had a good look. I'm just as nosy as my friend here, but I'm a bit more discreet about it.'

They waved me off with cheery '*Félicitations!*' towards Calais Centre Ville, where I thought I would have to take shelter for the night. But the sky began to clear and the rain abated. Suddenly, miracle of miracles, a watery sun broke through the clouds! I had already lost three afternoons' cycling out of four and was running behind schedule, so I decided to risk another drenching. I found the seafront, turned left along the Corniche and began my ride down La Côte d'Opal.

The stretch of coast between Calais and Boulogne was unknown territory and I was completely bowled over by its wild beauty. We tend to arrive at one port or the other and rush away across France, without realising what we're missing. I sped along the flat with the north-east wind behind me as far as Sangatte, where groups of swarthy men were mooching miserably around the nondescript streets. They were refugees from the Red Cross camp – Eastern Europeans, Middle Easterners and a sprinkling of Tamils or Sri Lankans. Huddled against the unaccustomed cold in their zipped-up black leather jackets and uniform jeans, they were all waiting for their chance to breach Tunnel security and get across to England. Then a serious climb led up to Cap Blanc-Nez and a spectacular view from the cliff tops over wild grey waves with leaping white horses. By the time the silvery sky dissolved into rain, I was near enough to Escalles to swoop down the steep cliff road into a comfortable Logis de France. I had only done about 12 miles (20 km), but at least I had made a start without getting a soaking.

That evening I went to the local shop to get myself organised for breakfast. An elegant young man in a cashmere sweater swung the door open for me with great panache: *'Bon soir, madame!'* The French are still polite. They still have style rather than 'attitude'.

I used to love my French breakfast, when it consisted of a fresh baguette with butter and jam and a croissant. It was inexpensive and perfect in its simplicity. But then they complicated it. They added orange juice (which I don't drink, as I've read that it's bad for my rheumatism), yoghurt and cereals (which I don't like), and cheese and cold ham (which I like, but not first thing in the morning). Prices have soared accordingly – and all for a pile of food that I don't want. So now I carry Nescafé and an electric boiler, buy a large packet of pain d'épices or similar, and eat and drink exactly what I like for my breakfast, when I like, in my own room. I find it most convenient, as I can save time by packing my panniers while my second mug of coffee cools. And I save a small fortune. Superb three-course French dinners at around £10 are a real bargain, but fancy breakfasts at £5 are not.

Wissant, Cap Griz-Nez, Wimereux, Boulogne and a score of long windswept beaches under perpendicular cliffs, carved by the Channel from the same block of white limestone as Dover. I passed a few tumbledown German pillboxes, relics of their Atlantic Wall, but it was the light that fascinated me. In the morning haze, the darker grey of the sea was scarcely distinguishable from the opalescent grey of the sky. Then a storm broke. Long jagged forks of lightning lit the clouds above Kent, which I could see quite clearly across the water. Thunder rolled, the sea turned to charcoal and the sky to industrial smoke. I cycled along, miraculously dry, beside a dense curtain of rain which never quite reached the shore. I felt very smug. That was at least one downpour I had missed! Had I chosen Newhaven–Dieppe instead of Dover–Calais, I would have been riding along in the middle of it all. Towards the mouth of the Somme, the land flattened into dunes and marshes where long-legged birds waded and fished among the reeds. The Opal Coast was deserted and I had its oyster-grey beauty all to myself. The only solid colour in the landscape, apart from my red waterproofs and orange bicycle, was the yellow of rapeseed and gorse.

The nature reserves and pine woods near the resorts were well provided with cycle-paths. Three sturdy women on Dutch sit-up-and-begs came wheeling along in the opposite direction and we all waved, but they were the only other cyclists. I heard a skylark singing, before it was drowned out by seagulls, screaming in panic at the start of yet another violent storm. On a hill outside Étaples, I passed a campsite in a field right next to a World War I cemetery. It was waterlogged and I thought how sad it would be to wake up in a tent in the rain, in the middle of a sea of mud, with nothing but crosses in view. *'Demain il faut continuer en bâteau'* (tomorrow we shall have to continue by boat), said a gloomy fellow-guest at my hotel.

It was not a joke. He was driving to Abbeville, one of the main cities of Picardy, which had been drowning in the waters of the Somme for more than two weeks. At home, I had seen English floods every day on the television news, but there had been no mention of France, where the flooding was in fact far worse. That evening I watched a television interview with a woman in Abbeville, who said that life had gone back to the Middle Ages. The sewerage system had broken down, and she had to put pans outside her door to catch rainwater for cooking, as the supply from the taps was polluted. Fortunately, I was sticking to the coast, which was unaffected. The ceaseless rain poured down on me, but at least it soaked into the fields and didn't climb up to my axles.

Le Touquet was once the height of fashion, a serious rival in elegance and high life to the Riviera. It is still a resort of luxurious shops, where silks, satins and sinful furs ooze temptingly in the windows. 'Sales-resistance' is my middle name, but even I found the displays so alluring that I had to slow down to gaze. If I had a fortune and were the spending type, I could squander it in Le Touquet with ease. In Le Tréport the sun came out and lit up the charming pink, green, mauve and yellow houses around the harbour, and as I toiled up the steep cliff out of the town, I looked back on a changed sea. By the shore it was pale sage green and the charcoal further out was striped with deep olive. I crossed the Bresle into Normandy and wheeled into the Tourist Office in Dieppe around noon on 5 May, just in time to get the last available hotel room.

Armistice Day is on 8 May in France, and 7 May was our spring Bank Holiday, so the town was seething with French and British, celebrating 'Le Long Weekend' with Dieppe's famous sea food. I pushed my bicycle along the crowded quais, past restaurants where the patrons sat with pincers in their hands in front of astonishing pyramids of shells – mussels, whelks, winkles, clams, spider crabs, cockles and round objects with spikes like miniature mines. (For those who enjoy such creatures and struggle to identify them on French menus, I have included an extremely useful glossary which I picked up in Dieppe. You will find it at Appendix C.)

I was lucky to find a bed in Dieppe and I decided to hang on to it until Wednesday. It was a very comfortable bed in a small, neat hotel, which was fortunate, as I had to spend most of the long weekend reclining on it. I had done something to my left knee. It felt as if I had banged it, but there was no sign of a bruise, so I guessed it was my old hockey injury come to haunt me again. Whatever it was, it was so painful that I had to stop cycling altogether and hobble round Dieppe on foot. I mingled with the pedestrians in the elegant Grande Rue, shopping in the *charcuteries*, *traiteurs* and *fromageries* for delicious picnics, which I ate in my room with my leg up.

'Come on. Let's push the boat out!' said an Englishman to his wife in the supermarket. 'Let's both have new toothbrushes!' Oh, the wildness of the English abroad!

It actually stopped raining that weekend, but the bunting flapped in an icy wind. The flags of their British, American and Belgian allies flew alongside the French tricolor, with the Canadian maple leaf in pride of place. There is a special bond with Canada, as men of Dieppe were prominent in its exploration; and 5,000 commandos, mostly Canadian, were killed or captured in the disastrous Dieppe Raid of 1942.

The Côte d'Opal had now become the Côte d'Albâtre, which the French Impressionists and Pointillistes had made their own – so much so that it was difficult to see it through any eyes but theirs. They loved the bathers and the beach huts and the ladies strolling along the promenades under their parasols. They loved the cliffs and the sea but, above all, they loved the light. Now that pitching an easel on the spot has become the norm for landscape painters, it seems amazing that it was not until the latter part of the nineteenth century that the idea occurred to anyone. When Monet abandoned his studio and had a rowing-boat rigged out with an easel and paints, it was still such an unusual event that Manet painted a picture of him, *Monet Working in his Boat* (1874). For Monet, light was 'the principal person' in any picture and he was fascinated by what he called the 'envelope', the trembling capsule of light around solid objects, rather than the objects themselves. In this, he was the true successor to William Turner. In fact, their paintings are sometimes so similar that I muddle the two. The excellent art gallery in Dieppe Castle has an interesting pair of paintings of the nearby Falaises du Pollet: Boudin paints the cliffs white, with a matching white beach, while Pissarro, at a different time of day, in a different light, paints them in subtle gradations of pink. There is a charming view of Dieppe by Sisley and a number of very gloomy Sickerts, which made me think that he must have stayed in the town in the same sort of weather that I was experiencing. His houses were dark brown and his sky charcoal, except over the Église de St Jacques, where it was browny-mauve. The day I visited the castle, I stood on the cliff-top battlements and saw a translucent blue-green sea, shading to cream towards the shingle beach. It was calmer than I had seen it since Calais and dotted with colourful spinnakers under a shimmering sky. It could have been a Monet or a Dufy. But the glamorous TV weathergirl in her gold lamé evening gown predicted a return to wintry showers.

When I set off again, my route was coloured green by Michelin, and that invariably means hills. I rushed down steep, twisting lanes of beech and oak, where the wind pelted me with cannonades of acorns, to reach some clean, deserted, out-of-season beach in the shadow of the chalk cliffs. Then I toiled up an equally steep, twisting lane to reach the next stretch of green cliff top. It was a breezy, exhilarating ride. The Charolais cattle were fat and contented, knowing they were safe in their fields. Notices were plastered everywhere. '*Halte au carnage! Vaccinons! Sauvez notre élevage!*' The French farmers were making it quite clear that, however feeble their English counterparts, *they* were not going to stand for the wholesale slaughter of *their* cattle.

The tomb of Braque in the little cemetery at Varengeville-sur-Mer was a real eye-catcher, with one of his trademark doves picked out in blue and white mosaic. It stood outside the village church, where his Stem of Jesse, a stylised indigo and turquoise tree on a blue ground, filled the east window with a subaqueous morning light. Braque's colours are clear and Mediterranean, in contrast to the greys, with streaks of pearl and soupy green, which so fascinated the Impressionists. There were plenty of elderly, rather sedate, English wandering round in Varengeville, looking for the Lutyens house and the Gertrude Jekyll gardens.

In Veules-les-Roses I stayed in an accidental hotel. It had started life as a large family seaside home, but late one evening an English family came knocking on the door. 'It was dark. It was pouring with rain. They were tired and depressed, and the children were crotchety,' said Madame. 'They were searching for a hotel and I knew they wouldn't find one this side of Dieppe, so I thought I'd better take them in. That was the start of bed and breakfast and, since then, I've developed the place into a hotel.'

This conversation was carried on in French, which Madame spoke effortlessly, but my ear just caught something. Evidently hers did too, because she narrowed her eyes and scrutinised me carefully. 'You're not French, are you? Are you Belgian?'

I was immensely flattered to be taken for a native French speaker, if not for a Frenchwoman. 'No. I'm English.' Then I added, with some hesitation, 'I've got a feeling you're not French either.'

She laughed. 'No. I'm from Pembroke. I married a Frenchman.' At that, we both switched delightedly to English. It's always such a treat, even after a short time away from home, to abandon outlandish tongues and sink back into the familiar for a nice gossip.

In Fécamp, the gloomy monastery brooded over the grey, miserable town. It's not surprising that the Benedictine monks there invented the eponymous liqueur. They needed something to cheer themselves up! I was about to cheer myself up with dinner when I realised that the proprietor of my small seafront hotel had given me the wrong back-door key. I went downstairs at 7 p.m. and found myself locked in an empty hotel. No dinner. And what if there was a fire? I would have to leap out of my upstairs window. I had just about come to terms with all this when I heard the back door open. I shot downstairs and met my rescuer, the local doctor on night duty; he had a room available in the hotel, where he could take the occasional nap and recharge his mobile. He was just dropping his overnight bag in this room before he went out again on a call and he agreed to leave the back door unlocked until nine o'clock, so that I could pop out for a quick meal. The proprietor treated me to breakfast next morning, as an apology.

The wind freshened as I cycled south west until it was blowing such a gale that even the towering climbs from the beaches were a relief from the buffeting I got along the cliff tops. What should have been the most exhilarating bits of the ride turned into a penance. I had pulled my woolly hat right down over my ears, but the wind was so fierce that it tore it off my head and sent it spinning across the grass. Sometimes cycling on the flat was such hard work that I had to get off and walk, leaning into the gale to give myself a bit of rest. Above Étretat, I cycled out to the Cap d'Antifer, trying to find the perfect spot to take a photograph of *the* Monet view, that archway gouged out of the cliffs by the sea, which he painted in all lights and weathers. I was nearly blown off the cliff top, and that was the end of Monet and his colours! All I cared about then was turning the pedals round to get myself off this high ground, where there were no hedges and not a single tree to shield me. I timed myself across one open stretch and found that it took me a whole hour to cycle 5 miles (8 km). Except in the notoriously windy Gobi Desert, I have never been quite so relieved to see buildings again. A terrific downhill swoop, with the scent of roasting coffee in the air, took me through the suburb of Ste. Addresse to the seafront at Le Havre, where the wind gave me a brutal slap in the face as soon as I wheeled out of shelter. In the Port de Plaisance, the rigging of a thousand yachts clacked against the steel masts with the din of a million glockenspiels. It had taken me seven exhausting hours to cover 36 miles (58 km). 'You're lucky to be cycling in France,' they told me when I staggered into a hotel. 'In England they're having 80 mph gales' (130 kph). I was supposed to feel grateful for small mercies.

If I was finding the weather a trial, it was even worse for a group of young Indians. Bundled up in anoraks, scarves and knitted gloves, they were struggling, with no French at all, to find pure vegetarian food in the supermarket. I nearly offered to help, but they seemed to be managing somehow, and I felt too zombie-like to bother after my battle with the wind. Next morning, when I was feeling brighter, I found them sitting at breakfast in my hotel, so I went over for a chat. They were management trainees from the Indian subsidiary of a French firm, sent over to Le Havre to learn the ropes at Head Office. I offered to interpret for them if they had any problems, but they said politely that they were 'very comfortable'. Then, as I was paying my bill and loading my bicycle, one of them came up and asked me where he could buy an English newspaper. Another came and asked about vegetarian food. Then the flood gates opened. They crowded round, asking me everything from where to hire bikes to how to get their laundry done – not 'dry cleaning', but 'wet cleaning'. They were worried about money, as the French franc was so expensive for Indians exchanging rupees. They told me that everything they put on their credit cards would be paid by their firm, but all cash expenditure had to come out of their own pockets and they were running short. When I explained all this to Madame at the hotel, she couldn't have been kinder. She volunteered to take them round to the laundrette, show them how the machines worked and put the coins in the slots herself; and she offered to buy them English newspapers and hire bicycles for them, adding all these small charges to their hotel bills, so that they could pay with their credit cards. By the end of all this, Madame and I were firm friends and she took me on a tour of her hotel. I had slept in a modern room, with curtains in bold primary colours and posters of Miro and Chagall on the walls, but I soon saw that every room was decorated in a different style, and all were elegant. Interior décor was clearly her passion, which she was able to indulge on a grand scale in a multi-bedroomed hotel.

Appropriately enough, I spent my last day on the coast of opal, alabaster and silvery light looking at paintings in the Musée Malraux. Monet grew up in Le Havre, and it was a picture he painted there, entitled *Impression, soleil levant*, that gave the name to the Impressionist movement. The Impressionists used to meet at Mère Toutain's, just across the Seine estuary in Honfleur, where Monet's teacher, Boudin, spent his life. Dufy was born in Le Havre, and every nineteenth- and twentieth-century artist anyone has ever heard of, English or French, painted in the area. So the quality of the 'local art' on display in that provincial museum is phenomenal. It puts the national collections in many world capitals to shame.

3. THE SEINE

All travelling becomes dull in exact proportion to its rapidity.

John Ruskin

As soon as I turned the corner and began to pedal east, I was out of the interstellar wind which had plagued me since Dieppe. First the refineries and factories of the Seine estuary provided shelter, then the avenues of trees which shaded the cycle-path along the Canal de Tancarville.

According to Napoleon, Le Havre, Rouen and Paris are just a single city with the River Seine as its main street. This conjures up visions of a built-up, crowded landscape, but nothing could be further from the truth. Across Normandy, the river loops through forests and apple orchards like a coiling snake (its name is said to derive from the Celtic *squan*, meaning to curve or bend). The main roads run in a straight line, taking the traffic directly across from the outer curve of one loop to the outer curve of the next, which leaves the inner curves virtually traffic-free. Right up to St Denis on the outskirts of Paris, I found tranquil riverside paths, where a farmer on his tractor or a couple of fishermen out for the day were the only human company. Looping the loops made for a long ride – 50 miles (78 km) between Caudebec-en-Caux and Rouen, for example, while the main road zipped across the two loop-tops in less than half that distance. But I was not in a hurry. Like Ruskin, I enjoy slow travel. After a season of rain, the grass gleamed with emeralds and I loved the sunlit glow of the Norman stonework and the richness of the changing landscape. It was the perfect ride and I wished it could last for ever.

The river rises in a forest glade at the foot of a Burgundy hill and flows 482 miles (775 km) to its estuary. The reason for its loopiness is that its fall over this distance is a remarkably small 1600 feet (488 m). When it enters Normandy near Vernon it is only 46 feet (16 m) above sea level, yet it still has almost half its entire length to travel before it reaches the Channel. I never thought I could get excited about geomorphology, but the contours of the land and the way they have been shaped by the sinuous Seine intrigued me. The current flows slowly along the inside of the loops, depositing stones and silt on gentle slopes which are sometimes farmed, but more often left as woodland or flood plain. At the outer edge of the bend, where the force of the stream runs into the banks, it has eaten them away over the centuries to form sheer limestone cliffs, like the ones on the coast. Before I cycled there, I pored over the map for hours, to see where I could switch banks and give myself an easy ride inside the lower bends. But when I got there, I found the roads along the inside were often far away from the river, to allow for seasonal flooding, whereas the roads on the outside banks tended to run along a narrow strip of land between the cliff face and the water. They kept me nearer to the river, which I was trying to follow, and were no more strenuous to cycle than the lower banks. So I decided to stick to the right, mostly northern, bank of the Seine and enjoy two totally different landscapes. One hour I was riding through forested national parks or monastery orchards weighed down with apples, watching cranes and herons fishing in the reeds. Then I rounded a bend and came up against starling-haunted cliffs. I found I could polish off two loops a day, two stretches of inside and two of cliffside, all as comfortable to cycle as sitting in my armchair at home.

The waterway itself was my theme – which was just as well, because France and Italy in particular are impossibly rich in art, architecture, music and literature. What could I write about the monuments of Paris or Venice that had not been written hundreds of times before, and written with far greater knowledge and sensitivity than I could ever aspire to? I had to be very selective about what I stopped to see, otherwise I would still be cycling to Egypt now. I decided to be a magpie and just peck at things that glittered. In Caudebec-en-Caux, I popped into the Église de Notre Dame, Henry IV's favourite bit of flamboyant Gothic as well as mine, where the sixteenth-century glaziers showed the Children of Israel crossing a literally crimson Red Sea. And the next day, I called in on the magnificent ruins of the monastery at Jumièges. If I had been a mediaeval Benedictine (perish the thought!), that is the monastery I would have chosen, supposing I were given any choice in the matter. Built in a fertile loop of the Seine, with protective hills behind and a sweeping view of the Forêt de Brotonne across the river, its twin towers preside in majesty over its fecund acres of farmland and orchard.

I had two literary calls to make as well. In Villequier I paused in the riverside park to pay tribute to the hunched-up, grief-stricken statue of Victor Hugo, brooding over the Seine at the spot where his daughter Léopoldine and her new husband were drowned in the tidal bore. It used to run with devastating ferocity, until it was tamed by nineteenth-century engineering works, which also deepened the river channel. I watched the resulting spectacle over dinner. No matter how many times I visit Caudebec, the sight of giant oceangoing vessels gliding through the town, darkening the riverfront restaurants with their bulk and almost scraping the windows, never ceases to amaze me.

Villequier was a duty call, as I have never really got on with Hugo. But in Croisset, a suburb of Rouen, my visit to Flaubert's little pavilion was an act of devotion. Here, in a corner of his mother's garden, he wrote *Madame Bovary* and his other masterpieces. The house has been rebuilt, but the pavilion still stands. I imagined him crossing the modest garden every morning after breakfast, regular as clockwork, to begin his day's writing. 'Be regular and orderly in your life, like a bourgeois,' he said, 'so that you may be violent and original in your work.' I followed him into his pavilion and stood at his writing desk, looking out on his view of the Seine. It is dominated now by factory chimneys, but I was interested to note that there were plenty of factory chimneys in a painting of that very same view, dated 1874. Flaubert's characters, like Flaubert himself, lived in towns and travelled by steamer up and down the Seine between Paris, Rouen and Le Havre. Open country was not the source of his inspiration.

I was not expecting any Egyptian connections along this stretch of the river, so I was pleasantly surprised to come across a Quai Napoleon, where a monument in a small garden commemorated the landing of Napoleon's mortal remains in 1840. They had travelled up the Seine in a black frigate, on their way from St Helena to their grandiose resting place in the Dôme des Invalides. This may seem like scratching around for associations, but it was in fact Napoleon's invasion of Egypt which sparked off the European craze for all things pharaonic. 'My eldest boy rides on a sphinx instead of a rocking-horse and my youngest has a pap-boat in the shape of a crocodile. My husband has built a water-closet in the form of a pyramid and has his shirts marked with a lotus,' wrote one 'Priscilla Plainstitch' in 1821, when she saw Belzoni's exhibition of Egyptian sculpture in London's Egyptian Hall. Egyptian architecture was too gigantic in scale to have much influence on the design of buildings, but crocodiles, sphinxes, winged discs, scarabs and lotus capitals could be added with amusing effect to otherwise conventional forms.

The last half-loop into Rouen was a nightmare, with factories lining both banks of the river. Trucks rattled and roared along the quais. Cobbles, stretches of railway track, then more cobbles. But I battled bravely into the peace of Rouen's pedestrian centre and hurried past its handsome mediaeval churches to greet my gentle friend, the second biggest cat I know. I was bitterly disappointed. The giant tabby had retired from his post at the reception desk of the Hotel des Carmes, along with his owners. To console me in my loss, the new proprietor, a keen young man, took me on a tour of the hotel to show me the improvements he had made and enthuse over his plans for the future – one bathroom to be refurbished each month. He was the second hotelier to share his dreams with me in one week. Do I strike them as an artistic person, fascinated by interior décor? I hardly think so, in my baggy cycling trousers, anorak and trainers. Is it because I'm a woman and supposed to be interested in such things? Or is it because I'm on my own and an easy victim? Whatever the reason, I listen admiringly and reap my reward in terms of nice rooms and willing service.

Rouen (Roman Rotomagus, the port they established at the lowest point where the Seine could be bridged) has all the splendours you would expect of the capital of Upper Normandy. It nestles in an upper bend of the river, protected by high encircling hills. There are newly restored half-timbered houses and magnificent Gothic churches. Joan of Arc was burned at the stake there and the heart of Richard Lionheart is entombed in the cathedral. Monet and Turner both produced a series of paintings of the towering West Front, catching the changing light of hours and seasons. Géricault was born in the city, and Poussin just upriver at Les Andelys. The stunning collection in the art gallery reflects all these local ties. As for literature, what school can compete with Rouen's Jesuit College (now renamed Le Lycée Corneille), which counts Pierre Corneille himself, Gustave Flaubert, Guy de Maupassant and André Maurois among its Old Boys? No wonder the city had Ruskin in raptures!

The weather had at last turned pleasant and I enjoyed wandering the sunlit streets and squares, doing nothing very much. I came across anti-war demos. *Non à la guerre! Non à la Busherie!* (a clever play on Bush and butcher). At first, I was surprised at the large number of elderly American tourists. Then I realised that they were on pilgrimage to Omaha and Utah Beaches, where the American 1st Army landed and suffered heavy casualties on D-Day. 'They need to go there,' said an Australian woman. 'It's their Gallipoli.'

I visited a sports doctor, as my knee was still troubling me. 'I get masses of Americans coming in for treatment,' he said. 'At home, they go everywhere in cars and they're just not used to walking. So when they come to Rouen, which is all cobbles and flagstones, they fall down like ninepins! I can't tell you how many nasty knees and sprained ankles I have to deal with.'

The Seine is a down-to-earth workaday sort of river. Tourists neglect it in favour of the Loire, its more fashionable, castle-crowned sister, but the Seine is truer to the diversity of French life. It makes no secret of its factories and executive housing estates, all with easy access to the Paris motorway. Yet it waters some of France's richest, most unspoilt agricultural country. It flows through France's artistic heartland. And in Paris, it has its hour of glory, when the capital's most majestic buildings jostle for space along its banks. Surprises lurk round every one of its snaky bends. On a flat stretch, I passed a huge Renault plant. Then, half an hour later, I was cycling under cliffs, watching paragliders leaping into space in flashes of rainbow colour. At Château Gaillard, late one afternoon, I stood on the battlements of Richard Lionheart's massive fortress, looking down from its dizzy escarpment on the breathtaking view of the Seine. Early next morning, I was in Giverny, in the tranquil valley of its tributary, the Epte, wandering beside the willows and waterlilies of Monet's garden. In Porcheville, near the refineries and cement works, I saw the first North Africans of my ride. It was Saturday afternoon and the men were mooching disconsolately through the bleak expanses of a high-rise housing estate. There was not a woman in sight. By contrast, in Meulan, just a little further upsteam, there was bustling life and jollity. It was the annual cheese festival. Jugglers, buskers and balloon-sellers worked the lanes between the cheese stalls, and there were tables and benches in the squares, where appreciative crowds were taking a glass or two of wine to enhance the flavour of their purchases.

On Sunday morning, in the Forêt de St Germain, I crossed an agricultural park and the grounds of a water-cleansing works, before riding past the elegant mansions and racecourse of Maisons-Lafitte. There were cycle-paths all the way. The Sunday cyclists were out in force, dressed in their lycra motley, like clowns on their day off. Red, yellow, blue, green, orange, purple – even a few tiger stripes! The jockeys' silks looked drab by comparison. From Croissy-sur-Seine as far as Bezons, the riverside roads were closed to traffic on Sundays. I was planning to stay in Argenteuil, which I knew from Impressionist paintings, but it was no longer the idyllic riverside village where Renoir's buxom, pink-cheeked girls danced with their lovers under lanterns. Its dingy streets were overshadowed by brutal tower blocks. I hurried on through the outer suburbs of Paris, until I came at dusk to a Campanile hotel opposite the Île St Denis. '*Quelle belle idée!*' said the receptionist, when I told her I was following the Seine. She got out a map to advise me on my route into Paris and gave me her very best room, on the top floor, where I had a fantastic view of the sun setting over the river. The hotel was beyond budget, but well worth the extravagance.

Then came my big day, the day when I cycled proudly into Paris. St Denis and Clichy were heavily industrial. I was caught in a rainstorm, but it struck when I was conveniently near a bus shelter, so I was able to sit it out under cover. Then came the smart suburb of Neuilly, with its houseboats and river views, followed by the Bois de Boulogne (my second racecourse in two days) and the wooded hills of St Cloud opposite, both rich in literary associations. Another great Renault factory filled the next south bend, and then I was in the city proper, pedalling along the Rive Droite.

The first landmark to come into view was the Tour Eiffel. I stopped to take a photograph of it, with Condor posing in the foreground, just to prove that I had actually cycled through Paris. Les Invalides, La Place de la Concorde, the Tuileries, the Louvre, the Île de Paris and Notre Dame – the cavalcade of French history passed before my eyes. But it was not a ride for the faint-hearted. A bus-lane ended without warning at a point where two fast traffic lanes joined from the right, and I suddenly found myself in the outer lane of three, with speeding cars on both sides of me. Then I got on to the Georges Pompidou freeway by mistake and had to cower by the embankment parapet for almost half an hour, until a gap appeared in the traffic. Then I sprinted across the three lanes to an exit road and joined the quieter street above. I was nearly deafened by the cacophony of horns. (Why do motorists do that? I obviously knew that I was in the wrong place and was doing my best to get out of it.) By the time I reached the Gare de Lyon at the east end of Paris, I was distinctly trembly at the knees. If you know exactly where to go, Paris is quite a good city for cycling. But if you don't know your way around the cycle-paths, minor mistakes can be a disaster.

When Napoleon invaded Egypt in 1798, his objectives were to block one of Britain's trade routes to India and establish a base for French imperial expansion eastwards. He soon defeated the Mamelukes at the Battle of the Pyramids and rode in triumph into Cairo. But he left his fleet unprotected in Abu Qir Bay. That was his undoing. Nelson located it and pounced, destroying 200 ships. Napoleon's army was trapped, prisoners in the land they had conquered. Realising his weakness, the Ottoman Sultan declared war on him and Napoleon returned quietly to France. His abandoned troops soon surrendered to a combined Ottoman-British force. Napoleon's dreams of an eastern empire were shattered.

In the short term, his military adventure was a fiasco, but it had far-reaching effects. Like Alexander the Great before him, Napoleon added an army of savants to his soldiery. One hundred and sixty-seven eager young scholars – historians, geologists, botanists, astronomers, civil engineers, linguists and mathematicians – were all set to work measuring, collecting, drawing and analysing. They discovered a magnificent forgotten civilization, half buried under the desert sands, Pharaonic Egypt, 'the cradle of the science and art of all humanity', as Napoleon called it. They discovered the Valley of the Kings and marvelled at the scale and splendour of the pyramids and temples. Abandoned by Napoleon, the scholars knew that time was running out. They carried on working feverishly. When they were captured, the British allowed them to keep their written records, but they were forced to surrender the material finds still in their possession, including the invaluable Rosetta Stone. In 1802, Napoleon ordered the Imperial Press to begin publishing. For twenty years, four hundred copper-engravers worked ceaselessly to produce the complete record of Egyptian antiquities and natural sciences in *Description de l'Egypte*. The study of Egyptology was born.

Fate dealt unkindly with the French, robbing them of so many priceless Egyptian treasures, when they had put so much work into their discovery. But their honour was preserved. After a frantic international race, it was a Frenchman, Jean-François Champollion, who first deciphered Egyptian hieroglyphics. The Rosetta Stone might repose in the British Museum, but it took a Frenchman to unlock its secrets!

The French occupied Egypt for less than four years, but they won the hearts of the educated inhabitants. A special bond with France was created, which was maintained even when Egypt was under British occupation. French was still the European language of choice and wealthy Egyptians sent their sons to university in France. They copied French fashions, took their holidays in Paris and Nice, and employed French architects and town-planners. It was a real love affair.

Its most visible token is the Luxor obelisk of Ramses II in La Place de la Concorde. '*En presence du Roi Louis Philippe 1er cet obelisque transporté de Louqsor en France a été dressé sur ce pedestal par M. Lebas Ingenieur aux applaudissements d'un people immense.*' The base of the obelisk has engraved diagrams, touched with gold, illustrating the method used by M. Lebas to raise the obelisk to the vertical. The feat was achieved in 1836, over forty years before Cleopatra's Needle was raised on the Thames Embankment. Both obelisks were presented by the Turkish Viceroy of Egypt, Mohammed Ali Pasha. King Louis Philippe gave a gift in return, an ornate clock (which has never worked) to embellish Mohammed Ali's grandiose new mosque in Cairo. There is no record of a return gift from the Prince Regent.

I walked through Les Jardins des Tuileries towards La Place de la Concorde and was dazzled by my first glimpse of the Luxor obelisk. The original gilding on its peak has been restored, and on that sunny morning it glittered against the clear sky. Taller than Cleopatra's Needle, it dominates the vast formal space at the very heart of Paris, whereas our poor Needle is almost invisible, dwarfed by the Shell-Mex building and cut off by traffic.

I had planned an Egyptian day – the Egyptian Collection in the Louvre and the nineteenth- and twentieth-century rooms in the Musée des Arts Decoratifs, where I hoped to find lotus lamps and Pharaonic chairs. But my bad luck held. The Louvre closes on Tuesdays and the rooms I wanted in the other museum were closed for refurbishment. So I just wandered along the Seine, as people do in Paris, past the magnificent buildings lining its banks, looking in the shops and drinking coffee at pavement cafés. The Paris quays were another favourite subject of the Impressionists and it was difficult to see the play of light and shadow through the trees with any eyes but theirs. The Seine in Paris must be the most beautiful river basin in the world. As in Rouen, there were lots of elderly American couples, walking along hand-in-hand like aged infants, picking their way carefully over the cobbles. In the Place du Châtelet, I had lunch by a Napoleonic fountain. His victories were listed on a column above four very peculiar sphinxes, who looked as if they were vomiting water. Then I strolled down the Champs Élysées and suddenly had one of those moments of sheer happiness. The sun was shining, I was alive and free, I had leisure, enough money to travel to Paris and the energy to enjoy its delights. What more could anyone want?

The mornings were growing misty, but the fine weather held. I crossed to the Rive Gauche at Austerlitz and followed the Seine closely through the outer suburbs, where the planes descending on Orly Airport roared overhead. It was an uncomplicated exit from Paris. Back on the right bank, I was soon speeding along riverside paths through the Forêt de Sénart. By late afternoon, I had reached the fringes of the Forêt de Fontainebleau. The great beefy Madame at my hotel had just fallen downstairs and broken her arm. It must have been an almighty crash! She let me have a room, but she was too encumbered with plaster and sling to prepare it for me. I went out shopping and came back to find a little stick-thin man with a weasel face changing my bed. Could that be Monsieur?

In Fontainebleau, I spent half the morning sheltering from torrential rain in the Palace. It was Napoleon's favourite residence, his '*vraie demeure des rois*'. Every square centimetre was extravagantly gilded and ornamented in Empire style. It was the décor of a megalomaniac, so suffocating that even the rain outside was preferable. I escaped into the huge, magnificent forest, once a royal hunting ground, and cycled its paths and peaceful roads for hour upon magical hour.

Near Moret-sur-Loing, where Sisley lived and painted for twenty years, the Seine spread out over shelving ground into a complex network of channels, weirs and pools. We were nearing the end of our journey together, some 350 miles (560 km) from Le Havre. One farewell stretch beside a railway line and we were in Montereau. I felt quite a wrench when my familiar Seine flowed off to the left, to its source in Burgundy's Côte d'Or, while I had to take the right fork, down the River Yonne.

It had been so easy to stay within sight of the Seine. The Yonne was more difficult. I often found myself far away from the river banks, puffing through a chain of small villages, mostly called something or other 'sur Yonne', and all on hilltops. I had got out of the way of climbs on my comfortable ride along the Seine and I resented the struggle. Muttering grumpily to myself in the rain and the failing light, I pulled up at the first hotel I saw, just outside Pont de Yonne.

It was one of those small hotels that survive in rural France but nowhere else in Europe. It had brown lino on the floors, candlewick bedspreads transparent with washing, and no private facilities. Two elderly sisters were the proprietors. They were short, stout little ladies, almost cuboid in shape, and extremely determined. When I arrived, they were playing cards in the bar with a couple of men, while the other male regulars squinted at the game through clouds of cigarette smoke. Fortunately, they took to me, referring to me as '*la petite femme*', though I was head and shoulders taller than they were. They joined me for dinner in the bar, because they wanted to know if Prince Charles would marry Camilla. They were very keen on our Royals, especially Prince William. 'We cried for hours when Diana died.'

I said I would be leaving at about 9.30, and at 9.28 exactly one of them was on the phone, asking if I was ready to go. They were off to do the weekly shop (6 litres of moules, etc.) and were decked out in their best clothes. 'You should get some different shoes,' was their parting shot. 'You can't cycle properly in those.' Pont de Yonne is very near Sens, the ancient home of a fierce Gallic tribe, the Senones, who crossed the Alps and dared to attack the fledgling city of Rome. The Romans repelled their first assault, because they were woken by the honking of geese, but the Senones were not ones to give up. They went back three years later and entered the city in triumph. I watched the two solid little sisters march over to their elderly Renault, shoulders back and determined chins in the air, and I knew exactly what the Romans had had to contend with.

The Yonne was my link between the Seine and the start of the Burgundy Canal at Migennes. I followed its murky waters across flattish arable land, where the fields were vast and there were no trees to protect me from a blustery south wind. It was not an attractive river. It flowed impressively enough under its six wide arches through Joigny, the first of Burgundy's wine centres, and left the town prettily enough along a road shaded with fine copper beeches. But rivers have characters, like people and animals, and this one failed to win me over. I was glad to finish my short stretch and embark on my next major waterway.

4. THE BURGUNDY CANAL

Two roads diverged in a wood and I –
I took the one less travelled by,
And that has made all the difference.

Robert Frost, 'The Road not Taken'

Imagine a tranquil path, shaded by poplars, where the only sounds are the rustle of leaves and the cries of waterfowl. This path runs through smiling valleys of maize and sunflowers, past peaceful hills where sheep graze, and climbs into the dense green clefts of wooded mountains. It travels for 155 traffic-free miles (250 km) through the loveliest countryside in France, with castles on crags, ancient monasteries and some of the world's noblest vineyards. Hidden from view, it passes through only one city, Dijon, and that secretly, through a park and a *port de plaisance*. Too good to be true? No. This 'less travelled road' exists and it runs beside the Burgundy Canal.

The Burgundy is France's most ambitious man-made waterway. Other French canals were cut across relatively easy terrain, but to link the Seine with the Saône and the Rhône, the Burgundy Canal had to scale mountains. Its highest point is an amazing 1,240 feet (378 m) above sea level and it takes 115 locks to get up there.

It is France's beautiful white elephant. As far back as François 1er, the kings of France dreamed of a waterway which would carry traffic from the Atlantic to the Mediterranean. Work started on a number of occasions but had to be abandoned when the money ran out. Then in 1783, in the epic age of canal-building, the Duchy of Burgundy decided to cut three canals from the River Saône – to the Seine, the Loire and the Rhine. According to the waterside monument in Dijon, the first stone of the Burgundy Canal was laid by the Prince de Condé in 1786. In 1808, the first barge from the Saône arrived in the Dijon Basin, but it was not until 1833 that the first vessel arrived from Paris, to great jubilation. The Burgundy Canal was one of the splendid achievements of the Industrial Age, but it came just a little too late. Like the Pony Express across America, it was soon made redundant by the railways. Bargees found its ladders of locks exhausting and time-consuming, so industrialists switched to trains and other, easier canals as soon as they were able. Today, there is virtually no commercial traffic on the canal, but it has been saved from dereliction by the increasing number of holiday boatmen who have discovered its gentle charms. For the long-distance sailor, it still offers a sheltered passage across France from the English Channel to the Mediterranean, but it requires patience. The maximum speed is about 6 mph (10 kph), progress at night is banned and there are all those locks to contend with! I would rather brave the Bay of Biscay myself.

The Canal begins near the great railway marshalling yards of Laroche-Migennes. The Yonne turns south there and its merry, chattering little tributary, the Alençon, comes into view. This was my first clear-water stream. It came tumbling down from the mountains on its pebbly bed and I followed it south-east along the canal into the heart of Burgundy.

From the canal basin, two lines of dense trees marched off into the distance, rigid as an exercise in perspective, casting gloom over the water. I cycled round to the first lock in Migennes to join the towpath. There was a decent gravel surface on the right bank as far as the second lock, where I crossed over and followed the metalled left-hand path for a mile or so. After that, both sides deteriorated to gravel and mud, interspersed with large loose stones and lakes where the potholes lay. It was yet another drizzly morning under a grey sky. The canal ran straight as a die. The soggy path was flat and deserted. No boats, no other cyclists, no fishermen, no waterfowl or swans, just one solitary man in a raincoat, loitering. He looked like every parent's dread, and he was a little unnerving even for a grown-up cyclist. There was a railway-line on one side and thick bushes and trees on the other, so I was shut off from the countryside. I felt vulnerable. As I struggled and skidded along, the spooky emptiness got to me.

I had so looked forward to cycling along the Burgundy Canal. It looked idyllic in photographs, but they were always taken in sunshine. With rain filling the puddles, I decided that Hell was a muddy green corridor. I hurried back to the second lock, where I could join the nearest road. It would take me through towns and villages, where there were people going about their daily lives, and give me a variety of scenery, not one interminable ruler, screened off from the world by bushes.

It was quicker along the roads and I enjoyed the map-reading challenge. In places, the nearest tarmac was in fact the towpath, widened. In others, the climb to a village was so steep that even the soggy path, far below, looked tempting. As I cycled further into Burgundy, past Tonnerre and Ancy le Franc, the flat lands of the great river basins began their ascent into seriously hilly terrain.

At Chassignelles, on a rare fine morning, I gave the Burgundy Canal a second chance. There were still puddles, fallen leaves and muddy sections, but on the whole the chalky gravel of the higher ground was firmer under-wheel. And the canal was more open-sided, with wide views of maize fields and sheep-dotted hills. I was still the only cyclist, but the locks were getting closer together as the canal climbed, so I was always in sight of a lock and a safety exit from the path. Lock-keepers were scarce. Many of the old lock-cottages are now holiday homes and one keeper has charge of a number of locks, riding back and forth between them on his little Mobilette. As the day wore on, the sunshine brought out the local anglers, some with as many as six rods in a row. Two mountain-bikers came breezing down from the summit and I stopped for a chat with a gnarled old countryman, who was grazing three sheep beside the towpath. The menace of the lower, waterlogged reaches seemed a world away and I began to enjoy the ride.

Between Poullenay and Charigny there was a real lock-ladder, thirty-one locks in six miles! I overtook a barge that was making its laborious way through them – about ten hours' work, according to the *Navicarte Regionale* – and I was happy to be on two speeding wheels. No matter how steep the encircling hills, I was always on ground as level as the water, until I came to a lock, when a burst of speed or a bit of a push took me up the short, sharp rise to the next flat stretch. It was a painless way to climb a mountain.

But it was too good to last. The rain came down again and the path deteriorated. There is no overall canal authority responsible for the upkeep of the towpaths. 'It's the local councils who look after them,' said a lock-keeper. His Alsatian had just given me a nasty fright and he had come out of his cottage to apologise and pass the time of day. 'Some councils are more serious than others. Most of them try to keep one path clear, the one near the lock-keeper's house, so we can drive our cars. But there are plenty of lazy devils around. Just look at those brambles over there! You'll have to take the D970.'

Burgundy hides its towns and villages in the folds of the hills. I could pass within a mile of sizeable cities and still not notice them. When I did pass through a village, it was often squat and unattractive. Unlike the white Caen stone of the Normandy abbeys, the dingy grey of the Burgundy churches did little to raise the spirits. It was all heavy – the rain, the stone, even the food.

The local cuisine is designed for hearty meat-eaters. I'm a pretty good eater myself, especially after a day in the saddle, but Burgundy was too much even for my ostrich digestion. The starters were meals in themselves – two boiled eggs in wine sauce or a giant slice of rich pâté being the local favourites. Desperate for some greenstuff, I lit up one evening when I saw 'Burgundy Salad' on the menu. When it arrived, it was a few miserable lettuce leaves, smothered in bacon bits and crôutons, topped off with a poached egg. '*C'est autre chose!*' said the waiter, beaming proudly. That heap of protein was followed by a delicious, but button-bursting, boeuf bourgignon, a huge slice of apple pie (which I had to pass over) and a fantastic cheese board, all washed down with a dense, velvety Burgundy. After a few evenings, I could face these gargantuan meals no longer. I shopped for bedroom picnics of plain ham, bread and apples.

A final twelve-lock ladder, and the Burgundy Canal reached its summit at Pouilly-en-Auxois. There it disappeared into a dank, narrow 2-mile (3,333 m) tunnel without towpaths. In the old days, it took solid legwork to push a barge through and, even today, when barges have engines, it is only the bravest bargees who venture into the blackness. Most pleasure cruisers ply the canal from the Seine to Pouilly-en-Auxois and back again, or steam up and down the popular section between Pouilly and Dijon. The canal runs under the town and a double line of trees, with stone airshafts at intervals, marks its path. A busy traffic roundabout crowns its apex. I followed the avenue of trees to Créancey and saw the canal emerge in a wild, overgrown bit of woodland. A notice said that the tunnel was excavated between 1826 and 1832, six years' labour. Just beyond it, I chatted to the lock-keeper at the great basin of Éscommes. In the days when traffic was heavy, the barges used to assemble there to go through the one-way tunnel, two convoys a day in each direction.

The lock-keeper and his friend in a little white van advised me on the route ahead. There was fine smooth gravel as far as La Répé, then the right bank became the D18. The little white van kept popping up, to make sure I knew the way. It was a breezy downhill ride from the densely wooded mountains around Pouilly-en-Auxois, through a narrow steep-sided valley, which gradually widened out towards the riverbed below. What should have been a sweeping, majestic view across the Côte d'Or was marred by mist and rainclouds on the distant hills, but the sun broke through overhead and, for once, I was cycling in the dry.

At Pont d'Ouche, the canal made a dog-leg turn to join the fast-flowing little River Ouche on its north-easterly run towards Dijon. On the sharp bend, I met four elderly Americans, cycling a little tentatively. They were passengers on a hotel barge, which was plying the canal between Dijon and Vandenesse-en-Auxois, and they wore identical navy-blue windcheaters bearing the logo of their tour company. The barge carried enough bicycles for all its passengers and provided maps with suggested rides.

'But where do you stay at night?' they cried in horror, when I told them I was cycling the canal on my own.

'In hotels. There are plenty around.'

'But what are they like?'

'They vary, like hotels everywhere. I always find somewhere reasonably comfortable.'

'Aren't you scared?' they asked. 'We cycle round a lot in the daytime, but it's good to know that we've always got the barge to go back to in the evenings. Private showers, sitting area, a nice meal, nice folk to talk to. How do you start looking for some place around here?'

'Well, there's a hotel over there for a start. Just across the road. That looks OK.'

'How do you know it's OK?'

'I go and look.'

'Rather you than me!' they chorused.

I passed their barge a little further along the canal. The rest of the bicycles lay in a neglected stack on the aft deck, while the four wives sat with the rest of the passengers and peered at France through the safety of the lounge windows. I expect they thought their four cyclist husbands were madly daring. To me, they were wise old men. They had not travelled far before and there they were, dipping their toes into France. On their next trip, they might dare to inch a little further out into the stream.

At Pont de Pany, on the approach to Dijon, I was startled to find the right bank of the canal turning into a motorway. The left bank was flooded in stretches, but at least it had been cleared of brambles. I battled my way along, using my Indian monsoon technique – just pedal like mad and hope there are no sharp nails down there. At Velas, Lock 45, the towpath was suddenly, magically, transformed. A smooth designated cycle-path, all beautiful floodless, mudless tarmac, sped along under my wheels and I entered Dijon in style.

Out in search of dinner, I first tried the attractive-looking restaurant in the hotel next door and was deafened by the shouting. It was the next group of Americans bound for a barge on the Burgundy Canal.

'Where y'all from?' yelled a voice from the deep South. 'Georgia? Son of a gun! So are we!'

Americans, particularly Americans on holiday, are like warm, exuberant puppy dogs. I knew, if I stayed, I should be swept up in the general sociability and I didn't feel strong enough. I had just cycled all the way down to Dijon from Pouilly-en-Auxois, only about 37 miles (60 km) admittedly, but hard going, with research to do on the way. I was in need of peace and quiet.

I was unlucky. I chose a small Italian restaurant, where my table was dangerously close to that of a university lecturer-cum-business consultant. He soon engaged me in conversation and talked about the solution of company problems until I was cross-eyed. I could make no contribution at all to his harangue, because I found him so difficult to follow. I suppose I should have felt flattered that he thought me capable of discussing the limitations of Cartesian logic when seeking business solutions. Like Red Riding Hood's grand-mother, he had a mouth overfull of large, dangerous teeth. He flashed me wolf-like grins and pushed his spectacles up over his wiry hair whenever he made a telling point. He was fifty times more exhausting than any group from Georgia. But I gained one interesting piece of information. I am *de l'âge canonique*, old enough for the Vatican to allow me to keep house for a priest!

The next morning, a cold, clammy fog had settled over the city, so I kept myself warm in the magnificent Ducal Palace. I returned in imagination to the clear light of the Normandy coast. There were Boudin studies of Honfleur and two paintings of the famous sea-arch at Étretat. In the one by Courbet, wild seas came crashing through; Monet's was blue and peaceful. My fellow-Nottinghamian, Richard Parkes Bonington, was represented by *Normandy Coast at Low Tide*, where the sky was reflected in pools of silver, dissolving on the sand into beige and grey, with flashes of blue and white. I emerged from the Musée des Beaux Arts into a murky drizzle. Dijon is a noble city. A strategic post on the Celtic tin route from the Seine to the Adriatic, it prospered under its powerful dukes, who at times were wealthier and more influential than the kings of France. There are fine mediaeval and renaissance buildings, shops to tempt the rich and discerning, and gourmet food to die for. But nowhere looks at its best in the rain. I gave up sightseeing and spent the afternoon reading.

Egypt being one of my themes, I was delighted to find that the monument to the opening of the Burgundy Canal was a fine obelisk. The Luxor obelisk given by Mohammed Ali to King Louis Philippe had just arrived in Paris when the canal was completed and the Duchy of Burgundy must have been swept along on the wave of popular enthusiasm for all things Egyptian. The obelisk towered over the *port de plaisance*, dwarfing the trees in the waterside park.

When I left the obelisk behind me, it was actually a sunny morning, though the towpath was still muddy after the rain and I had a strong south wind to contend with. Would the weather never be kind? Canals are cuts in the earth, following the low ground between hills, so they are usually sheltered. But the last lap of the Burgundy Canal crosses a plain, where the wind whistles through the maize. It was a sociable ride though. There were groups of long-distance walkers along the path. I don't usually care for walking, as I find it too slow, but booted feet can negotiate puddles and stones far better than wheels. Perhaps I should enjoy a walk along the canal, provided I had company to ease the boredom on the flat, straight bits. I rested a while and watched a man training his young labrador to jump in and out of the canal on command. The puppy loved the water and was always eager to jump in. Getting him out was quite a different matter, especially if he saw ducks. There were anglers crouching on little camp-stools under wide umbrellas and I stopped for the occasional chat. They were fishing for carp and pike, but only one had had any success. His catch lay beside him on the grass, under the predatory eye of a tall grey crane.

At St Jean-de-Losne, the Burgundy Canal reaches its destination, joining the navigable River Saône. I celebrated the end of the muddy towpaths with a picnic lunch on the lawn of the last lock-keeper's cottage. He kindly brought me a plastic table and chair. It had taken me the whole morning to cycle the last 18 miles (30 km) from Dijon, but I was not totally put off the canal. I had just been unfortunate. In such a wet season the towpaths were always soggy under-wheel, even when it was not actually raining. In a dry, sunny summer, the ride would have been a spectacular doddle. One day, I shall travel again down that less travelled road and hope for better weather.

5. THE RHÔNE

I doubt whether I ever read any description of scenery which gave me an idea of the place described.

Anthony Trollope, *Australia and New Zealand*

The Saône is the Rhône's most important tributary, a significant river in its own right, but for me, it was just a three-day ride. As I set off downstream, I reflected on Trollope's view. The river was famous for its scenery, and if it was a waste of time writing about that, what else was there to write about? The weather? I had decided to stop moaning about the weather, unless it was really extreme. I would accept rain as the normal condition of my life and say no more about it. Wine? There was no time for an oenophilic tour of the Burgundy vineyards and, in any case, there was nowhere on my bike to store purchases. I could only hope to meet the region's fine vintages at dinner. People? Western Europe is not America or the East. The French are self-contained, as we are, and conversation rarely bubbles up spontaneously. When my bicycle draws up to a hotel in Turkey, for instance, everyone bursts with curiosity. Who am I? Where am I from? Where am I going? What am I doing? Why? In no time, they know my life history and I know theirs, and we are drinking tea together. In France, I wheel my bicycle before the glazed eyes of a receptionist, who goes through the room formalities, showing little interest in me and none at all in Condor. Conversation has to be nurtured, and I have to do all the nurturing. People who have ventured no further than Western Europe may have been sure of their creature comforts, but they have missed out on the real camaraderie of travel.

I had such a struggle with the south wind that it was late afternoon by the time I arrived in Verdun sur Doubs. There I came up against that great Continental hazard, the hotel closing day. Two of the three hotels were having their weekly day off and the gîte was about 9 miles (14 km) out of town, further than I felt I could cope with. So I ended up in a costly 'hostellerie' out of the exclusive *Chateaux and Grand Hotels of France* booklet. The cheapest menu was almost £30 for two courses, without wine – very expensive by French standards – and consisted of local specialities. I had moved out of the region of ducks and geese and was now into snails, frogs' legs, perch and pike, none of which I fancied. I excused myself, telling the eager young chef-proprietor that I was too tired after a hard day's cycling to do justice to such exquisite fare. I staggered across the road to the Atac supermarket and bought a picnic supper of sandwiches, fruit and wine. After a lot of nurturing the next morning, the pleasant young man began to talk. He told me that he dreamed of walking the pilgrim road to Santiago de Compostela. I had cycled that road a few years back, so we actually had an animated conversation. He said he couldn't wait for his retirement. Then he, like me, could have adventures on the road. He gave me a reduction on my bill.

The Saône is a calm, domestic sort of river, with pleasure steamers and families in motor boats. My road ran close to the water, through peaceful villages and ancient towns with fine Romanesque churches. It was holiday country and I mingled with anglers, strollers and other cyclists along the quais. Every small town seemed to be making an effort to lure tourists with some unusual attraction – an international police museum, a fire brigade museum, or a festival of sheep. I liked the idea of sheep partying! At Chalon sur Saône, another obelisk stood in the town centre, this one celebrating the opening of the Canal du Centre. I was seeing obelisks everywhere.

I crossed and recrossed the river, seeking out the nearest roads. On one or two stretches, this meant that I had to cycle along the notorious N6. I kept passing life-sized black cut-outs, sinister men with crimson saltires slashed across their chests, and I realised that they marked accident black spots. They came thick and fast as I travelled down the highway, which was perhaps not surprising, considering the area. St Amour, Macon, Chardonnay, Juliénas, Morgon – the signposts read like a high-class vintner's catalogue.

The British are said to be the world's greatest dog-lovers, but the French are rapidly catching up. In fact, in one respect they have gone beyond us. One day, in the depths of the country, I spotted what I thought might be another obelisk poking out above the trees. It was not quite the right shape, being cylindrical, but it was in such a rural spot that it couldn't possibly be a factory chimney. What was it? I went to investigate. It was the chimney of a pet crematorium. Beside the building was a Wall of Remembrance, where the urns containing the ashes of little Fido and Puss were laid to rest in niches, each marked with name, dates and a touching verse. Once I was aware of them, I began to see pet crematoria all over the place. I was reminded of the time I stayed with friends of friends in Albuquerque and shared the spare room with the ashes of Trixie and Spot.

It was the Tour de France. Every morning there were highlights of the previous day's stage on television, so whenever it rained, I stayed in my hotel room till check-out time, watching other people cycling. Their endurance astonished me. After 120 miles (200 km) of racing, when they had *only* another 12 miles (20 km) to go, they started their sprints to the finish. Where did they find the energy to sprint after that distance? And to do it day after day, sometimes over mountains? It must be the toughest, most gruelling sport in existence. It certainly put my own poor cycling into perspective. I watched in admiration. I particularly liked the aerial views, when I could see the long mass of cyclists flowing round the bends, like a beautiful multicoloured serpent.

Lyon is the transport hub of the south, a monstrous tangle of speeding motorways. I still remember the terror I felt when I once had to drive round the Périférique, the city's unofficial Silverstone. The signs were bewildering. Trucks and cars flashed in and out of the exit lanes, dodging in front of me and hooting with the rage of drivers who knew exactly where they were going, while I was just struggling to stay alive. I was not looking forward to entering that urban jungle on a bicycle.

But the day I cycled into Lyon was one of my best cycling days ever. After a night in the Saône-side town of Belleville, in a hotel with the delightful name of 'L'Ange Couronné', the Crowned Angel, I crossed over to the left bank of the river and picked up the tranquil D993. It followed the course of the Saône through sunny, stone-built villages at the foot of wooded hills. Even on the outskirts of Lyon, the country was amazingly rural. The mountains of the Mont d'Or loomed across the river, but I was cycling on the flatter bank, past slopes and islands luxuriant with trees. One of these islands, L'Île Barbe, so charmed Charlemagne that he built a library in its woods. There was hardly time to register surprise at this easy ride. By mid-morning I was in Lyon itself, and there was not a motorway in sight. I rode through the stunningly beautiful gorge, gouged out by the Saône between the hills of Fourvière and La Croix Rousse, and I was on the city quais. My road had led me simply and painlessly into the very heart of Lyon. I reached Quai Tilsit, opposite the cathedral, turned left and wheeled my bicycle down the Rue Victor Hugo, Lyon's lively pedestrian centre.

It was love at first sight. Lyon may be France's second city, an important industrial and banking centre, but there is none of the harshness and stress associated with its northern equivalents, cities such as Birmingham and Stuttgart. The Lyonnais are relaxed and affable. They know how to enjoy themselves in a civilized way over the pleasures of the table. (It is no accident that Rabelais, the creator of such celebrated eaters as Gargantua and Master Gaster, should have practised medicine in Lyon. It was a famed gastronomic centre, even in the Renaissance.) In the evenings, they stroll past the elegant shops – not just peering at fripperies like silks and handbags, but buying books, pricing antiques and having earnest conversations in dusty little workshops for the repair of ancient clocks, or the restoration of tapestries. The affluent drink aperitifs in pavement cafés, while groups of students loll around outside, putting the world to rights over slices of pizza. It has the feel of an old university city rather than a commercial powerhouse.

Its charm lies in its geography, at the confluence of two majestic waterways. Here the River Rhône, flowing westwards down from Switzerland and the Alps, meets the south-flowing Saône. Together, over the centuries, they have built up a broad peninsula, the Presqu'Île. It was such a magnificent situation that the Romans made it their capital of the Three Gauls. For strategic reasons, they founded their city, Lugdunum, on the right bank of the Saône, where they could command the confluence from the towering height of Fourvière hill. The mediaeval city straggled down from the same summit, but as Lyon grew in wealth and importance, the silk weavers crossed the Saône to the Croix Rousse district and the centre of gravity moved to the Presqu'Île, round the monumental Place Bellecourt. This is the area where I stayed, in the modern centre of things, near the Place Ampère. A military band played jaunty music in the square, presided over by a statue of the great physicist himself, whose amps are the measure of all our electrical currents. He was flanked, I was pleased to see, by two male sphinxes. Brothers of the four in the Paris Place du Châtelet, they were vomiting water in the same unlovely manner. It seemed incongruous that creatures born of Egypt's sand should decorate fountains.

The city grew up around the Saône, because the banks of the Rhône were a problem. When the Alpine snows melted, the Rhône rushed brimming and turbulent through the city, flooding the low-lying ground. But eighteenth- and nineteenth-century engineering got the better of it. Canals were dug to siphon off the seasonal surplus and the Presqu'Île, protected now by high embankments, was extended southwards from the Place Bellecour to form the new district of Perrache, named after one of the chief engineers. What used to be flood plain on the Rhône's left bank became valuable building land, and the final phase of Lyon's development moved eastwards in a burst of vehicle factories, chemical and engineering plants and workers' housing. The present-day city is so agreeable because it is really two cities in one. Its industrial engine is completely separate, across the Rhône, from its leisurely, citizen-friendly heart.

There was so much to see in Lyon that I knew I would have to go back to explore it thoroughly, with a different budget, a different wardrobe and a different agenda. With only two days to spare, and a passion for museums, how could I possibly decide between them? There were too many enticing options, from Roman remains to the museum of silks and fabrics. So I visited none of them. I concentrated on the rivers. I rode the cable car up to the esplanade in front of the Basilica of Notre Dame de Fourvière, where I got a splendid view of both the Saône and the Rhône, as they made their stately progress under the city's bridges. But best of all, I took a cruise.

I boarded the *Navig'inter* boat by the Pont Napoleon, opposite La Cathédrale St Jean, and chugged down the Saône to the confluence. The two great rivers merge at a long, narrow spit of pale sand. The Hindus worship at the place where rivers meet. To them, a confluence is so holy that a bathe in its waters washes away sin; and if the ashes of the dead are scattered there, they are purified. Not being a Hindu, I have my doubts about all this. But I have to admit that the merging of rivers is an impressive, almost mystical sight. Small rivers are lively. They join forces eagerly, chattering as they grow in strength and tumble together down the steep mountainsides. In the Karakorams, I have followed the new-born Khunjerab from its trickle out of a snowfield, through rocky gorges, to its merger with the fledgling Hunza. I rode beside their combined stream as it raced down over rocks and stones to join the wider Gilgit, which in turn crashed with a roar into the mighty Indus. Small mergers are noisy, but when the confluence is the meeting of two great rivers, each one wide and powerful in its own right, their coming together is majestically silent. That afternoon in Lyon, there was not so much as a ripple over the sandy spit. The water flowed softly, as smooth as satin. What was remarkable was the change in colour. As we rounded the bend from the brown Saône into the Rhône, we sailed out on to dark, jewel-green waters.

Cruising along the Rhône past the fine avenues of plane trees, the nineteenth-century esplanade and the prosperous bourgeois architecture, we arrived at Le Pont Lafayette. Its sturdy central piers were ornamented with classical statues, a female nude on the west pier and a large, bearded male on the east. The young, voluptuous female was the Saône, half-recumbent and langorous. Her senior, the River Rhône, struck a more vigorous attitude, grasping a staff in his left hand. Both rested their right hands on the heads of lions, which were so benign that they seemed to be smiling; and both were surrounded by fishes and bunches of grapes. The city's symbol and the produce of its teeming river basin came together in two allegorical tableaux. This bridge was our turning point. The boat described an arc, then steamed back down the green Rhône to the confluence and the brown Saône.

My fellow passengers were mostly British. Paris had been swarming with elderly American couples. In Lyon, it was the British who were walking along hand-in-hand. They both wore sandals, drip-dry clothes and those detachable sun-flaps which fit over spectacles. He generally carried the backpack. 'Did you hear the carillon?' asked the guide as one group piled back into their coach. 'Yes, marvellous – merveuse. Is that how you say it?' They were tentative, timid and anxious to please, and my heart went out to them.

I had moved a long way south from Calais and when the sun shone, it burned. So I set my alarm for 6.30, to get a good start in the cool of the morning. And guess what? I woke up to rain. But

I set out from Lyon all the same, squeaking along in my waterproofs. I crossed the Rhône by the Pont Lafayette, cycling over the heads of the two river gods, and was immediately in the other Lyon, the one the tourist never sees. There were poor districts, where the unemployed, many of them North African, were trudging through the rain to the shops. Then came smarter suburbs, villas with gardens and modern apartment blocks. Further out still, on the very fringes of the Greater Lyon conurbation, I passed through huge industrial zones. Manufacturing has moved out to these new conglomerations, to have easy access to the motorways and airport, taking the jobs away from the inner working-class areas. Because of the canals, there was no route out of Lyon along the Rhône itself, but I did run parallel to the Canal de Jonage. When I joined the river itself, out in the country towards Anthon, it was an even purer green. It was the green of conifers, of spruce trees, whose needles almost verge on blue. There was not the slightest hint of yellow, brown or olive. I have seen many beautiful rivers. The deep sky-blue of the Indus, as it flows down from the mountains of Kashmir, takes a lot of beating. But I think the loveliest colour of all is the true, unsullied green of the Rhône.

As usual, I took the longer routes, following every bend of the river. Sometimes I would come to a fork in the road, where one sign pointed to, say, Belley by the tourist route and the other would be the route to Belley advised for heavy vehicles. These 'tourist routes' invariably climbed mountains, so I found myself in the unusual situation for a cyclist of deliberately picking out the roads with trucks on them. Fortunately, there were very few. Most were zooming along the motorways, leaving me to travel alone along tranquil tree-shaded lanes.

The Rhône began its climb into the Jura. There were wooded mountains, but what should have been a spectacular landscape was hidden in cloud. Le Grand Colombier was covered head and shoulders, and disconsolate families in raincoats and shorts wandered round the mountain resorts, waiting for the sky to clear. The evenings were grey and cold.

On my worst day (a day so extremely dire that I think a moan about the weather is fully justified!), I had a great climb up from Frangy in pouring rain, then a steep descent into Bellegarde, on which I maddeningly lost all the altitude I had struggled to gain.

Then another great climb, at the top of which the heavens opened even wider and a hurricane blew. I sheltered for over an hour in the only available place, under the narrow eve of a wayside telephone station, but that simply directed the torrents into a few soaking streams, instead of allowing them to fall thinner and wider. When it calmed down to a drizzle and a mere gale, I continued down the mountain and found myself at the mouth of a 200-metre tunnel, with no alternative route for cyclists. There was nothing for it but to cross my fingers and sprint through.

There were traffic lights controlling the flow of vehicles in alternate directions. I waited for the one on my side to turn red, then darted into the tunnel. If I pedalled like crazy, I might just get through before the next wave of traffic came up behind me. Travelling through a tunnel in a car, with the windows tightly shut, gives no idea of the monstrous, reverberating din of trucks on the unprotected ear. As vehicles surged towards me out of the gloom, I thought my eardrums would burst. There was no lighting in the tunnel and I had no lights on my bicycle. I just had to pray that no oncoming car would be mad enough to try to overtake a truck in the dark. I had moments of sheer, blind terror before I broke through into daylight, a split second ahead of the next stream of cars. My heart was pounding like a sledge-hammer and once I was out in safety, my knees turned to jelly. I had to get off and prop myself up against a wall, until my pulse slowed down and I stopped trembling. Had I known how terrifying the noise would be, I would have waited at the entrance, all night if necessary, for some kindly lorry driver to give me a lift through.

I got over the next hill, then had to take shelter under a bridge through the worst of another downpour. The rain clouds had drifted so low that they were now lying as mist over the road, making cycling dangerous. I had been aiming for Geneva, but I had to give up at Farges, just a few miles short. When I stripped down for a hot shower, I found that the rainwater had penetrated my waterproofs and soaked right through to my well-hidden passport and credit cards. It had been another frustrating day, when I had covered less than 20 miles (32 km), despite an early start and the best intentions.

The first time I cycled round the world, I crossed the Jura and reached Lake Geneva at Lausanne. I had never seen such torrential rain. On my present trip, I crossed the Jura by another route and came down to the lake at Geneva. The weather was identical. Is it always like that in the Jura, or have I just been unlucky?

I had so looked forward to my first visit ever to Geneva, but dripping red waterproofs and a sodden woolly hat were hardly the clothes to be seen in. It was such an opulent city. Rolls Royces and Ferraris swept past its commercial banks and glittering boutiques. Sheltering my camera lens as best I could from the downpour, I took a few photographs of the Rhône as it glided out of Lake Geneva under a series of wide road bridges. Then I slunk away on my modest bicycle, feeling like a pauper at the feast. Grey water, grey sky, grey buildings. It should have been possible to see the Alps, but the clouds hung down so low that I was lucky if I could see the nearest hill. I rounded the end of the lake and soldiered on. At least there were decent cycle-paths along the lake shore.

Yvoire, the first place beyond Geneva, was a 'mediaeval city'. Picturesque to the point of parody, it seethed with day-trippers. I took one look at its quaint cobbled streets and shops full of tourist tat, and decided to carry on to Thonon. There the hotels were all full. I was just about to turn away in despair from the last possibility when Madame took pity on me.

'I do have one small room,' she said, 'but I hardly like to offer it to a lady. It doesn't have a bathroom.'

'A lady like me, out in the pouring rain on a bicycle, late in the evening, would be glad of some straw in a cowshed, provided it was dry! A private bathroom is the least of my worries.'

She led me out to a dear little wooden chalet in the garden, my haven in the storm.

When I wandered across to the dining room for dinner, I saw why all the hotels in Thonon were full. It was a holiday resort, where people stayed for a fortnight 'en pension'. The restaurant reminded me of *Monsieur Hulot's Holiday*. The pensionnaires all greeted one another ceremoniously and enquired about their day. Most were elderly French couples. The women were wearing smart dresses and were well coiffed. They talked cheerfully to the women on adjacent tables, while their husbands, dry old sticks in cardigans, sat silent. The women were the energetic partners. They had probably suggested the holiday, picked the resort, booked the hotel and done the packing for both of them. All the old chaps had to do was drive the car.

Having photographed the Rhône's exit in Geneva, I wanted to take corresponding photos of its entry at the east end of the lake, but the river forms a wide delta there and its main stream was not clearly defined. I gave up trying to get a good view and began to cycle away. There was a horrible grating noise and I could scarcely turn the back wheel. I inspected it carefully. There was nothing visibly wrong. Perhaps the brake was catching. I am not a good mechanic, but that never causes problems, as I always manage to break down near a bike shop. This time an excellent cycle emporium was just five minutes' walk away. I explained my difficulty. 'Wheel your bicycle across the shop and let me look at it,' said the mechanic. 'Hm. Would it have anything to do with this, I wonder?' he enquired mildly, waving the unattached hook of one of my bungees, which was catching in the spokes. It was utterly shaming. How could a round-the-world cyclist be so incompetent?

Switzerland is a wonderful country for cycling. It took me by surprise, because I always think of the Alps when I think of Switzerland, and they are only for Kings of the Mountains. But first I rode along the low southern shore of Lake Geneva, then I followed the Rhône as it wove its way through the Valais, a smiling plain of vines and apricot orchards. I had never dared imagine that Switzerland could be so flat. According to my map, the Dents du Midi towered over the Valais on one side and Les Diablerets on the other, but I never got a good view of them. Yet I had two sunny days, and enjoyed my ride along superb roads with light traffic. Motorists were extremely polite, always stopping at pedestrian crossings. There were cycle-paths everywhere, swept clear of glass and nails, and as well maintained as the car-lanes. Many were dedicated asphalt tracks, which ran through fields and copses, well away from the exhaust fumes of the road. For once, I was not cycling on potholed poor relations. Martial, the chef-proprietor of L'Auberge de Vouvry, my first Swiss hotel, went in for road-racing. According to the chatty young man at reception, he had already cycled 2,000 miles (over 3,000 km) that season as part of his training. His dashing red and yellow racer kept my orange Condor company in the basement. I had a light supper in the brasserie, as Martial's main restaurant was one of the 'Grandes Tables de Suisse', far too grand for me and my cycling wardrobe. So I didn't meet him until he came over to my table at breakfast time.

'I've been looking at your bike,' he said. 'Very nice. I've brought it up from the cellar for you. It's just outside the door. I gave it a quick check-over first and I thought the back tyre could do with a bit more air, so I've pumped it up for you.'

Now that's what I call service from the proprietor of a hotel!

Despite the well-swept cycle-paths, I was bowling along with the wind behind me when I got a slow puncture in my front tyre. Right on cue, a Firestone tyre specialist appeared across the road. The young mechanic had obviously lived all his life with cars and had no idea how to change a bicycle inner-tube. His boss came out of the rear office, watched him with wry amusement for a while, then took over and changed it expertly himself. He had grown up in the days when boys went to school, and young men did their courting, on bicycles. My problem solved, I managed to speed into Sion before the next storm. Thunder rolled over the invisible mountains and lightning split the flying clouds. 'We've walked from Chamonix,' wailed four American academics in my hotel, 'and we haven't seen a single mountain yet!'

It was time for some serious thinking. I planned to follow the Agène, a tributary of the Rhône, up to the Nufenen Pass. Its source lay just below the col. I saw from the map that I could cycle up beside the river (or push up beside it!) almost the whole way. On the other side, just below the col, rose the River Ticino, which would lead me down to the Po Valley. I was following rivers across Europe, so the Nufenen was my perfect pass. It would allow me to climb over the Alps without losing sight of water for more than a mile or so. But I was having misgivings. My friend Valerie had motored over the Nufenen Pass on her way to Italy, so that she could reconnoitre my route. She reported that there were hotels in Ulrichen, at the bottom of the ascent, but after that, there was nowhere at all to stay until I was well down the other side. The climb was less than 10 miles (16 km), but it was extremely steep and there were few people up there, even in good weather. To attempt it on my own in cold, rainy conditions and poor visibility would be downright stupid. I had to find a bad-weather alternative.

The best of a second-rate bunch seemed to be the Simplon Pass, as there was a railway line from Brig through the Simplon Tunnel to Domodossola. There I could join the River Toce and follow it down to Lake Maggiore. I hated the idea of taking the train through the Alps. It would be a major defeat, a break in my chain of rivers. But I had to be sensible. In dangerous mountain weather, it might be the best I could do. At Sion Station, they told me it was impossible to take bicycles on the Simplon trains, as they were international expresses. I doubted it. In such a cycle-friendly country, I felt sure there must be some provision for bicycles, even if they had to be despatched through the tunnel by goods train. Failing all else, I would just have to cycle up to the Simplon road tunnel and hang around in hopes of a lift in a truck. But the weather might still break. Always an optimist, I decided to wait until I got to Brig and assess the situation then. At least I had found an alternative route, which was not too far from rivers.

I spent an extra day in Sion, chatting to the mournful Americans while the rain poured down. Then, to our astonishment, we woke to a fine morning. I flew past them on the road to Brig. They were stomping out of town in their walking boots, weighed down with packs the size of small apartment blocks, while I was light as air on my speeding machine.

In Brig, I discussed my predicament with the helpful woman in charge of the tourist office. She confirmed what I had suspected all along, that there were plenty of local trains which took bicycles through the Simplon tunnel. But she enthused about the Nufenen Pass.

'The weather forecast for the next few days is excellent, for a change, and the Nufenen is spectacular, especially the Valle Bedretto on the other side. It's so beautiful – an experience not to be missed. But I don't know about climbing up there on a bicycle.' She gave me a doubtful look. 'It's very, very steep. You would need to be really *in forma* to attempt it.'

It turned out that, like most non-cyclists, she had no idea of a bicycle's potential. She was quite astonished to hear that I had cycled from Sion that morning, an easy 36-mile run (58 km) along the flat. Her eyes popped.

'If you can cycle as far as *that*, and be in Brig by lunchtime, you'll have no problem at all with the Nufenen. Go for it!'

Brig to Ulrichen was a serious climb, from 2,234 to 4,420 feet. (681–1,347 m) in the short space of 23 miles (37 km). The valley narrowed between gorges, until there was only just room for the road and railway to squeeze in beside the river. The Rhône was now a rushing torrent, frothing and foaming over the rocks. It was no longer the deep jewel green of the valleys, but a beautiful grey-green with a hint of blue, what the Greeks called *glaucos*, the colour and intensity of Pallas Athena's eyes. Ulrichen stood in the middle of a grassy plateau, so broad that I needed my bicycle to explore it. It was a village of wooden houses, each one quainter and more rickety than the last. Clouds of brilliant red geraniums spilled down from every window-sill and there were gnomes in the gardens. It was real Hansel and Gretel country. I expected Snowwhite or the Wicked Witch to pop out of a little wooden door at any moment. The mystical spot where the Agène flows into the Rhône was lost in a campsite. I cycled as far inside as I dared and saw that even the tents were little fairy-tale cottages, with windows and frilly curtains.

The other guests in my hotel made me realise how many opportunities I had missed in my childhood and how far I had to travel now to catch up. There was an English family, parents and two teenaged boys, who arrived in climbing boots, all four of them draped in serious-looking ropes and crampons. They spent the evening poring over maps and mountaineering books, discussing the best way to approach a particularly difficult climb. And there was a Swiss boy of about ten, on a walking holiday with his grandmother. They had a wonderful, easy relationship. They too were hunched up over a map, crunching apples as they planned their next day's walk. Coming from a family whose idea of a holiday was a week in Mablethorpe, I thought how very fortunate those boys were to be introduced to such a challenging activity as mountaineering by their parents. They would grow up with the confidence to tackle anything. As for a mountain-walking grand-mother – when I thought of my own two, lovable as they were, and tried to imagine them striding through the Alps in corduroys and boots, I almost laughed aloud! Our lives in Nottingham were so very different.

My own challenging day dawned bright. I managed to cycle out of the village, but that was about as far as my pedals would take me. After that, it was a steady walk. The Agène soon changed from the chattering little stream I had seen in Ulrichen to a swift torrent, cascading over rocks. My road climbed past farm buildings, until the wooded hills became too steep for cultivation. It was a relief when the broad Agène Valley broke the climb and I was able to cycle for a while. The landscape reminded me of Scotland. The trickle of river flowed across a wide, treeless expanse, with bare slopes rising above it on all sides. The only difference was the height of the surrounding mountains. It was daunting. I could see my road snaking up from the valley, and I counted thirteen loops. There was little traffic, but I watched the occasional coach slow down on a hairpin bend, drive gingerly round it, then lurch up the next straight incline. If buses were finding it so difficult, what would it be like for me? I had a snack and a drink, resting in the sunshine on a red and white fence. Then I braced my shoulders and set off.

At 15,530 feet (4,733 m) the Khunjerab Pass over the Karakorams is the most taxing pass I have ever crossed on my bicycle. The Nufenen was a mere 8,130 feet (2,477 m), which put the climb into perspective. If I could get over the Khunjerab, the Nufenen should be a doddle. The two final ascents were roughly the same length and, as far as I could judge, of the same steepness. But there the similarity ended. The Khunjerab is so high that people suffer headaches, nausea, nosebleeds and sometimes total disorientation. I was lucky. I suffered none of those, but I did find it extremely difficult to breathe in the thin air.

Up the Nufenen, I plodded steadily, enjoying the spectacle as more snow-capped peaks came into view at every bend. The hours passed and I began to flag, but I was in no hurry. The days were long and I knew that I could whizz down the other side in a flash. Provided I reached the summit by five o'clock at the latest, I should be safe. It gave me tremendous satisfaction to look down from the higher loops on the road-serpent winding below. That was all conquered territory. But then the shock came. I rounded the twelfth bend and saw that the thirteenth loop was not in fact the last one. The road ran behind the shoulder of a rock and continued to climb. By this time, I had reached the snowline and though I was not gasping, Khunjerab-style, I was getting a little short of breath. I adopted my Khunjerab technique – count one hundred paces, take a short breather, then count the next hundred.

The pass was motorbiker heaven. They overtook me in droves, racing round the loops, leaning into the curves and roaring along the straight. I was beneath notice. The overtakers who greeted me were all cyclists. '*Forza! Avanti! Coraggio!*' They all seemed to be young Italian men. It was obviously a matter of pride for them not to get off and push, even if the climb was killing them. They drank in the saddle and scattered tubes labelled 'Liquid Energy' by the roadside.

I finally reached the col at 2.15. It had taken me just over five hours to tramp up the road from Ulrichen. Feeling quite vain and infinitely superior, I queued in the Nufenen café with the groups who had come up by coach. I probably buy just one ice cream a year and this was the day I fancied it. I took my Magnum out into the sunshine and licked it in front of one of the most spectacular views in Europe. The moment was all the sweeter because it was unexpected. I never dreamed, in stormy Sion, that I would manage to cross the Alps that summer on my bicycle. But I'd made it, against the odds, and beautiful Italy lay before me, just two days' cycling away.

6. THE TICINO

There is probably no pleasure equal to the pleasure of climbing a dangerous Alp; but it is a pleasure which is confined strictly to people who can find pleasure in it.

Mark Twain, *A Tramp Abroad*

I had climbed my dangerous Alp and now I was ready for my reward. I leapt on to Condor and took off. The road zigzagged down the mountain. It began with a sharp dip from the rocky summit, a few tight bends round crags and boulders. After that, it descended far less steeply than it had risen, curving back and forth across the mountain's wide, grassy shoulder until it disappeared into the fir trees far below.

I had just rounded the first steep bend when a tiny stream came splashing down the rock beside me. I looked up and saw the new-born Ticino trickling out of a snowfield. It disappeared into a drainpipe, emerged on the other side of the road and cascaded merrily down to the next level. After that, we played leapfrog. I cycled round the tight bends and crossed it as it tunnelled under each flat stretch of road. We both broke free together. The precipitous crags gave way to gentler grassy slopes and the little Ticino tumbled into its straight run for the valley, while I released my brakes and flew like a bird. I was still freewheeling when I swooped down to the treeline and the sublimely beautiful Valle Bedretto. By this time, I was beginning to feel weary. Unbroken downhill cycling is easy on the legs, but hard on the concentration. I decided to leave my ride through the Valle until the next morning, when I would be fresh enough to appreciate it. I turned off at one of the first villages, a small mountain resort, where I found an *osteria*.

Villa was still in Switzerland. It looked Swiss, but the people spoke Italian, and they had that wonderful Italian warmth and curiosity. I was no longer a stranger, of no interest at all, provided I paid my bill. In the *osteria*, which was also the village café, my arrival on a bicycle caused a stir. And when they heard that I had cycled over the pass, which here was called not the Nufenen but Il Passo della Novena, their admiration was quite head-swelling.

I had been dreaming of Italian food. So far, in the French and German cantons of Switzerland, I had been disappointed with the cuisine. There seemed to be only one way of cooking meat or fish – smothering it in breadcrumbs and frying it. As for the salad, unless I remembered to tell the waiter that I wanted it *'nature'*, it was served in a sea of disgusting salad cream.

La Signora was apologetic when I went down for dinner. 'It's a quiet season with all this rain we've been having. There aren't many people around, so I'm afraid the menu's a bit limited. What about starting with a nice big salad from the garden, and then a good spaghettata? And some wine, of course.' Pasta and salad with Italian olive oil. It was exactly what I needed after the day's exertions. To round it off, she presented me with a bowl of home-grown strawberries. Perfect.

Apart from one small hill in Airolo and a few man-made humps such as railway bridges, my ride downhill continued for an amazing 40 miles (63 km). I sat in armchair comfort, while the glorious scenery rolled by. It was like being at the cinema, with fresh air thrown in. The rainy season had been kind to the Valle Bedretto, watering its green slopes and forests so that they glittered emerald in the morning sunshine. Tiger lilies grew wild beside the railway-track and when I got down to Pollegio, I saw my first oleanders, a sure sign that I had reached the balmy south. At one point, I looked up to my left and saw the terrifying spectacle of the San Gottardo motorway issuing from its tunnel near the peak of a mountain. Drivers who take that road cheerfully should see it from down below! It swings right out from the mountainside and hovers in space, supported on one lone concrete strut. I was glad to be down in the valley, gliding safely through a deep wooded cleft along my tranquil, almost empty road.

All day, I had the River Ticino for my companion. It took in other mountain torrents as it raced down the valley and soon swelled into quite a self-important little stream, bustling down over the rocks. Far too grand now for drainpipes, it swept under its very own stone bridges. I watched it grow with a proprietorial eye. After all, I had seen its very beginnings, and it was only right that I should take a benign interest in its progress, like an indulgent godmother. By the time we reached Bellinzona, it was already a significant river. It widened still further as it crossed the Magadino Plain, then spread into a broad delta to enter Lake Maggiore.

That was the last I saw of it for a couple of days. Locarno, the name of so many dance halls in my childhood, was a spacious lakeside city, with promenades and flowering trees – a little like Evian, but less relaxed. I kept getting lost in its traffic-ridden centre, among convoys of buses run by FART, but I found my way eventually to Ascona, wheeled my bike through its quaint cobbled alleyways, thick with discos, and came out on to cycle-paths along the lake shore.

I crossed the frontier at Valmara and spent my first night in Italy in Cannobio. There was a large party of Russians in my hotel, trying to order their dinner in broken English. The waitresses had had years of practice in speaking German, but they had to keep rushing over to my table for help with their English. 'How do you say *piccante?*' 'Spicy.' They rushed back to the Russians. 'Spicy,' they said, and the struggle over the menu card continued. I wondered if the Russians understood 'spicy' any better.

'My name is Anna too,' said the proprietress. 'And this is Camilla,' she added, when a dignified grey tabby appeared and began to wind itself around my legs. I like people who introduce their cats in a respectful manner.

Another wonderful day's cycling in perfect weather took me through a chain of smart resorts. In Verbania, it was the Friday market. I stopped to buy some new cycle mitts and the stall-holder was dazzled. She shouted to all her neighbours that I had cycled from London. '*Che coraggio! E da sola!*' I was again mobbed by admirers.

The western shore of Lake Maggiore became wilder and steeper as I travelled south. In the deep bay where the River Toce feeds into the lake between Verbania and Stresa (the river I would have followed, had I been forced to take the Simplon Tunnel), lie what are considered to be the lake's jewels, the Isole Borromee. Isola Bella, once nothing more than a bare rock, was transformed into a garden paradise by Count Carlo III Borromeo for his wife Isabella. Importing soil from the mainland, he planted orange and lemon trees, camellias, magnolias and evergreen shrubs around a Baroque palace. I am not an expert on gardens, so when I saw the queues for the boats in Stresa, I decided to admire the islands from a distance. I was more interested in the idea of the Borromeos. Princes of the Counter-Reformation, the family held the See of

Milan almost as a right. One of them, Carlo (soon to be canonised) took it over as 'administrator' even before he entered the Church, at the ripe age of 22. He was made Cardinal for the purpose by his Uncle Medici, Pope Pius IV. The Borromeos were never popes themselves, but they had uncles who were! The family has held on to much of its fortune. They still own the Isole Borromee, along with the fishing rights on Lake Maggiore.

In Sesto Calende, at the foot of Lake Maggiore, I joined the Ticino again. It flowed out of the lake, calm, wide and green – the same deep jewel green as the Rhône. It was a very different river from the turbulent stream that had flowed in, and I wondered how geographers had decided that it was still the same Ticino. From my hotel balcony, I watched a group of children, perhaps eight or nine years old, having a lesson in canoeing from a man in a motorboat with a megaphone. There were joggers and cyclists on the riverside paths. Serious anglers in waders stood in the shallows, with rods a mile long, and swans and coot drifted serenely down the sweetly flowing stream. It was an idyllic spot. That evening, from the terrace restaurant, I had a ringside view of the fireworks at the local festa, as I tucked into my most delicious meal for weeks – aubergines stuffed with mozzarella, followed by thin, tender fillets of grilled pork, served with grilled tomatoes and a fresh salad. A coachload of corpulent Russians arrived in the middle of my meal and swooped like a flock of gannets on to a table of champagne and caviare, the prelude to a daunting set menu.

Joining the riverside path, I was able to follow the river past Sunday crowds enjoying the sandy banks. I was set upon by two Jehovah's Witnesses. Determined women, they cruised along beside me, driving me so far on to the grass verge that I was obliged to stop or fall into the Ticino. When I pretended not to understand Italian, they offered me tracts in a choice of English, French and German.

I have often arrived in Italy at Milan's Malpensa Airport, without realising that it lies right on the edge of the extensive Parco Regionale della Valle del Ticino. Few of the guidebooks mention this fact, which must make this wildlife conservation area Italy's most beautiful secret. I skirted the airport, then swooped down a steep hill through woodland, back to the river at Vizzola Ticino. There I found a smooth asphalt path, running through the park beside the Navigazione Grande, the canal that leads into the industrial heart of Milan. The canal runs parallel to the Ticino for something like 20 miles (32 km), and its former towpath was thronged that sunny day with cycling, line-skating families. If only the path along the Burgundy Canal had been as smooth! I thought back to that stony, potholed horror, waterlogged in the rain, and shuddered.

Shortly after my picnic lunch, I saw an astonishing sight. There were boys surfboarding and capsizing in kayaks – on a canal! An electricity generating station near Turbigo was creating such turbulence that the water rose up in giant waves. Boys plunged in and rode the crests across the canal with all the aplomb of California surfers.

At Abbiategrasso, the Navigazione Grande turned east towards Milan, while I continued along the Ticino Valley as far as the village of Bereguardo. There I put up at a restaurant, which had a few bedrooms as a sideline. The owner had the most terrible black teeth I had seen in years and long, greasy grey hair, thinning on top. His shining silver Audi was much more impressive than his person.

'You do want the room just for sleeping in, don't you?' he asked suspiciously. I wondered what else he thought I might do in it. Set up in business for men with a kinky taste in grandmothers? He led me up a bleak concrete staircase round the back of the building. Although it was late in the evening, I was beginning to think that I would perhaps have to soldier on to Pavia. But the room was tidy. All its five beds had clean sheets and, as it was Sunday, there were no truck drivers for me to share the bathroom with. Surprisingly, there was quite a good original oil painting of the Ticino and a Salvador Dali print on the walls.

When I went down to dinner, I was so glad I had plucked up the courage to stay. The proprietor had got used to me by that time and turned quite affable.

'Just my luck!' he said. 'I *would* have roast beef on the menu when an Englishwoman comes to dinner! You're the roast-beef experts and you'll probably think mine is inedible.' As Lombardy is Italy's rice-growing region, we started with a wild mushroom risotto. It was delicious, a risotto to die for! Then, rather nervously, he served my roast beef 'Italian style'. It turned out to be cold, thinly sliced and cooked to perfection with a pink centre and a brown outside. It was served with lemon quarters and salad, and he seemed a little surprised when I asked for mustard, but he made it freshly for me. Half a litre of red wine, a litre of San Pellegrino and a crème brûlée brought my bill, including the room, to just under £10, 'between friends'. Then he offered an extra drink all round, so that everyone in the restaurant could toast my cycling exploit 'from London!'

I had had seven days of splendid weather and now I was in Italy, my spiritual home, where the summer sun always shines. After weeks of waking up in the morning, looking anxiously out of the window, wondering if the rain would be light enough to make cycling bearable, I jumped out of bed with confidence and fell into my travel routine. Two mugs of coffee and a bun while I packed, then an early start. I breezed along with no worries, no appointments, no responsibilities, no timetables. Everything I needed in the world was hooked on to the back of my bicycle. Life was so simple. All I needed to think about was the road ahead and where I would spend the next night. At one time, I had begun to doubt that I would ever reach Egypt. Now the land beckoned invitingly. Between the Ticino and the Nile lay months and months of exhilarating, carefree cycling. Life was as good as it gets this side of paradise.

My solitude ended in Pavia, Roman Ticinum, as my friend Heather arrived from London with her Brompton to join me for ten days. This raised my standards – more gastronomy and more expensive hotels. Alone, and penalised for single occupancy, I have to look for modest places to stay. Sharing, I can move upmarket. And alone in the evenings, I'm usually so hungry that I rush into the first presentable restaurant and take pot luck over a crossword. Sometimes I eat superbly and sometimes the food would challenge a dog. In company, we always dine well, because we seek out the best restaurants and try the local specialities. Dinner becomes a civilized and leisurely experience.

Museums and monuments become more rewarding too, when there is someone to exchange ideas with. Outside Pavia, we visited what is perhaps the pinnacle of Renaissance architecture in Italy, the Certosa di Pavia. Begun by Gian Galeazzo Visconti in 1396 and completed a century later by the Sforzas, this opulent monastery was built to house their tombs. It was such a magnificent complex that even the contemplative Order of Carthusians lived there in style. No monastic cells for them. Each of the twenty-four monks had a smart little terrace house with two living rooms, a bedroom, a chapel, a spacious loggia overlooking its own garden and an elaborate chimney in the style of a church campanile. The houses faced on to a green cloister the size of two football pitches. Today's ten monks live in holier simplicity. We were shown round the splendours of the monastery by one of these Carthusians, who break their vow of silence on a rota to escort visitors. Like the Taj Mahal, the monastery dazzled as a whole and enchanted in detail. There were beautiful starry ceilings, the taps in the small cloister were upended bronze dolphins, whose tails were turned to produce water, and the font had a granite obelisk on an inlaid marble base as its centrepiece. Before we even entered the building, we were captivated by the façade, a feast of inlaid polychrome marble, stone swags and curlicues, statues, friezes and fascinating marble roundels, each one carved with the portrait of a noble Roman. It was here that I made my first Cleopatra connection since leaving London. One of the roundels was a portrait of the young Octavian, who defeated Antony and Cleopatra at the Battle of Actium. Another portrayed him later, as the mature Emperor Augustus.

The Italians, like the French, all take their holidays together. They rush to the sea like lemmings. The weekend Heather arrived, the newspapers claimed that 60 per cent of the population was on the move. This is tiresome for tourists, as half the restaurants and shops are shut '*per le vacanze*' just at the time when they are most needed. Pavia and Piacenza were both pretty dead, though they had a few fine buildings. We walked the empty streets to the cobbled Piazza del Duomo in Pavia, which was dominated, as its name suggests, by the cathedral, a building constructed in the strangest ridged brickwork we had ever seen. Heather described it as 'a knitted cathedral', and that's exactly what it looked like – plain knitting. The other feature of the square was an equestrian statue, notable because some wag had taken a brush and painted the horse's prominent testicles a bright sulphur yellow. Piacenza's main square also had its horses, fine spirited bronzes, unpainted this time, bearing the martial figures of two Farneses.

More interesting to me were the rivers. My little Ticino, which I had followed down from its source, was about to lose itself, merging its waters with those of the River Po. It flowed along its final stretch, past Pavia's municipal gardens, under a covered mediaeval bridge (bombed during the war, but faithfully restored), then along a highway shaded by trees. Just beyond the outskirts of the city, the long Ponte di Becca spanned the confluence. I took pictures of the Becca, the pointed spit of sand which marked the mystic spot. We debated, in our usual pedantic way, why the spit was 'Becca', a feminine noun, when *becco*, the beak of a bird, which it so clearly resembled, was masculine. Unable to solve the puzzle, we cycled across the bridge and took the road to Piacenza.

7. THE PO

The traveller who has gone to Italy to study the tactile values of Giotto, or the corruption of the Papacy, may return remembering nothing but the blue sky and the men and women under it.

E.M. Forster, *A Room with a View*

For such a great river, the Po is surprisingly shy. It hides itself away across flood plains, behind curtains of trees. We picked out minor roads as near to the banks as possible, but we were still nowhere near the water's edge. Even through villages with names such as S. Cipriano Po or Arena Po, we still had no view of the river. In fact, we had no view of anything at all. Endless fields of maize, higher than our heads, bounded the lanes on both sides, obscuring everything in that flat, featureless world but the soaring campanile of the next village church. Piacenza was on the river, but the ancient walls, which still define the city's limits, were far away from its banks. It was not until we crossed the bridge to enter Cremona that we saw the River Po again.

Cremona is one of my very favourite Italian cities – not for its art and architecture, or its violin-making, but just because it's a beautiful place to *be*. The main square, the Piazza del Commune, is a heart-stopper, with the stunning west front of the cathedral and baptistery on its religious side and opposite, on its secular side, the Gothic brickwork of the Palazzo del Commune and the Loggia dei Militia. Yet it is not the individual buildings which dazzle, stupendous as they are, but the magnificent, breathtaking whole. The square is an enormous, beautifully balanced space. It is the largest drawing room in Lombardy, given over entirely to pedestrians and cyclists. Here the Cremonese take coffee or ice cream with their friends, or simply stand around in groups, beside or astride their bicycles, discussing politics and exchanging local gossip. They sit on the marble steps of the cathedral, reading their books and newspapers. In the late afternoon, the café tables round the edges creep out into the square, until the vast expanse is a sea of tablecloths. Then, at nightfall, comes the moment of high drama. The floodlights are switched on and the white marble of the cathedral comes alive, its statues stepping from the surrounding shadows and its giant Gothic lantern illuminating the sky. There is no finer view from a restaurant table.

The entire city centre is traffic-free, so everyone cycles. Whole families go around on bicycles together, like ducks on a pond, the parents leading the ducklings in procession. If the children are very small, they share one bicycle, a toddler perched behind and a baby on a seat attached to the handlebars. Old men in shorts glide past at a stately pace. Old ladies go shopping, a box on the rear carrier and string bags dangling. Business executives hold their mobiles in one hand, while they gesticulate wildly with the other. Kids do wheelies and lovers hold hands. Dogs sit up proudly in bike-baskets. The Cremonese are so relaxed on their bicycles that they often ride along with their arms folded. I have even seen them reading as they go.

We loved Cremona, but it played a miserable trick on us. It produced a storm. Thunder, lightning and torrential rain kept us penned up for hours in our hotel, along with the decorators, who were painting the exterior yellow. 'We shall all be living in a yellow submarine,' joked the owners. 'We've had so much rain this summer. The work's weeks behind schedule.' The streets were soon ankle-deep in water, but it was simply because the drains were unable to cope. Fortunately for Lombardy, there are so many nature reserves along the Po and so much pristine flood plain that the river has plenty of room to spread out, unlike the rivers of Northern Europe, which burst their banks and rush through towns and villages like liberated prisoners.

In a lull in the storm, we picked our way across the flooded cobbles to explore Cremona's elegant shops. Heather needed something new to wear at a family wedding and found the ideal outfit. I needed some new socks, which I bought in the Wednesday market. The stall-holder assured me that they were made of pure Scottish cotton!

After another day when we failed to see the Po, we turned inland from Casalmaggiore to visit Sabbioneta, the ideal city, built from scratch by Vespasiano Gonzaga in the latter half of the sixteenth century. A true Renaissance disciple of the Greeks, he was inspired by their view that 'Man is the measure of all things'. So he planned a city 'built to the measure of man'. It is one of Italy's minor gems. Its hexagonal walls still stand, surrounded by open country and enclosing regular streets on a grid pattern. The Ducal Palace is the most imposing building, but it is the Garden Palace, where Vespasiano lived in the summer, which is the real delight. It has some of the most delicate frescoes ever painted. There is a Roman column in a square, supporting a Roman statue of Athena, and the Arts are represented by a classical theatre, similar to Palladio's Teatro Olimpico in Vicenza. It has a foyer, a deep stage with wooden buildings constructed as a street, changing rooms for the actors, busts of the Greek gods round the auditorium and a painted loggia, high on the walls, crowded with *trompe l'oeil* musicians and spectators. Vespasiano transported villagers from the countryside to live in this first Garden City. What they thought of their compulsory transfer to this centre of classical culture is not recorded. At its height, there were 2,000 inhabitants. Unfortunately, it was subject to flooding by the Po and, after the death of its founder, the people drifted back to their old homes, leaving a ghost city. Today, the streets are deserted, except for tourists and the few shops and cafés which cater for them.

Gonzaga's classical city built to man's measure is a Mediterranean ideal. Not for them the Romantic obsession with landscape. Men and gods are their only concern. If the northern artists of the nineteenth and twentieth centuries had lived on the Po and Ticino, the world's art galleries would be awash with their water and the light that plays on it. But the Italians have always painted people. At first, they were exclusively the people of the Bible – the Holy Family, the saints and the prophets. Then came the Renaissance and the rebirth of interest in all things classical. The Greek pantheon and the heroes of Greece and Rome were added to their list of subjects. They learned from Greek sculpture, helped by their own experiments in anatomy, how to model the human form in action. Their static holy groups were transformed into living people, acting out with vigour the events and disasters of their lives. But landscape was stylised background, just a few rocks and a tree against a blue sky. Canaletto painted the regattas and lively crowds of Venice, with a few white flecks on a blue ground to show that the gap between the buildings, the Grand Canal, was a waterway. It was left to northern artists such as Turner, Manet and Whistler to paint 'Venice at dawn ... wobbling in a thousand fresh-water reflections, cool as a jelly' (Lawrence Durrell).

From Casalmaggiore, we had planned to go on to Mantua, but Sabbioneta was so interesting that we spent the whole morning there. The noonday sun was strong when we left and the Brompton is not really a long-distance, cross-country bicycle. We faded out in a café in S. Matteo di Chiaviche, far from the nearest hotel. The proprietor took pity on us. He telephoned Nizzoli's restaurant in Villastrada, where he knew they had a few rooms, and booked us in. As we cycled there across low-lying farmland sectioned by dykes, we had no idea of the wonders which awaited us.

The hotel annexe, where we were shown to our bedroom, was the sixteenth-century priest's house, attached to the church. We slept in the former oratory, which was heavily shuttered and overwhelmed with ponderous dark wood furniture. Every inch of the wall space in the room and down the staircase was hung with paintings of Signor Nizzoli, pumpkins, nudes, sly peeping cats, frogs and snails, all amusing and all originals, signed by devoted clients. An old wooden sign creaked outside our window: La Locanda del Peccato di Gola (the Inn of the Sin of Gluttony).

The restaurant was equally bizarre. The centrepiece of a ceiling fresco was Nizzoli in his chef's hat, surrounded by dozens of tiny chef Nizzolis flying on broomsticks. Every shelf and table had a ceramic frog or snail; and the walls were a riot of frogs, snails and pumpkins – pumpkin people, pumpkin houses, pumpkin cars. Signor Nizzoli specialises in pumpkins and has written a book devoted entirely to pumpkin cooking. Needless to say, we began our absolutely delicious dinner with the local speciality, tortellini stuffed with pumpkin!

We had a rather broken night, because the church clock chimed the quarter hours with a great clang, and our bedroom was right next door. The booming church bell joined in at 6.30, with the call to early Mass. There was a storm in the night too, which rattled the shutters and beat against the window panes. In the morning our bicycles out in the courtyard were streaming with water. My Brooks leather saddle felt as soggy as a sponge and Heather tipped an impressive cascade from the canvas bag on her Brompton. While she was trying to dry it out in the hall, Signor Nizzoli arrived with his little terrier to pay us a courtesy call. With an air of mystery, he produced a pair of huge keys from his pocket and unlocked a heavy door. Behind it stood an iron gate with a fearsome lock and chain. This was his Holy of Holies. It was his shrine to Vittorio de Sica. The great neorealist film producer, perhaps best remembered for *The Bicycle Thieves*, was a local boy. He often came from Rome to visit his family and when he did, he regularly dined at Nizzoli's. The shrine was a photographic record of de Sica's career, with pride of place in the exhibition going to pictures of the cinematic giant embracing Signor Nizzoli and enjoying his frogs and pumpkins.

Cyclists are so privileged. Had we been in a car, we would have driven straight to Mantua. We would have checked in at a normal hotel and gone to a normal restaurant for dinner. We would have flashed past the little town of Villastrada without even noticing it, and would have missed the most extraordinary, fantastical place on our trip – and, incidentally, missed the best dinner! Serendipity rides a bicycle.

We left in a light drizzle, which turned to steady rain as we crossed a bridge of boats near the mouth of the Oglio. We were in the middle of another magnificent park, the Parco Regionale del Oglio Sud, cycling along an embankment on a good asphalt track. Just as we left the Oglio delta and reached the River Po itself, there was a cloudburst. Sheets of rain as thick and opaque as shower curtains obscured the landscape. The only building in sight was a restaurant. It was closed, but there might be an outbuilding where we could shelter. We rushed over, left our bicycles under a leaky awning over the terrace and huddled in the front porch. The door opened and we were pulled inside by a man who spoke strange Italian. (We learned later that he was Romanian.) He brought us towels, made us coffee, then gave us a lemon sorbet. Still the rain came down in sheets. I have never known rain of such intensity last for so many hours.

Heather was seriously worried, because her new wedding finery was travelling on the back of the Brompton. I suggested she fold her bike and take a taxi into Mantua, where I would meet her when the storm abated. But a young Italian arrived, the brother-in-law of the Romanian, and he had a better idea. He knew some Germans who were staying in a nearby Agriturist. They were on a fishing holiday and had a pick-up truck. He would borrow it and drive us both into Mantua. I was reluctant, as I always am, to accept a lift on a cycle trip. It seems like cheating. But we had already sat in the restaurant for two hours and the weather still showed no sign of improvement. The two men ganged up on me and Heather refused to leave me there on my own, so in the end I yielded to pressure. The bikes were loaded on the truck and the three of us squashed together in the cab with all the luggage, including the famous wedding dress.

The rain on the road was terrifying, with floods in the hollows and visibility almost nil. We reached Mantua safely, but our greatest challenge was still to come. I defy anyone, who is not a radar-carrying native of Mantua, to find any building in that nightmare of one-way streets. We had made the mistake of booking a hotel in advance, so we were not able to leap into the first presentable place we saw. We had to circle the city to find the San Lorenzo. The poor young man got soaked to the skin, running in and out of the cab to ask the way. When we finally located the hotel, we had to tour the neighbouring streets for another half-hour before we could find a legitimate way to approach it. Mercifully, after all this, Heather's dress came out of its plastic bag crushed, but unharmed. A night on a coathanger and it was as elegant as ever.

Mantua, to our relief, was out of the Lombardy region which prides itself on its donkey stews and roast horse. We were in more acceptable ham and pork country. So we lunched on pasta with minced piglet, then spent the rainy afternoon in the Gonzagas' Palazzo Ducale. The torrents had kept away the crowds and we were amazed to have the celebrated Mantegnas in La Camera degli Sposi completely to ourselves.

In other rooms, we remarked on the large number of horses painted most realistically from behind, their anuses lovingly defined. There were flocks and flocks of cherubim with dimpled bottoms. And when we went to a car-hire depot to pick up Heather's zippy little Fiat, we noticed that all the pin-ups on the walls were photographed from behind, buxom girls in G-strings, sticking out their bottoms and ogling provocatively over their shoulders. Are Italians bottom-fixated? we wondered.

Returning with the hire car which was to take Heather back to Malpensa, we went round the city in circles again, flustered by honking drivers. We knew exactly where the hotel was, but the bafflement was getting there. Suddenly, I spotted a bus, the No.1

Circolare, which I knew stopped in our square. 'Follow that bus!' I cried. We sped along behind it, like gangsters in a bad film, wheeling round in wide arcs, in and out of back streets, until we pulled up with a flourish in its wake, outside our own front door. Never drive in Mantua!

Getting out of the city was easier on a bicycle, as I could ride against the traffic or push. It was still raining when I left, but another night in the San Lorenzo was out of the question. Single occupancy was far too expensive and also, to my great indignation, I was being charged for leaning my bicycle against their garage wall. In all my years of cycling, it was only the fourth time I had ever been charged. I was incensed.

Mantua is on the River Mincio. I followed its parallel Canale Bianco to rejoin the still invisible Po, which I crossed at Ostiglia. The sun came out as I cycled through Truffle Valley. Unfortunately, it was not the season for those rare, delicately perfumed tubers. It would be piglet or pumpkin again with my pasta. I entered another unexpected chain of national parks and wetland reserves, where an asphalt cycle-path ran along the top of an embankment. There were tall grey cranes, casting disdainful eyes on the lesser marsh birds, and I even caught the occasional glimpse of the River Po. In my Sermide restaurant with rooms, the boss led me into his garage (no charge this time!). He was curious to know where I had sprung from and exclaimed *'Non è possibile!'* when I told him I had come from London and crossed the Alps. I overheard him later, relaying everything to his wife in the kitchen. *'Madonna! Mamma mia! Madonna!'* was all she could manage to utter. They were spell-bound, eager to be involved in the adventure, if only by wheeling my bike, carrying my bags or treating me to a really special dinner at a discount. I was back in the real Italy, among real warm-hearted Italians – a world away from the greedy, indifferent flunkeys of our Mantua hotel.

More riverside cycle-paths, stands of poplars, sugar-beet facto-ries, rice and maize, and finally a wide tree-lined avenue to the centre of the city of Ferrara. It claimed to be a city for cycling, but I still didn't take to it. I know the red-brick battlements of the Este fortress are magnificent, but their scale and grandeur are menacing. I walked into the great echoing space of the cathedral and felt cowed. There were palaces and museums on every corner and huge cobbled squares, which were hard on the feet and tyres. Ferrara is not a city 'made to the measure of man', but a city made to overwhelm him. I was glad it was Monday, the day when the Castello and museums were closed. I had every excuse just to wander round in search of the absurd, like the stone griffon outside the cathedral, which had wheels instead of legs. My spirits lifted as soon as I cycled out of town down the Via Pomposa.

Ferrara was built on rising ground near the point where the River Po divides into two main channels and the myriad streamlets and canals which form its delta. I followed the southern branch, the Po di Volano, until it split near Ostellato. The canal I took next was famous for its huge shoals of eel. Its banks were certainly thick with anglers. Some had elaborate contraptions consisting of four or five rods with a net suspended between them, a bit like the cantilevered Chinese nets in Cochin. At the end of the canal I came to Comacchio, a delightful miniature Venice, all canals and bridges. It was the local festa, with fireworks, a funfair and a festival of boats. People in mediaeval costume paraded from the town hall to the lake, preceded by heralds with trumpets and a percussion band. Had I stayed on in Ferrara to see that forbidding Castello, I would have missed all the fun.

Thalassa! Thalassa! I reached the Adriatic Sea at Porto Garibaldi. I had been invited to spend a few days with my friend Minne at her seaside home in Lignano, and I was looking forward to a holiday from travel. To get there by train, I had to go back to Ferrara. I cycled north across the Parco Regionale del Delta del Po, another haven for egrets, herons, avocets and the like. Again, there were tranquil cycle-paths through marshland and woods, and along a narrow neck of land between the sand dunes and a great lake. I spent an hour in the peace of Pomposa's Romanesque Abbey, then cycled on to Codigoro, where they kindly held up the train when they saw me tearing out of the ticket office. Travelling back to Ferrara, I paid less for myself than for Condor. I was relieved to find the next day that the bike charge was still the same, though my own ticket to Latisana was considerably more.

My abiding memory of that riverside ride across Italy is the amazing network of regional parks, which extend almost the entire way from the Alps down to the Adriatic Sea. We tend to think of the Italians as people who go out and shoot everything in sight, including songbirds. But these days nothing could be further from the truth. They have discovered ecology and are putting all the passion of new converts into the conservation of natural habitats. Their parks are a delight. There are forests, Alpine valleys, wetlands, lakes, saltmarshes and dunes. Most of them are traffic-free and all are crisscrossed with well-maintained paths. If you cycle, walk or ride, you will be in paradise – provided it doesn't rain. So go there!

8. ADRIATIC ITALY

Chi lascia la via vecchia per la nuova,
sa quel che perde e non sa quel che trova.

Italian proverb

'When you leave the old road for the new, you know what you are losing, but not what you will find.' The proverb could go further. Even when you are travelling the old road, you can still meet with surprises. I thought I knew the area round Venice inside-out, but this time I was looking at it from a different perspective and the kaleidoscope twisted.

My long river journey, which began at Le Havre, had ended at the Po delta. Now I had to follow the sea coast all the way to Egypt. It would not be easy. In fact, when I set out again after my holiday with Minne, I was out of sight of the sea throughout my very first day. Lignano stands on a broken coastline of lagoons, marshes and river deltas, so I was well inland, cycling through flat fields of maize, until I came to La Salute di Livenza. There, I could join the Livenza River and follow it to the sea at Caorle. It was a green river, but its green was a mixture of lime and olive, tinged with yellow, not the clear spruce green of the rivers which rise in the Alps. Inland, my road ran through small towns, unchanged for a century or more. Loud-mouthed men, most of them old, shouted witticisms to one another across the café tables. There was not a woman in sight, unless she was serving in a shop. When I came to Lido di Jesolo, just a few miles away, I was in another age, almost on another planet. Women in bikinis stalked the streets and joined the men in the cafes. I even saw one fishing – a sport usually practised only by men, if you can call such an idle occupation 'a sport'.

Strictly speaking, I could have gone back on the train and resumed my cycling at Porto Garibaldi, the point at which I originally reached the Adriatic. It would not have been cheating, as I would not have been skipping any part of my direct route. But I was cycling the extra distance because my friend Katherine was coming out on the European Bike Express to join me in Cavallino. She arrived with my tent. It was high season along that popular holiday coast and accommodation might be a problem.

The Venetian Lagoon was my big surprise. As a student, I once spent a month in Venice on an art and language course. I explored the city's palaces and churches on foot and learned to find my way unerringly through its twisting alleys; and I got to know the well-visited islands of Murano, Burano and Torcello, north-east of the city. But now Katherine and I were crossing the lagoon in the other direction, towards Chioggia, and this was a different world.

We cycled from Cavallino along the thin tongue of land to Punta Sabbioni, where we wheeled our bicycles on to a vaporetto bound for the Lido. It crossed the wide channel, called the Porto di Lido, which is used by liners approaching the city of Venice. At one time, it could be closed off by giant chains to prevent enemy ships from entering the lagoon. This crossing was the nearest we came to the city. Our view from the deck would have thrilled the Impressionists – all those domes and campaniles dissolving in the mists of morning.

Most people, including myself in the past, head straight across the Lido for the beaches on the Adriatic shore. This time, Katherine and I turned right out of the vaporetto station and cycled along the Venice side of the narrow island. Elegant villas and apartment blocks lined the road, which was shaded by mature plane trees. It was a prosperous suburb of Venice. The lagoon side of the island was tranquil, tourist-free, and had proper streets where residents could drive their cars. We cycled the length of the Lido to the car-ferry at Alberoni, and made the five-minute crossing of the Porto di Malamocco to Pellestrina.

Malamocco itself is now no more than a fishing village on the Lido, but it was once the capital of the confederation of lagoon islands. It gave its name to one of Venice's most decisive battles. In 810 it was captured by Charlemagne's son Pepin, who then made the mistake of trying to sail across the lagoon. His fleet ran aground on the mud flats, where the sea-faring Venetians destroyed his floundering ships and massacred their crews. But the Venetians learned their lesson. They promptly moved their capital from the Lido to the safer islands of Rivoalto across the lagoon, where the city of Venice still stands today.

If the Lido was a very thin island, Pellestrina was thinner still. It was no wider than a piece of string. There was a road along its spine. A bus chugged along from one ferry to the next, while we cycled between umbrella pines, with a view of the lagoon to our right and a mighty stone sea wall atop the dunes to our left. Except for the two small villages of San Pietro and Pellestrina, the island was given over to sand and scrub. It was inhabited exclusively by the fishermen who trawl the lagoon bottom for clams and those other strange shallow-water creatures that appear in Venetian fish-markets. It is work with diminishing returns. Overfishing and no-go zones round industrial Marghera have reduced the once plentiful catch to such an extent that fish farms have had to spring up to fill the void. Farmed fish is cheaper and it's safe. If you ate the fish from Marghera's chemical effluent, you would light up at night!

From Pellestrina, we took our third ferry across the Porto di Chioggia. This was the safer end of the lagoon for fishing and had a workaday look about it, still hauntingly beautiful, but less desolate. There were wooden shacks on stilts, small battered boats tied to piles, and fishing nets draped from poles, every one with a hopeful seagull perched on top. We sailed past groups of divers. They were busy shoring up underwater structures and attending to light buoys and channel-markers, essential in those treacherous waters. Half the lagoon is Laguna Morta (Dead Lagoon), mud flats except at the high spring tides. But even the navigable Laguna Viva (Live Lagoon) can deceive those who were not born to its shallows.

Between them, the three islands of Lido, Pellestrina and Chioggia create an almost continuous sand-bar between the Adriatic Sea and the Venetian lagoon. Running from north to south, they guard the city of Venice against the fury of the sea. They are fascinating places, yet they are unvisited by tourists, except for the Lido beaches. Pellestrina, in particular, is a wild, unspoilt, unique ribbon of land, protected by its inaccessibility. The only convenient way to explore it is by boat and bicycle. It was a great find, the highlight of an exhilarating morning.

The River Brenta flows between Chioggia and the mainland, but there were no more boats. The busy S.309 from Venice swerves out over the lagoon to the island, then bridges the Brenta on its return to the mainland. We had no choice but to follow it, cowering on the hard shoulder as the trucks of Mestre and Marghera thundered past. It was such a relief to be able to turn off when we reached the northern limit of the Po delta, the mouth of the Po di Venezia.

From Ferrara, I had chosen the southern branch, the Po di Volano, so it was very satisfactory to be able to complete the Po, as it were, by inspecting its other main branch. We crossed it by a long bridge, which gave us an amazing close-up view of a giant liner under construction in a dry dock, and stopped for the night a little way upstream in Taglio di Po.

We were back in the wonderful nature reserves of the Po delta. The next morning, we rejoined the main road south, but left it early, branching off by the quiet Po di Goro and cycling through the oak and juniper woods of the Bosco di Mesola, an ancient forest planted by the Etruscans. Through fields of artichokes, we reached the coast at Volano, and I retraced my wheel-prints down the narrow neck of land between the sea and the wetlands of the Valle Bertuzzi. As it often does, the landscape looked quite different from the opposite direction. Going north, I had been scanning the marshes for the first sight of the great tower of Pomposa Abbey. This time, I was intent on staying as close as possible to the sea and was far more aware of the striped umbrellas and multicoloured shards of the windsurfers. We passed through the string of seaside resorts north of Porto Garibaldi, where I had first hit the coast. After that, I was off into the unknown.

The Lido di Estensi was so elegant that it was impossible to resist. It was founded by the Este Dukes of Ferrara as a salubrious seaside retreat, away from the malarial swamps of their dismal city. The main avenue was, not surprisingly, the Via Ducale. It was a thoroughfare of patrician grandeur, quite unlike the main drag of any other seaside resort. Its pristine flagstones ran between rows of obelisks, with triumphal arches at each end. To parade up and down in the late evening, when the boutiques were glittering and the grandiose structures gleamed white in the moonlight, was to be transported to another, more lavish age.

Our hotel was not lavish, though. It was very much an Italian family hotel, where everyone was on full board. The vestibule was cluttered with pushchairs, buckets and spades. There were babies sleeping in prams and dogs tearing round the gardens. The very young and the very old were most in evidence. There were at least four groups which seemed to be Darby and Joan clubs. The food was simple and substantial – generous helpings of pasta, followed by grilled fish, salad and crème caramel – just the menu for hungry cyclists.

I had left the rains and rice paddies of Lombardy far behind. Now the problem was heat. We started cycling early in the mornings, to catch the cool sea breezes. As the sun warmed up, its power was intensified by the dazzle of the sea to our left. We were following the coast, so there were no shadows, no buildings to shield us from the glare. The beach resorts were milling with people and hotel rooms were hard to find. But the thought of baking in a hot tent was unbearable. We stopped cycling early to begin the desperate search for a hotel, splitting up to double our possibilities. Our best find came one day when we were on the verge of despair, after about twenty failures. We were offered an inexpensive glorified beach-hut, belonging to a booked-up hotel. It had its own patio garden and deckchairs by the sea. We could lock our bicycles safely inside and enjoy the hotel swimming pool.

We had one cultural day, when we cycled through Ravenna. At the Church of Sant' Apollinare in Classe, just south of the city, we arrived during the celebration of Mass. The priest wore green, white and gold vestments, which exactly matched the green pastures, pretty white sheep and gold cross and stars of the mosaics in the apse behind him. I always find early Byzantine churches uplifting. They are light, airy, colourful places, which stress the positive side of Christianity. Christ is shown in His glory, as the Pantocrator, the Ruler of the World, not as the tortured Jesus in agony on the cross. In my favourite Ravenna church, Sant'Apollinare Nuovo, mosaic saints and martyrs process all the way down the nave to Christ on his heavenly throne. They are all dressed in white, all with golden haloes and all looking immensely cheerful. Each one carries no more than a discreet symbol of his martyrdom, a miniature spear, cross or grid-iron. It is the end result, the triumph of faith, which is celebrated, not the suffering which led up to that triumph. In Western churches, particularly in Spain, we are battered by the horror and the joy gets overlooked. As I wandered round Sant'Apollinare in Classe, turning all this over in my mind, I came across the sarcophagus of a little Roman girl. The touching inscription said that she had died at the age of 1 year, 6 months and 9 days, *contra votum*, contrary to the prayers of her parents.

Rimini marked the start of what the Italians call 'La Costa Tedesca', the German Coast. Rimini, Bellariva, Marebello, Rivazzura, Miramare, Riccione, Cattolica – miles and miles of beach umbrellas, divided into rigid hotel blocks by colour. Green stripes for the Excelsior, orange for the Venezia, yellow stripes for the Costa Azurra and blue for the Capri. Different colours, but the same umbrellas and the same sun-worshipping bodies on beach loungers.

As we cycled south, the hazy shadows of the distant Apennines slanted towards us, gaining definition, until the mountains met the coast at Cattolica in a solid mass of headland. The main road to Pesaro ran along a valley behind it, but we were sticking to the sea, so we pushed our bikes up a steep, crooked little path from the beach to the start of the cliff ride, one of those wriggling roads marked green in Michelin, which always means hard work! It was hot and exposed up there, but we had the scent of wild roses and pines, and such clear views that we could almost see across the blue Adriatic to Croatia. At one point, we looked north along the coast and saw those coloured slabs of umbrella stretching all the way back to Rimini.

We whirled down into Pesaro and then we were back on the flat. Sometimes the railway ran between our road and the sea, and sometimes we cruised along the beach. We had reached the olive belt and there were vines, peach orchards and cicadas singing day and night. Our life fell into an easy routine – an early start to get 20 miles or so under the wheels before the day heated up, a break for coffee and a bun, more cycling, a break for a sandwich lunch, then the search for a hotel. Katherine is a good cycling companion, because she goes at about the same speed as I do and has just about the same staying power. There is never the problem of one of us needing to stop while the other still feels daisy-fresh.

Once we were established in our hotel, Katherine rushed into her swimsuit and off to the beach. She lives by the sea in England, but still can't get enough of it when she's travelling. It was too hot out there for me. I holed up with the curtains drawn, to enjoy the delicious cool of our room over books and a siesta.

The Adriatic Coast was my holiday on the way to Egypt. I had nothing to do but admire the blue of the sea and the sky. When I cycled this way on my first journey round the world, I was following the Roman roads. Rimini was the start of the Via Emilia to the Alps, and Fano the start of the Via Flaminia to Rome, so I had work to do in both cities, inspecting the Roman remains. This time, I just swept through Rimini and Fano, enjoying the here and now, not pondering over the then. Senigallia had a fortress and elegant arcaded buildings fronting a canal, but I simply glanced at them and passed on. The Montefeltro family was not part of my brief. It was all very restful.

On the outskirts of Ancona, we were showered, literally, with a gift of figs by a man plucking them high up on a wall; and in the gloomy port itself, we met a dog with the extraordinary name of Quando (When), a yappy miniature Schnautzer that made noisy work of guarding our bicycles on the hotel terrace. A tremendous climb out of Ancona brought us to another of Italy's magical regional parks, the Riviera del Cornero. Mount Cornero rises precipitously from the sea to a height of 1,877 feet (572 m). The headland it creates is splendidly unkempt. We cycled through yellow broom, purple thrift and wild pink sweetpeas. Clouds of white butterflies settled on our handlebars and swooped through our wheels. There were the usual fields of maize where the land flattened out a little; but there were also great swathes of purple lavender, whose fragrance in the heat was so intense that we were almost intoxicated. We reached our summit fairly soon at the village of Pietralacroce, then cycled an undulating road with spectacular views over the sea and the inland hills. A wild plunge down the mountainside above Numana and we were back at sea level and the start of another hundred miles or more of beach umbrellas. Most of the resorts were pleasant enough, but unexciting. The only one with any claim to graciousness was San Benedetto del Tronto, a sort of Lido of the south, where the palm-shaded promenade with its elegant hotels seemed to stretch forever beside the long white strip of sand.

We had struggled over two rocky headlands, but they were no more than tiny blisters on the coastline compared with the one that lay ahead of us, the giant Gargano Promontory. This wild region of Puglia, like a rocky spur on the boot of Italy, had a heart of ancient oak and beech forests. A few fishing villages dotted its periphery, connected to the outside world by a green Michelin worm of a road, 100 miles (161 km) long. The whole promontory was a national park and we should probably need our tent. It would be our greatest challenge yet.

On our way to the promontory, we climbed a particularly steep hill in the noonday heat and came to a dead end at the mouth of a tunnel. It was 360 yards long (330 m). There was no footpath inside and no alternative route round it. I had frightened myself to death in a 200-metre tunnel in the Jura – 330 metres was just impossibly dangerous. We cycled back to the small Ortona headland and pushed our bikes up the mountainside into the town. There was a sheer drop from the city wall, which dwarfed the port below. We looked down like eagles from a crag.

There are cyclists who ride up mountains for fun, for the excitement of defying gravity. Katherine and I are not like that. We cycle mountains only if they stand in our way. We don't deliberately seek them out. We had had an exhausting day and were starting to wilt at the thought of those Gargano cliff tops in the blazing heat. My policy was to stay by the sea, so I refused to consider the gentler road behind the promontory, through Foggia. But would we be able to manage that desolate route round the promontory?

A brilliant solution to our problem was presented by the son of the hotel owner, a charming young Jesus lookalike, bearded, tall and skinny as a telegraph pole. He told us there was a daily ferry from Ortona to the Tremiti Islands; and from there we could take another ferry to Manfredonia. We would still be rounding the Gargano Promontory by the sea, but we would be spared the arduous road. He rang the Adriatica office and booked our tickets.

The sea around the Tremiti Islands is crystal-clear, the cleanest, most translucent sea water I have ever seen. We landed on San Nicolà, where Katherine was soon in her bathing costume, swimming from the pebbly beach. I was pleased to be there, because I had found another of my extremely tenuous connections with Cleopatra. The Emperor Augustus, who defeated her and annexed Egypt to Rome, used the islands as a place of banishment. His scandalous granddaughter, Julia, was one of the reluctant inhabitants. The tradition continued for centuries. Political prisoners crowded the islands' gaols, while the free population shrank alarmingly. As a remedy, the Bourbons forcibly exported a consignment of Neapolitan women, seized in the city's taverns. The descendant of one of those unwilling imports must have been serving in our seaside bar. Grumpy, squat and lumpen, in a hectic nylon dress, she slammed our seafood risotto on the table with a sour expression, which perfectly matched the flavour of the cooking.

While Katherine bathed, I climbed up to the town, with its small piazza and pine-wood park. Its stronghold was a monastery with charming animal mosaics on the floor – rearing horses, stags and mysterious fish. Between spells as a prison island, San Nicolà had a sacred history. In ancient times the Tremiti Islands were known as the Islands of Diomedes because the Greek hero is said to have settled there after the Trojan War. When he died, his followers built a temple in his honour on San Nicolà. According to Pliny, Aphrodite rewarded their loyalty by changing them into seabirds, so that they could sprinkle the temple every day with sea water from their beaks and fend off invaders. Diomedes' temple was replaced by the Christian monastery, an offshoot of the Benedictine Montecassino.

On the way to Manfredonia, our high-speed motor launch rounded the Gargano Promontory and we got a close-up view of the horrendous crags we had missed. There were watchtowers, lighthouses and a few beaches at the bottom of clefts in the rock. At one time, these villages must have been accessible only by sea. Even now, the descent to them from the road above was vertiginous. We had saved ourselves at least three days' desperate cycling.

Manfredonia had refineries off-shore and fetid marshes behind. We cycled along the flat shadeless coast road into a headwind so strong that we were reduced to seven miles an hour. No wildlife could exist in the stagnant, sewage-ridden swamps. Salt flats followed and slightly cleaner lagoons with wading birds and swallows. At every intersection, unbelievable queues of cars stretched into infinity, all intent on a family Sunday on the beach. Heaven knows what the bathing was like!

We had now reached the torrid south with a vengeance. Every day was hotter than the last and the burning wind from the south east sprang up regularly each morning at ten o'clock. Like the blast from a baker's oven, it seared our skin and parched our throats. Although I was wearing long trousers, I developed an ugly heat rash on my thighs, and my back and arms burned through my shirt. I envied Katherine her darker colouring. She tanned so easily, while I just went blotchy and itched.

The day we cycled into Bari, the sun glared in our faces and the wind blew stronger and hotter than ever. On the outskirts of the city, I almost passed out and had to crouch in the only shade I could find, the shadow of a rather smelly petrol-station loo. That decided us. We had been debating whether to finish our Adriatic ride in Bari or Brindisi. Either port would do for my crossing to Greece. But two more days in that blast furnace, just to cycle past a string of holiday beaches, were not to be contemplated. We would end the misery in Bari.

Katherine's trip was over now. She went back north on the train, to pick up a flight to London. I took a day or two off in Bari, enjoying its leafy squares and doing some essential shopping. Then I booked my passage to Igoumenitsa and my first serious meeting with Cleopatra.

9. IONIAN GREECE

Fair Greece! Sad relic of departed worth!

Lord Byron, *Childe Harold's Pilgrimage*

Greece went badly, even before it started. I was robbed in Bari on my way there. It happened like this. I was setting out for the docks to catch the night ferry to Igoumenitsa. I wheeled my bicycle from its hiding place in the back yard of my hotel and propped it against the front wall. Right beside it, on the marble steps up to the vestibule, I dumped all my belongings in a heap, ready to be loaded. Among them was an extremely small backpack, which I found so useful because it was black suede and smart enough to double up as a handbag for evenings out. In the split second that I took my eyes off my pile of luggage to attach a pannier to the rack, a sneak thief snatched that little black bag and disappeared. He was so quick that I saw nothing. Fortunately, I was wearing all my money, my credit cards, my passport and my ferry ticket in a body belt, so the items in the bag had no monetary value whatsoever. There was my journey log to date (not my full notes, but my daily record of route, distance, weather and expenditure), my address book, reading glasses, a book of *Times* crosswords, a black and a green biro, a sunblock stick, my comb, lipstick and nail file, and a prosciutto roll for my supper. The thief must have been a very disappointed man! It was such an expensive-looking little bag that he must have expected wads of money, if not a few diamond necklaces. As for me, I was hopping mad at the inconvenience. I was particularly annoyed about the address book because I usually kept it with my stationery in one of my panniers, but I had taken it out that afternoon to catch up on postcards in the shade of one of Bari's delightful squares. So the one time I had it in my little bag was the time the bag was stolen. I pedalled down to the docks in a fury.

Having lost my nice prosciutto roll, I needed drachmas to buy supper on the ferry. 'You're the one with the bicycle,' said the purser. They don't miss much, I thought. Later that evening, as I was watching the starlit waves, he came to join me for a chat at the rail. His English was excellent, and he was my first listener, so I'm afraid I treated him to a long lament about the robbery. He was most sympathetic, as he had recently been a victim in Bari himself. His car had been broken into and his mobile phone stolen. As he had his entire telephone directory programmed into it, his dismay at the inconvenience matched mine at the loss of my address book.

'Bari's always been notorious for theft. And now Greece is going the same way. It used to be a safe place. Now you can't be too careful. It's all those Albanians and Romanians flooding in. They've got nothing and they're all light-fingered.'

People everywhere blame their neighbours for their problems – Greeks and Turks, French and British, Spanish and Portuguese, Brazilians and Peruvians, Canadians and Americans. I thought the purser was playing the usual game of 'blame your neighbour', until I travelled through Greece and saw the scale of the problem. The Greeks are more prosperous than they used to be. The European Union has been good to them, so their country has become a magnet for bombed-out, poverty-stricken migrants from the Balkans and the Middle East. Greece is one of Europe's front lines.

The change in Greece's fortunes was evident on the ferry. When I crossed over to Igoumenitsa in 1987, on my first ride round the world, most of my fellow passengers were Greek *Gästarbeiter*, returning home for the summer holidays. They drove proudly off the ferry, their German Fords groaning under the weight of washing machines, television sets and electric mixers, gifts they had scraped and saved for in their years as factory-hands on the Ruhr. In 2001, it was a different picture. There were few Greeks on the ferry, as Greece is now a net importer of labour. This time, the passengers were mostly Turks, taking the short sea-crossing to Igoumenitsa before driving the fast new road over the Pindos Mountains to Thessaloniki, Thrace and home. They were now the ones sporting the German number plates, and they were the proud owners of the little Fords loaded with kitchen equipment. I listened to the families with interest. The groups of adults spoke Turkish among themselves and used a mixture of Turkish and German when they shouted at their over-excited children. The children played together exclusively in German.

Igoumenitsa too had changed. In 1987 it was just a drab, dusty dump of a port, to be rushed through as quickly as possible. In 2001, I cycled off the ferry into a bright, cheerful modern town with a pedestrian centre, smart shops and pavement cafés. What a transformation!

I booked into a hotel there for two nights, because I had to assess my losses and replace as many stolen items as I could. I sent a fax from the post office to my friend Priscilla, who has keys to my flat, asking her to go round there and find my old address book – not to risk posting it to me, but to give me crucial information by fax and phone. The reading glasses were not a problem, as I always carry an old pair, but I had to go shopping for notebooks and other odds and ends. Then I lunched on a delicious spinach pie in hot flaky pastry straight from the baker's oven and slept through the heat of the day. After the sweltering humidity of the Adriatic Coast, it was a real treat to be in the drier atmosphere of Greece; and the air conditioning in my bedroom was the icing on the cake. It was a Japanese Hitachi unit high up on the wall, which I could switch on and off myself by remote control. I could even adjust the temperature for my total comfort. I was in paradise.

Before I set off on my bicycle, I spent a bit of time rearranging my luggage. I had stopped using a handlebar bag after mine was stolen on a train in Varanasi Station and I had gone over to the small black rucksack for my immediate needs. But after Bari, I felt that *all* small bags were a provocation and decided to dispense with them in future. It was not easy to find handy places for the oddments I used to carry in my little black bag, but I eventually found hidey-holes for all of them and set off in the cool of the morning.

There was a long climb out of Igoumenitsa, but as I toiled up the mountainside I was rewarded with a stunning view of the harbour in its wide bay below and the glittering sea, with the misty shape of Corfu on the horizon. Cycling down the Adriatic Coast, there had been nothing to shield me from the dazzle of the rising sun on water. On the rugged coast of Epirus I had every mountain and tree in Greece between me and the sun's rays. Pink and white oleanders lined my shady road, and myrtle, sage, wild figs and olives flourished on the ragged slopes where cicadas sang. When the sun finally cleared the mountain peaks in the late morning, the scent of pines was intoxicating. Epirus is wild, untamed country, with a history of banditry, but its mountains held no terrors that perfect July day, not even from traffic, as the trucks from the early-morning ferries had all passed me in convoy on the outskirts of

Igoumenitsa. I had the mountains and sea to myself. The southern cape of Corfu melted into the distance and the green hills of Paxos and tiny Antipaxos came into view. After all my cycling over the past few months, I was taking even the steepest climbs with ease, and was amazed to find myself in Mesopotamo by the early afternoon, at the turn-off for the Necromanteion of Ephyra, a little-visited Oracle of the Dead which I had longed to see for years.

Scholars have a merry time arguing about the location of Homer's sites, but I like to think that he knew this coastline well and described it accurately in *The Odyssey*. Ithaca lies off-shore, not far to the south west, and if Homer knew Ithaca, he would surely have known Ephyra too in the valley of the Acheron River. According to the Greeks, it was one of the entrances to the Underworld, and Circe's description of it in Book X of *The Odyssey* certainly fits the spot. She tells Odysseus to sail north across the River of Ocean until he reaches a wild coast, where there is a grove of tall poplars and willows sacred to Persephone. There the River of Flame and the River of Lamentation (the Kokytos), a tributary of the Styx, form an island round a rocky crag to pour their thundering streams into Acheron. We know that what used to be a great harbour in classical times has silted up, along with the lake around Homer's rocky crag, but the crag is still there above the main road, and the Rivers Acheron and Kokytos still flow around Ephyra. Odysseus made his offerings of honey, milk, wine and water, then sacrificed a young ram and a black ewe to the spirits of the dead, who came flocking round, drawn by the smell of blood, and made their prophecies.

I had a snack and a drink, then left my bike in the restaurant and climbed up to the ruins. Homer's willows still grow along the Acheron, but the poplars on the site have been replaced by cypresses, the trees associated with death throughout the Mediterranean. The Cyclopean walls of the sanctuary stand over the cave, which was the entrance to the Underworld and the scene of mysterious rites, where cunning priests played highly profitable tricks.

The buildings take the form of a maze, with black, windowless rooms. Those who came to consult the dead would have to spend the night in these grim surroundings. They were fed on hallucinogenic beans (archaeologists have found desiccated samples), then led in a state of total disorientation round the twists and turns of gloomy corridors, to make their offerings of blood and wine to the thirsty ghosts. The climax of the rite came when they were led down into the pitch dark of the cave, the very mouth of Hades. Excavations have revealed the most amazing iron and bronze hook-toothed wheels, exactly the same machinery that was used in Greek theatres to let down gods from the heavens, the classical *deus ex machina*. We can only assume that the priests used cranes and windlasses to dangle the dead before the terrified eyes of their gullible clients. Traces of sulphur show that these 'ghosts' were probably lit up in flashes of spooky light. It was not an oracle to consult for trivial reasons. The seekers must have been pretty desperate for advice to submit themselves to such terrors.

It was not far to Loutsa, where I was planning to spend the night, but the steep ascent from the Acheron Valley was an ordeal in the blazing afternoon sun. A bit of cycling, a bit of walking, then it was all I could do to stagger across to an olive tree and collapse under its shade. Once I reached the cliff top, the road retained its height and I realised that Loutsa and the other beach resorts were all in charming coves about 3 miles (5 km) down a dead drop. Cycling headfirst down one of the paths would have been scary enough; but I should have had a heart attack the next morning, trying to push Condor with all my gear back up the path to the road. So I struggled on and ran out of water. I was so desperate that I flagged down a Swiss car and begged. Then, as always seems to happen, just as I was reaching the limit of my endurance, I looked down another of those vertical cliff paths and spotted a restaurant advertising rooms, just a few metres off the main road. They had a vacancy and I was saved. After three cold drinks and a shower, I flopped down on my shady veranda. All energy spent, I idled away the rest of the afternoon watching the hotel puppy. He was pouncing on the heaps of leaves which an old man was trying to sweep and when the old man drove him off with his broom, he charged and somersaulted round the trunks of the lemon trees, chasing their flickering shadows.

The same puppy must have woken the entire hotel with his barking when I tried to slip quietly out of the gate at six the next morning. It was my big day. I should be meeting Cleopatra for the first time since I left her Needle at the end of April.

The mouth of the great inland sea, known as the Ambracian Gulf, was the scene of the Battle of Actium, the final showdown in

31 BC between Antony and Cleopatra on the one side and Octavian on the other. In the civil wars and foreign skirmishes which followed the assassination of Julius Caesar, Antony and Octavian had campaigned themselves into position as the two most powerful Romans. Octavian's power base lay in Rome itself and Rome's western provinces; Antony was pre-eminent in the eastern Mediterranean, where his marriage to Cleopatra had brought him the client states of the Pharaohs, as well as Rome's eastern provinces. Greece lay in the middle, between their two spheres of influence, so when the two men squared up for the final round of their contest, it was the obvious battleground. They fought in Greece, but the prizes were Rome and the wealth of Egypt. The victor would be the most powerful man in the world.

The road from my hotel climbed higher and higher along the cliff tops and I was looking forward to a fantastic panorama of the battle scene. But the coast road flattened out gradually and when I got past the overhanging mountains, there were tall trees and oleanders blocking my view of the water. A narrow promontory led to Preveza at the northern end of the entrance to the gulf and I sped along it with a wonderful following wind. To my left, I caught glimpses of the ruins of Nicopolis, the city Octavian founded on the site of his camp, to commemorate his victory in the battle, but I didn't stop to inspect them. I went straight to the docks in Preveza and joined the queue for the ferry.

The size of the Ambracian Gulf just took my breath away. I had expected a large expanse of water, but not this immense ocean. And the inlet from the Ionian Sea was even narrower than I had pictured it. The sandy spit of Actio, where Antony's forces camped, virtually sealed off the gulf. It was so near to Preveza that I was across on the ferry in ten minutes. When I saw the lie of the land, I was amazed that Antony and Cleopatra had stationed their combined fleets inside the gulf. They were rats in Octavian's trap. The land around the gulf was so marshy and mosquito-infested that they were dependent on supplies of food from Egypt. Octavian had only to seize the islands of Corfu to the north and Leukas immediately to the south to cut their supply lines. In the end, their ships' timbers rotting and their men dropping off like flies through disease and hunger, they tried to break out. If they could engage Octavian's fleet in the open sea, their own heavier vessels would have the advantage. The two fleets were fairly evenly matched in number, but Octavian's ships were lighter and more manoeuvrable – and he had the finest naval strategist Rome ever produced, the great Agrippa, as his admiral. The break-out was a fiasco. Exactly what happened is unclear from the accounts which have come down to us, but it seems they were harried by Octavian's fast little ships, disappointed in the wind they were hoping would fill their sails, and perhaps impeded by disaffected troops. When only a part of the fleet had managed to get through the narrow passage, Cleopatra's squadron of sixty ships broke through Agrippa's line and she sailed out to sea to clear the sandbanks. Antony hesitated, then followed. Cleopatra's purple sails disappeared over the horizon, followed by Antony's flagship. The men were devastated, thinking their leaders had deserted them. The rest of the fleet surrendered to Octavian and the army went over to him en masse. Antony and Cleopatra had staked all and lost. They fled to Egypt, where they committed suicide. Cleopatra's Kingdom of the Ptolemies became a Roman province and Octavian plundered the royal treasury to pay off his war debts. His victory was easy and complete. He assumed the title of Augustus and sole power over Rome and all its dominions.

As I was travelling from west to east, I came across Cleopatra's end before I discovered her beginnings. It means that I have to tell her story back-to-front, breaking all the rules of conventional biography. It's unfortunate, but it can't be helped. Either her life has to go backwards or my bicycle! (For those who are worried by this irregularity, I have listed the chief events of her life in chronological order as Appendix B.)

Until recently, the fine beaches nestling beneath the crags of this wildly romantic coast were a well-kept Greek secret, but now they feature in the holiday brochures. It was Saturday, changeover day for the package people, so the tiny airport at Actio was humming with activity. Charter flights were zooming in and out, and when I took the peaceful road along the south shore of the gulf, I suddenly came to a set of traffic lights where there was no traffic. They were red, so I stopped dutifully and gazed around me in puzzlement. Then I spotted a plane in the distance, flying low across the water. It was obviously coming in to land at Actio. As I stood at the lights, it came down towards the road and flew across just in front of me, clearing my head and handlebars by a whisker. I cowered down and covered my ears, while passengers grinned at me through the windows. It was too close for comfort.

The lakeside, which had failed to provide Antony and Cleopatra with food, was still poor marshy country, though the locals were doing their best with plastic tunnels of tomatoes, small patches of maize in the middle of scrub and tobacco leaves drying in sheds. I passed an old woman in black, who was driving a few sheep and goats to the lower slopes of the overhanging mountains; and a scrawny old man in a tweed suit and cap, with two goats on strings, waved his walking stick at me in greeting. The goats were so keen to get a better view of this lone cyclist that they tugged the poor old chap into the road and nearly pulled him over. I stopped at a village for a Coca-Cola and a most dignified, moustashioed elderly gentleman walked by, with an old-fashioned flat cap pulled down low over his eyes. He couldn't believe them when he saw me sitting outside the village café, with my bike propped against the tree. Too polite to stand and stare, he walked on a little way, then turned back and walked past again – and again, and again – taking discreet peeks. It was all very rural, a hidden corner of Greece which time had forgotten. The black dresses and tweed suits took me back half a century, to the days when the country was poor and tourists were a rarity. The man in the café spoke Greek and not a word of anything else, but his little boy waved to me shyly as I left and said 'Goodbye', so times were at last beginning to change.

In contrast to the old-fashioned innocence of the countryside, the lakeside ports of Vonitsa and Amfilohia showed modern Greeks at their brashest. I have never seen so many BMWs, Audis, Mercedes, Ferraris and Alfa Romeos in one place. As for the yachts – they were the sort where white-coated waiters served drinks under awnings, while their employers eyed the exercise machines on the aft deck and promised to start getting themselves into shape tomorrow. The quayside fish restaurants were expensive and I kept bumping into Greek Canadians, holidaying in western Greece and looking to buy property.

I had a choice of routes down to the Gulf of Corinth, both of them more or less beside water. Having explored the southern shore of Cleopatra's Bay of Actium, I could take the rugged coast road from Vonitsa to Astakos (Greek for crayfish), then cycle across a wild promontory, where the only path was far from the sea and looked on the map like a frenzied worm on a bad day. The alternative was to climb over the Acharnanian Mountains from Amfilohia, then follow the chain of lakes, rivers and irrigation canals across agricultural land. The wild coast was tempting, but exposed and not very sensible in the heat of midsummer. So I chose the second. It was shorter and flatter, and there was a market town halfway along it, where I guessed there would be hotels.

It was tobacco country and the chain of lakes, even the great Lake Ambracia, was sadly depleted to water the crop. I rode beside canals, then along the majestic sky-blue River Acheloos. In this unregarded corner of rural Greece, known as Western Roumeli, the roadside shrines were devoutly tended. Oil lamps burned in the little glass-fronted boxes before the icons of saints, and the sight of so many of them on the edges of tobacco fields did make me smile quietly to myself. I thought of all those saints protecting a crop which would hasten the arrival of smokers to join them in heaven! A road lined with delicate apricot-coloured oleanders ran between Lake Trihonida and Lake Lusomahia. Then I cycled over mountains and through a most spectacular gorge, to find the great expanse of the Gulf of Messalongi spread out beneath me. The usual town-twinning notice stood by the roadside, its Union Jack welcoming me to the Sacred City of Messalongi. It was sacred because of the heroic resistance put up by its citizens during a Turkish siege in the War of Independence, and the Union Jack was painted on the sign because Lord Byron died there (of malaria, not of fighting) in the same war. Messalongi is twinned with Gedling, which is near Newstead Abbey, Byron's Nottinghamshire home. Unfortunately, the name appears as 'Gelding' on the notice.

Exactly forty years ago, I visited Messalongi with my husband. We went there by bus from Delphi and everyone thought we were crazy. No one went to Messalongi in those days. I remember walking up a long, dusty main street with dingy shops. A gloomy hotel-keeper, whose droopy grey Balkan moustache matched his air of despondency, called out 'Hotel!' to us as we passed. He obviously had no hope of custom; and we laughed to think that anyone could contemplate *staying* in Messalongi.

Now there are elegant hotels along the edge of the lagoon, block-booked by groups, and the shops along the pedestrianised main street, the very street we walked along forty years before, are full of smart clothes, leather goods and computer games, just like the shops in any other prosperous town throughout the Western world. The supermarkets too have their shelves crammed with the same international brands. The only difference I noticed was the respect paid to a shopping priest. He had bought shampoo for his long grey locks and two dozen tins of sardines (for himself or his cat?). When he neared the check-out with his basket, everyone stood aside to let him go to the head of the queue. I doubt if you would see such reverence towards the local vicar in your neighbourhood Tesco. But apart from that little incident, I could have been in any supermarket anywhere in Europe. The Greeks are keen on their roadside slogans – 'Down with the dictatorship of the EU!' – but they would not be so well off without it. Their economy has thrived since they joined.

Messalongi was a furnace, where everyone inched along the walls like beetles, cowering in scraps of shade. Luckily, my modest hotel in the town centre had air conditioning and I had a lovely cool bathroom with real marble on the floor and walls. Marble is so common in that part of Greece that the road-builders find it cheaper to use than white paint. They lay it down in bars to mark the edges of the hard shoulders and carve it in deep corrugations to startle absent-minded motorists. Once laid, it lasts forever and is totally maintenance-free.

I waited until late afternoon before visiting the town hall museum, but as I crossed the square to the gleaming white mock-classical building, I was blinded by the glare of the light. Even at that time of day, the heat was still unbelievable. I was an egg frying in a pan. I scuttled into the shelter of the Byron Memorial and met with a heroine's welcome. '*O Lordhos Vyronos*' is a hero in Greece and I happen to have been born, like him, in Nottinghamshire. If the red carpet had not already been on the floor, it would have been laid for me that afternoon by the delighted attendant.

Byron arrived in Messalongi in January 1824. He was the most glamorous, the most aristocratic, and the richest of the Philhellenes dedicated to the cause of Greek independence. At the time, Messalongi was one of the few small pockets of land to be liberated from the Turks and it occupied a key position at the western end of the Gulf of Corinth. Byron stepped off his ship from Kephalonia with his usual panache, dressed in scarlet military uniform, with a guard of kilted guerrillas. He was greeted with a 21-gun salute and put in command of the town garrison, but everything went downhill from there. He spent a frustrating three months, plus a large slice of his wealth, trying to persuade the warring Greek generals, who were mostly mountain brigands from the wilder parts of Greece, to stop fighting one another and join forces against the Turks. In the end, he turned out to be more successful in death than in life. He died, appropriately enough for such a romantic poet, at the height of a thunderstorm, and his heroic death stirred up passions throughout Europe. Young men flocked to the cause, but it was not until the end of the Napoleonic Wars that England, France and Russia stepped in as 'Great Powers'. The Greeks got their independence in 1830.

After the death of Lord Byron, the Turks laid siege to Messalongi. The citizens resisted their firepower with astonishing valour for over a year, but when the Egyptian fleet under Ibrahim Pasha captured the lagoon, their supplies were cut off and, desperate for food, they decided to break out. In those days, the city was an island with the Gulf of Messalongi on one side and the lagoon on the other. A drawbridge from the city gate was the only connection between the town and the mainland. They let down the drawbridge and nine thousand men, women and children fought their way through what is now known as the Gate of the Exodus. All those who survived this wild dash were ambushed and massacred in the mountains by an Albanian mercenary force. The few defenders left inside blew up the city and themselves, rather than surrender to the Sultan's army. The city is now a national shrine, the Sacred City of Messalongi.

Inside the town hall, there are some vivid heroic paintings of the siege. In pride of place hangs a copy of *Greece on the Ruins of Messalongi* by Delacroix. Then there are the more lurid scenes painted by patriotic Greeks – women killing their children, rather than have them fall into the hands of the Turks, women hurling stones from the battlements, Bishop Joseph of Rogi exploding in a flash of gunpowder, citizens captured and hung, and the valiant Exodus, with Christ and his angels holding garlands for the heaven-bound martyrs.

Compared with all this, the Byron Memorial was tame, if more tasteful. It was dominated by his white marble statue, posing in front of a sky-blue screen. Copies of portraits showed him in a variety of Greek national costumes and there were pictures of three bronze clocks, which were evidently popular productions at the time of his death. One was ornamented with a figure of Byron in the arms of Greece; one with Byron reading *Childe Harold's Pilgrimage*; and one with the poet wandering pensively among Greek ruins. It was all beautifully set out and labelled in English as well as Greek, but they did seem to be scratching rather desperately for exhibits. A chunk of stone from Newstead Abbey, a set of Nottingham lace doilies with the Nottingham coat of arms, and even a photograph of Gedling's unlovely Civic Centre! But the people of Messalongi had done their best with what little they had and it was a collection assembled with evident love and pride.

When the air cooled down a little, I cycled to the Garden of Heroes, to visit Byron's statue, where some people say his heart is buried, only to find that it was being refurbished. Yet another of the things I had travelled months to photograph was under scaffolding! That always seems to be happening to me. I was annoyed and disappointed, but I found a garden bench and I was soon enveloped in the gorgeous scent of pine and eucalyptus. My frustration melted away into the evening air. A million cicadas sang to me and I had one of those moments of sheer delight, when I could think of nothing I would rather be doing than sitting in that garden on that evening in Messalongi.

A leisurely ride round the lagoon and I was back in my hotel, chatting to the owner. He was a young Cypriot, who had studied at Birmingham University, run a business in England for ten years, then returned with his English wife to Greece.

'When you had the whole of Greece to choose from, why did you settle in Messalongi?' I asked.

'By chance really. We started off in Athens, but we had friends here and came once or twice to visit them. We both took a fancy to the place, so when this hotel came on the market, I made an offer for it, and here we are. That was two years ago and we've never regretted leaving Athens. Such a noisy, crowded place! Here, we all go everywhere on our bicycles and the children are safe playing in the streets. It's small and friendly.'

He was my third new hotelier, and for the third time on my trip I was taken on a tour to see the refurbishment. Le Havre, Rouen and now Messalongi. I was becoming an expert in bedroom décor and the logistics of modernising bathrooms while keeping the hotel open for custom. But it was good to have a proper conversation, my first since I talked to the purser on the ferry. Greece was often a lonely place.

I had problems with the language. Modern Greek is similar enough to classical Greek for me to be able to get the gist of a newspaper article or understand a menu, but the spoken language defeats me. The consonants are amazingly liquid and the vowel-sounds completely different from the ones we used in school. So although I can construct grammatically correct sentences, no one can understand my pronunciation. I spent six weeks in Greece and I tried so hard with the language, but got nowhere. At the end of that time, I still couldn't get my meaning across to the Greeks, or get more than a glimmer of what they were saying to me. I found it quite depressing, when I had spent so many years studying the Classics. Perhaps I was carrying too much ancient baggage. I might have done better if I had had to start modern Greek from scratch like my other travelling languages.

Whatever the reason, I was failing to communicate. And the Greeks themselves were no help. I had so far met very few who could speak anything but Greek and, in any case, they seemed unwilling to take the trouble with a stranger. I had just come from Italy, where the people are splendidly exuberant and extrovert. Waiters in restaurants, chambermaids in hotels, bus conductors, people in cafés, they all enjoy talking, in whatever language. Hospitality spills over and the bicycle is a bonus in a country where *ciclismo* is a national sport. The contrast with Greece could not have been starker. When I think of their seaside resorts, I see arrogant men in white trousers, stalking along the waterfront clutching their flies, still arguing loudly, as they did in Byron's day, and shouting into their mobiles, while their brassy women concentrate on the shops. Greece has changed with prosperity. The old people are still courteous and genuinely interested in visitors, but commercial success has produced a younger, more boastful breed, obsessed with the trappings of wealth and influence. For these, a foreign cyclist, a pauper riding a lowly machine, is a worm beneath their notice.

So I led a solitary life in Greece, not helped by the timetable I had to stick to if I was to make reasonable progress. Once I left the fresher Ionian coast, the heat was overwhelming. I set my alarm for 5.30, when the stars were still bright and the bats were still fluttering outside my window. As the hotels were not serving breakfast at that hour, I had a mug of Nescafé and some sort of a bun in my room. I aimed to be out on the road by 6.30 at the latest, so that I could reach my destination between 10 and 11 a.m. In western Greece, I never had a problem with hotels, as they all had vacancies at that time of the morning. I checked in, restored my blood sugar with another mug of Nescafé and some sweet biscuits, then went out to do my odd jobs – shopping, getting cash from a hole in the wall, buying stamps at the post office. I was too hot and tired to feel hungry, so I lunched in my room on my favourite spinach pie from the baker's, or cheese triangles (tasteless, but they travel well), crackers and those huge misshapen, multicoloured Greek tomatoes, which taste heavenly, unlike our perfect red billiard balls. Then I showered and holed up for the afternoon, sleeping for two or three hours, like a good Greek, writing up my notes, writing letters, reading, planning my next day's route, until the cool of the evening, when I went out to sightsee and stroll around the town. The Greeks dine at a very late hour and by the time the restaurants started to open, somewhere around nine o'clock, I was absolutely ravenous. After 50 miles (80 km) of draining midsummer heat, I needed serious food much earlier. I usually ate my dinner in silence, served by a grumpy waiter, who obviously found me an inconvenience when he wanted to talk to his friends. Then back to the hotel and bed around 11.30, feeling uncomfortably full. Greek food is heavy and quite greasy. Even with my 'eat anything' ostrich digestion, I got through boxes of Rennies.

I was getting a bit bogged down in culture after Ephyra, Actium and Messalongi, three major sites in five days, and I felt for Madame de Sevigny, who said of sightseeing, 'What I see tires me. What I don't see worries me.' So it was in a kind of holiday mood that I set out from Messalongi for the seaside shore of the Peloponnese. I was relieved, too, to be leaving the formidable mountains of Western Roumeli for a few days' cycling along the flat, though there was still one massif left to climb. Of the 23 miles (35 km) from Messalongi to the ferry at Andirio, almost 16 were steadily uphill, as if the landscape were on some kind of a geological tilt. I dipped for a while to the Euinos River, in midsummer just a few puddles under an enormously long bridge, then up again through treeless rocks to the summit, where I had one of those views which make mountain-cycling worth all the pain – the Messalongi lagoon behind me, still veiled in morning mist, and the sparkling Gulf of Corinth ahead. They were building a bridge over the gulf, so I looked down on a vast construction site, where grey-coated olive trees rose like spectres from the dust clouds. Then I gritted my teeth against vertigo and hurtled down to the shore, with a sheer rock drop to my right. Once across on the ferry to Rio (free for foot passengers and cyclists), I cruised along in the shade through a string of quiet seaside resorts until I reached a dead end by some fish restaurants and had to climb up to the main road. There the heat hit me like a hammer and I was forced to stagger into the first hotel I saw, an expensive beach resort, way above budget, where I paid a small fortune for swimming pools, tennis courts, waterskiing and discos at night – none of them of the slightest interest to a weary sun-frizzled cyclist. I didn't even have the strength to go swimming.

I unloaded my bike and wheeled it away to a shed to lock it up for the night. It was only then that I realised I had stupidly left my keys, compass and the gold chain I always wear round my neck when I travel in the hotel in Messalongi. I rushed to the phone.

'Oh, thank goodness you've rung!' said the nice young man. 'The chambermaid found them this morning and we didn't know what to do because we didn't have a forwarding address for you. We were so worried.'

It was not the first time I had left something behind on my cycle travels, but it was the most awkward. In the normal way, I reckon that one day's cycling equals one hour in a bus. So, on previous occasions, I have caught a bus to my last night's hotel, picked up what I've left behind and got back in time for dinner. But this time, it could not have been more complicated. It took me the whole of the next day, eight hours from door to door, to reclaim my chain and keys from Messalongi: a bus to Rio town centre, a 4-kilometre walk to the docks, a pause for the ferry, a long wait for the Messalongi bus, a bus cancellation from Messalongi to Andirio, the ferry back, a bus to a strange terminal in Patras (there was no direct service from the docks to my hotel at Psathopyrgos), a walk across Patras to the main bus station and a final bus home. I could have kicked myself. Of course, it could have been worse. I could have lost my keys and chain. The smiling proprietor handed them over and beamed when I gave him a tip for the honest chambermaid. 'She *will* be pleased. She's saving up for a washing machine. Nothing has ever gone missing in this hotel,' he added proudly. I left his civilised place and returned to a bear garden. Last night's noisy crowd of Polish teenagers had been joined by three coachloads of teenagers from Italy, and the banging of doors and excited screams in corridors kept me awake till the early hours.

The first night, when my keys were missing, I had to keep my bicycle in my bedroom. It was a bit of a squash and I kept banging my shins on the pedals as I squeezed by. So the second night, with my padlock in operation again, I wheeled it to the outbuilding where the guard dogs were chained. One was a sleepy old St Bernard, the other a young German Shepherd. The girl from reception escorted me there, so that the dogs would realise I was not a marauder and know that the bicycle belonged to me. 'If anyone else so much as looks at that bike now, they'll be mincemeat!' she said.

At 6.30 the next morning, the two dogs were roaming free and Condor, still chained to a post, was splayed out on the ground in a peculiar position. As I went over to unlock it, the young German Shepherd crouched down with his ears back, wagging his tail and rolling his eyes sheepishly, as dogs do when they feel guilty about something. Not understanding, I unlocked the bike, leaned it against a tree and started to load it up. When the puppy saw that I was not angry with him, he came over to play. He worried my panniers and ran off with my cycling cap. I chased him and we had a fine game. When I cycled away, I was careful not to look him in the eye, because I heard him panting hopefully behind me to the main gate. Given the least encouragement, he would have followed me all the way to Egypt. It was not until the next morning that I saw the reason for the guilty rolling eyes. Bored stiff on his chain, and possibly teething as well, he had chewed the plastic flap on my front mudguard to shreds and even had a go at one of the brake cables.

It was a beautiful ride to Corinth along the northern shore of the Peloponnese. A motorway had syphoned off most of the trucks, leaving the old road which linked the seaside towns relatively free of traffic. At first, it climbed the foothills of the overhanging mountains and I saw the beaches way below. At Platanos, a sheer cliff was cut into three giant steps: the railway on the bottom, my road in the middle and the motorway roaring high above me. Then I was down on the seafront for a brilliant ride through pine-shaded resorts with a light breeze behind me. Posters advertised circuses, the old-fashioned sort with wild animals; and there were posters of glossy men, who might have been politicians or pop stars. It was hard to tell, as they all had the same slicked-back hair and gleaming capped-tooth smiles.

In Xylocastro I was accosted outside the post office by Kevin, a sociable Irishman who taught English in Athens. He had once been a racing cyclist, so he appreciated Condor's finer points. In the evening, he and his Greek wife Roula turned up at my hotel and took me out for an ice cream on the seafront. They were admirable people, concerned about the world's injustices and prepared to do something about them. For instance, they corresponded with people on America's Death Row. Sometimes the prisoners were reluctant, thinking they had nothing to write about, but 'Describe your day; tell us your daily routine; tell us what you can see out of your window' usually got them started, and they came to value the contact. One woman had taken to writing poetry and a young man, who was almost illiterate when he started to write to them, had improved so much that he had enrolled on a degree course. Prisoners can be on Death Row for twenty years, waiting for their appeals to go through the courts, so Kevin and Roula encourage them to do something with their time, to take control of their lives as far as is possible in their circumstances, rather than just sitting in their cells in blank despair. In one case, when they were convinced that a young man had been wrongfully sentenced at the age of seventeen, they campaigned through Amnesty International and got his case re-examined. But they thought he was dead, despite their efforts. He rang them and said that he was due to be executed the next day. 'If my reprieve comes through and I'm still alive, I'll ring you again tomorrow evening, without fail.' They sat by the phone and heard nothing. The next day, Roula rang the prison to enquire.

'I'm afraid I'm not in a position to give that information, ma'am,' said the Jack-in-Office at the other end of the line.

'For heaven's sake! This is a human being we're talking about. Can't you just tell me whether the boy's alive or dead?'

'I'm not in a position to say, ma'am.'

They still have no official information, despite writing to the prison governor, so they wait in waning hope for a letter.

I had never come across this particular type of quiet, unsung, unrewarded voluntary work before and I was fascinated to hear their stories and moved by their compassion. I felt guilty for weeks afterwards, because I was just gadding around on a bike, doing nothing to make the world a better place.

In Corinth (where currants come from, hence the word) there was an International Chess Congress and the four good hotels were all fully booked by chess-mad Eastern Europeans. But a German-speaking Macedonian working in Corinth persuaded the owner of a seedy D-category hotel to put me at the head of the queue for the one room soon to become vacant. I waited in the gloomy lobby with the proprietor, his son, the night watchman, the Macedonian, a woman with a baby and various men who just seemed to be sitting around, as men do in Greece. With the Macedonian as my interpreter, I told them all about my travels and was eventually given a double room at the single rate, because I had come so far on a bicycle! The room was over a 24-hour fast-food outlet, so pizza-delivery boys revved up their motorbikes under my window all through the night. It was the one and only hotel I stayed in where I had fleas in my bed, but I was grateful to have a bed at all.

I took a taxi up the sheer rock road to Acrocorinth, the ancient citadel perched on a 1,886-foot-high (575 m) pinnacle. My guidebook said that the watchtower on the peak of the mountain commanded views over the Saronic Gulf to the east, Attica to the north and Argolis to the south, as well as the Gulf of Corinth to the west. Acrocorinth controlled the approaches to the narrow isthmus from every direction, and it was easy to see why the city had once been so powerful. I took the writer's word for it. The struggle up through the ruins to the topmost peak on such a blazing afternoon was quite beyond me; and even if I had managed it, with my vertigo, I could never have climbed the rickety ladder up the tower.

'Bicycle' and 'from London' in Greek were enough to create a fan club of ancient men in the city square. They whiled away their day in the shade of the trees and looked out for me, waving their walking sticks, tottering over to greet me and giving me great hugs whenever I appeared. They were less keen on an insensitive hulk of a young man, who was marching round Corinth in a scarlet T-shirt with the Turkish flag emblazoned on the front. Kevin and Roula had told me that relations between Greece and Turkey had become much more cordial since the two countries had sent aid to each other in recent earthquakes. In fact, the Greek press was encouraging Greeks to go on holiday to Turkey, telling them that the Turks were kind, honest people. 'They look you in the eye and offer to help, without calculating what might be in it for them – an attitude unfortunately lost by the Greeks,' said one newspaper. But even so, the scarlet Turkish T-shirt was a bit too much. It drew sharp intakes of breath from the local lads sitting outside the cafés, and I wouldn't have fancied that silly young wearer's chances in a back street on a dark night.

With my nightdress securely sellotaped in a plastic bag to stop the fleas from jumping into the rest of my clothes, I set out for Athens in the cool of the morning and crossed the Corinth Canal. It was amazing to stand on the road bridge, which I had only seen from ships sailing below, and look down from my dizzy height into the narrow cleft. It was far more dramatic from above. I was not lucky enough to see a liner or a giant tanker come through, clearing the sides by inches, but I did coincide with a tug pulling some sort of dredger.

When the Corinth Canal was opened, it was an ancient dream come true. Slicing across the limestone ridge of the isthmus, it cut the journey from the Adriatic to Piraeus by more than 200 miles (320 km), and saved seafarers the often stormy journey round the southern prongs of the Peloponnese. As early as the sixth century BC, Periander, King of Corinth, had built a kind of stone runway, called 'the diolkos', to connect his port on the Gulf of Corinth with the one on the Saronic Gulf. Ships were unloaded and somehow hauled across the 4 miles of the isthmus. The Emperor Nero even began work on a canal in AD 67, but cutting through the limestone mass was too difficult even for his brilliant Roman engineers. It was not until 1893, after twelve years' toil, that the rock was hacked away and the Corinth Canal officially opened.

I cycled along the north bank towards Loutraki, as near as I could get to the canal, looking for traces of the diolkos, which I understood could still be seen. But I couldn't find them. All I saw was litter-strewn wasteland and nasty guard dogs. It was a fruitless detour, but at least it was a pleasant morning run along a quiet, cool, shady road. It was to be my last pleasant run for a very long time.

The old road to Athens began along a rocky shore, where a scattering of pines and wild olives clung bravely to the cliffs above shingle coves. I cycled east, into the blazing heat of the sun, but at least the motorway was high above me and the traffic was light – until I got to Eleusis. There the nightmare began. The old road merged with the motorway and I found myself on the hard shoulder of a highway crowded with speeding lunatics. Not content with their own four lanes in each direction, cars and even heavy trucks kept cutting in front of me, to overtake on the inside. Tempers rose with the heat, horns honked, brakes screeched and the exhaust fumes were so thick that I nearly choked. I have never been so frightened on a road. There was no alternative route and I had to concentrate so hard on keeping alive that the only way I could cope was by cycling for about ten minutes, then finding a safe spot to pull off, where I could stand with my eyes shut while my pulse slowed down to normal. Fortunately, as I was following the coast, I had only about an hour of this terror before I could fork right off the main Athens highway and take the quieter road directly to Piraeus.

I cycled along to the harbour, where Cleopatra would have seen her fleet riding at anchor, when she and Antony paused to sightsee in Athens on their way to disaster at Actium.

Piraeus was once a seedy, down-at-heel port, where no one would ever think of staying. But when I cycled along the front, I found a breezy promenade with palm trees, good shops and modern hotels. I had been intending to stay in downtown Athens, but why swelter in the heat of that chaotic, traffic-ridden city when I could live far more comfortably for half the price by the sea, and travel into the centre by metro in twenty minutes? Piraeus was a more manageable size too for getting jobs done. There were camera shops galore along the waterfront, where the assistants spoke English and I was able to get a small problem with my Olympus sorted out in no time. American Express recommended an optician, who fixed me up with reading glasses. (My good pair had been stolen in Bari, and I had lost my old reserve pair in my panic on the motorway that morning, so I couldn't even read my maps.) I was able to use the fax machine at my most accommodating brand-new hotel; and I found an old-fashioned Greek restaurant round the corner, where the dishes were all laid out for inspection, in traditional style, and I could choose from the pots. They even had a microwave there and served my choice of dish piping hot – something which rarely happens in Greece, where they think that food above lukewarm damages the stomach.

It was time for a rest from cycling, so I spent a few days haunting the museums in Athens and Piraeus and catching up on correspondence. The heat was so debilitating that I spent two hours in a museum and was finished for the rest of the day. Athens was noisy, seething with tourists and impatient Greeks; I was having trouble with the Syntagma Square branch of American Express over some missing correspondence; and I fell down with all my weight on my bad knee. I decided that Athens was quite the most unpleasant Western capital. In fact, when I tried to think of a worse one, I could only come up with Jakarta in the whole world. I felt lonely, stressed out and downhearted. Looking back on those days, there were only two bright spots. One was the elegant Goulandris Museum of Cycladic and Ancient Greek Art, where the violin-shaped marble women could have come straight out of the studios of Henry Moore, Brancusi or Modigliani. The other was my friendly hotel, where I was so well established that I was even asked to take a turn at reception one evening, while the owner rushed out to do her last-minute shopping. 'You needn't answer the phone,' she said. 'Whoever it is will probably ring again. And if anyone arrives, tell them there's a room and ask them to wait a couple of minutes.' My Greek was just about up to that and I earned a large ice cream for my trouble. I never knew the name of the owner, but she was a wise woman, who spoke excellent English. When I checked out of the hotel, she said, 'I don't know what you're looking for, travelling around on that bicycle, but I hope you find it.' A thoughtful variation on 'Safe journey!'

10. AEGEAN GREECE

Place me on Sunium's marbled steep,
Where nothing, save the waves and I,
May hear our mutual murmurs sweep;
There, swan-like, let me sing and die.

Lord Byron, *Don Juan*

As I was following the seashore, I had to cycle round the long loop of Cape Sounion. At first, the road was motorway, through the fashionable resort of Glyfada – though why it was fashionable, beyond proximity to Athens, I couldn't for the life of me imagine. Eight lanes of traffic roared between its apartment blocks and the beach, while planes from Athens airport screamed overhead. When the motorway ended, there was a string of seaside towns, where I could buy cold drinks and rest on park benches. It was a rugged coast. I climbed over ridges, then swept down to the shore, where the blustery wind was flecking the deep indigo of the sea with pure white foam. Every sea has its own particular colour. The Aegean is of such an intense blue, almost a bruised purple, that it must surely be Homer's 'wine-dark sea'.

I had hoped to stop for the night before Cape Sounion, but I suppose the beach resorts were too near to Athens to have hotels. The rich had their own weekend places, while the rest could easily drive to the seaside for the day. So there was nowhere for me to stay. I had to soldier on through the afternoon heat, across country that grew wilder and windier towards the cape, with no shade at all, nothing but myrtle on scrubby hillsides. I kept climbing round bleak headlands, always expecting Poseidon's temple to appear round the next bend, only to find that there was yet another bend and another crag ahead of me. At last, the sixteen striking columns of the temple came into view on the height of the promontory, dominating a cove of yachts and an expensive hotel, where my husband and I once had lunch in my earlier, more lavish existence. With no strength left to climb to the temple, I struggled on to a hotel, which turned out to be considerably further round the bend than I had reckoned. I had cycled almost fifty miles over punishing terrain and I was wobbling with fatigue. My bad knee hurt, my face flamed and my legs were burnt scarlet, despite wearing long trousers. A light supper of moussaka, salad and ice-cold wine, and I staggered to bed. Tomorrow I should begin my journey out of the furnace towards the cooler air of northern Greece.

Having cycled south from Piraeus along the western perimeter fence of Athens Airport, I found it quite depressing to glance to my left in Markopoulo and see planes again. Two days' toil and I was back where I started from, still beside the airport and still within reach of the local Athens buses. I slept under a flightpath, on a busy road junction where traffic roared until 4 a.m. when the planes started, but I was so desperate to find a hotel on that inhospitable shore that I would have taken a bed in a pneumatic drill factory!

In Marathon I came to a dead end, like the Persians who invaded Attica in 490 BC and lost 6,400 men in one of the most significant battles in world history. If Athens had lost at Marathon, there would have been no flowering of classical civilisation and no democracy. But they won a stunning victory, losing only 192 hoplites. I paid my respects at their simple grassy burial mound, then tried to move on towards Thebes. The Marathon police were discouraging. The mountain route through Grammatiko was horrendously steep and there were no hotels up there; and even if I managed to get through, I would end up on the Athens–Thebes motorway, where it was illegal for me to cycle. The only thing was to take the bus – but as there was no bus direct from Marathon to Thebes, I would have to go back into Athens. What a prospect, after so much effort to round the cape!

I went to the bus stop, but when the driver and conductor saw me standing there with my bicycle, they just laughed at me, shouted 'No!' through the door, without even bothering to open it, and sped off down the road. Greek charm! I went back to the police station and told them what had happened. 'Is that normal?' I asked. 'Or did I get a difficult driver?' 'It's normal. Buses don't take bikes.' In the mid-morning heat, I nearly exploded. Why send me to catch a bus when they knew very well that buses didn't take bikes? But I bit my tongue. There was obviously nothing for it but to cycle back to Athens and take the train to Thebes. Of course, it was an interesting ride, because it was the original Marathon course, the legendary 26 miles run by Pheidippides. He is said to have rushed into the market-place at Athens, gasped 'We've won!'

and expired on the spot. The truth is more impressive. It was the entire battle-weary Athenian army who raced that distance, to prevent the Persian fleet from attacking their undefended city.

A sunbaked ride through thickening traffic, a row with an unco-operative doorman at American Express, a struggle through the maelstrom of central Athens to the station, and at last I was on the 14.24 to Thebes. I shared a compartment with seven young Greeks (four boys and three girls), all shouting and smoking. They hurled bottles, cans, cartons, cigarette packets, matches and fag ends out of the window with gay abandon, adding to the million such items of litter which are a feature of the Greek countryside. The Greeks are the champion chuckers-away of Europe. Since they became prosperous, they have gone over entirely to 'designer water', even though their tap water is perfectly safe, and all those plastic bottles go flying out of car windows, until the whole of their ancient land is a plastic-coated tip.

The train passed through sheer mountain clefts, thick with myrtle, pine, olives and mimosa, and the motorway ran alongside through the same narrow passes. There was little sign of habitation, apart from the odd hut and a few goat tracks, so I was glad that I didn't have to cycle there. Attica was stark, sun-stricken and unproductive as land. But that may just have been the secret of the Athenians' success. As a settled agricultural life was out of the question, they had to find other, more strenuous ways to earn their living and make their mark in the world. They grew bold in war and even more formidable in intellect.

When the train drew into Thebes Station, I saw something I never thought to see in Europe – families living at the ends of the station platforms, as they do in India. They may have been gypsies, or they may simply have been the dispossessed of the Balkans and places further east, fleeing the despair of poverty and the bombardments of NATO. I expect they were hoping to move west, to England or Germany, where the streets are paved with gold. The lucky ones had the transport to get there. Families were crossing Greece in ramshackle pick-up trucks, with awnings to give shade to the children who were riding on top of the suitcases. These migrants slept out on grass verges at night, or camped in unfinished buildings, then moved on in the morning. A few stayed and made lives for themselves in Greece. I met a Punjabi petrol-pump attendant, who had lived near Athens for twelve years, and most of the hotels seemed to be staffed by Bulgarian chambermaids. But, broadly speaking, Greece was a transit zone, where the tide of humanity was moving west.

Modern Thebes is perched on the ancient acropolis, with the railway station on the fertile plain below, so it was quite a struggle to climb up to the town, but well worth it. I liked Thebes better than anywhere else in Greece. Traffic was banned from the city centre, where charming cobbled streets led up to a shady square. From the writing desk under my window, I looked out on an avenue of mimosa trees, half veiling a set of barristers' chambers and an empty shop. Perfect peace after the racket of Athens. I even had BBC World on my television and could catch up on the news. I found a workmen's clothing store, where I bought a pair of really heavy-duty black cargo pants to protect my legs from the sun. Then I gave my poor aching, sunburnt body a couple of days' rest.

Friends had told me that I was mad to be cycling in Greece in August, but I had taken no notice. After all, I had cycled across Greece from Igoumenitsa to Thessaloniki in 1987 and had no problems. What I had not taken into account was that my 1987 route lay across northern Greece, high up in the Pindos Mountains. In 2001, I was much further south, down on the blazing coastal rocks, in the hottest summer the Greeks had seen for years. To add to my woes, there were 'road improvements'. Where routes cut a path through savage mountains, it was much too expensive to hack out a completely new road and leave the old one intact for slower traffic, so the transport ministry were simply widening the old roads into shadeless six-lane highways. These wound their way across desolate, sunbaked terrain, where there were no villages, no filling stations, not even a goat. On one occasion, when I had run out of drinks, I was so hot, thirsty and desperate for shade that I crouched down in the shadow of a parked truck, while the driver revived me with cool water. I reached rock-bottom when the north wind blew, hot as the flames of Hades and so strong that I sometimes had to get off and push, even on the flat. Every day was an ordeal and every evening a weary round of seaside hotels, which were all booked up in high season. Their owners were doing so well that they didn't bother to say 'Sorry', or even 'No'. They just tossed their heads back.

This harrowing ride almost ended in disaster. I was cycling along at six o'clock one morning, before the road-builders had started work. They had built a new carriageway, but it was not yet open to traffic. It was the perfect place to cycle. I hauled my bicycle up the embankment and cruised for miles along the smooth, traffic-free surface. When it was nearing its end, I spotted a truck exit and set a diagonal course towards it. What I didn't spot was that the surveyors had stretched a length of fine wire, at about hub height, down the middle of the new carriageway. As this was Greece, no one had thought to wind a bit of red and white plastic round it, or put up a warning sign. I ran into the wire at top speed and the next thing I knew, I was still travelling at speed, but on my side with Condor on top of me. Fortunately, I had gone into the wire at an oblique angle; had I gone at it head on, I should have catapulted over the handlebars. I was badly shaken, but nothing was broken. As I struggled to extricate my gears and pedals from the wire, a stream of blood poured down my leg and formed a puddle round my trainers. I managed to get to Kamena Vourla, which was not far away, and found the pharmacy. My left leg had been saved by my Theban workman's trousers, because the deep striated cuts and grazes from my knee down to my ankle were all clean and gravel-free. I limped around the town's crowded hotels and managed to find a room in a small pension, where I painted my cuts and grazes with the chemist's iodine and spent the day on the bed with my leg up. I had cut my left elbow too, and that evening I developed the most magnificent bruises on my left shoulder and hip, and a spectacular livid lump on the inside of my right knee. I was a fine sight, especially as the scarlet heat rash had flared up again.

This whole ride to Egypt seemed to have a jinx on it – torrential rain in England, France, Switzerland and north Italy, a bad knee, a robbery in Bari, the dead-end at Marathon, accommodation problems, the Greek heatwave, and now this accident. Was I unlucky? Or was I lucky that nothing was worse? So many things had gone wrong, but none of them was a total disaster. I had even had my punctures near to tyre specialists!

Nagging constantly at my mind was the need to stick to my timetable. I had to be inside Syria by the end of October, before my visa expired, so I had very little leeway. Even so, I was longing for a break, and the accident gave me the excuse. Instead of cycling via Thermopylae and Lamia, then round a desperately mountainous headland to Volos, I decided to be kind to myself. I would do a day-trip to Thermopylae on the bus, then take the ferry from Agios Konstantinos across to Skiathos, one of the islands of the Sporades, and another ferry from there to Volos. My route would still stick to the sea and take the same length of time as cycling, but it would give me a much-needed rest.

When I was a child, I had a favourite book called *The World of the Ancients*. In it, I read the romance of Leonidas and the 300 Spartans, who died to a man holding the Pass of Thermopylae against Xerxes and his Persian hordes in 480 BC, and it was this heroic tale more than anything which inspired my love of the classics. Bad leg or no bad leg, I had to see Thermopylae. When I hobbled off the bus, I was in good company. All the villagers were old and lame, staggering along on sticks, and too deaf to hear what I was asking, so it was some time before I found the narrow track between the highway and an olive grove. It ended at a massive white marble monument, with a menacing statue of Leonidas on top. Financed by subscription from Greek Americans, the monument was flashy and vainglorious – just the qualities most despised by the austere Spartans. It could not have been more inappropriate. To add to my disgust, though I searched all over, I could find no sign of the movingly simple couplet by Simonides, which originally marked the tomb: 'O passing stranger, tell the Spartans that we lie here, obedient to their instructions.'

Kamena Vourla and Thermopylae are popular spas, where the sulphur springs are supposed to be good for rheumatism. Hence all the elderly on sticks and zimmer frames. My inexpensive pension was full of retired workmen, their wives and widows, all in Kamena Vourla to take the waters. They lived frugally, preparing their own meals in the communal kitchen and gossiping all evening on the verandah, instead of gadding around the town.

It was so hot that I propped my door open with a chair and sprawled out on the bed, wearing nothing but my large cotton square as a sarong. My neighbour opposite kept his door open too, so I had a good view of his thick flannel pyjamas, which were buttoned right up to the neck – in that heat! He was a doddery old factory-hand, who had worked for five years in Stuttgart and three in Worms. *'Viel Arbeit. Viel Geld.'* (Lots of work. Lots of money). At last, I had someone I could understand, and we struck up a friendship across the corridor. In the evening, he acted as my interpreter, which was a great help. Previously, I had got no further than showing the old ladies my wedding ring. Now I could tell them that I was in Greece for two months, but my husband was in London as he didn't cycle (my usual story). That caused great amusement. But when they heard that I was planning to continue into Turkey on my bike, they were so alarmed that two of the old ladies crossed themselves.

There was a terrific thunderstorm in the night, which cooled the air, but it was still raging violently when my alarm went off. I couldn't possibly cycle to Agios Konstantinos for the early ferry in such a downpour, so I turned over and went to sleep again. I was startled by a vision in green and white flannel pyjamas. My ancient friend had barged in, without so much as a knock on the door, to check that I was still there and not out on my bike in the storm. 'You're crazy enough!' he said. 'You could be struck by lightning out there.'

The sun came out later that morning and I was able to cycle on to the noon boat to Skiathos. I was so tired that I slept most of the way across. Skiathos town was a real tourist trap, where I heard British voices for the first time since Venice and bought a *Daily Telegraph*. I could have bought fish and chips and English breakfast too, had I wanted them. The rest of the island was a rugged mountain, green with shrubs. I was surprised to read that it was fifth on the popularity list with foreigners, after Corfu, Mykonos, Delos and Rhodes.

I treated myself to another day off in Volos, a pleasant, cosmopolitan port with fish restaurants along the waterfront. I had my gears tuned by an excellent cycle mechanic, had my hair cut by a German-speaking hairdresser, stocked up on snacks in the mouth-watering *delikatessens* and was served dinner by a waiter who had worked in Covent Garden for eighteen months. My leg was beginning to heal up nicely and I felt that life was improving.

Even the cycling took a turn for the better. For weeks, progress had been so difficult that I was starting to think it was time to hang up my cycling shoes. Now I was on the flat, bowling across the Plains of Thessaly, famous in ancient times for the breeding of horses. The old roads to Thessaloniki were still there, running beside the new motorway, through villages with shade trees, vegetable patches, vineyards and orchards. The morning was cool, the land was abundant and life was suddenly wonderful. I burst into boisterous Schubert, startling the birds with a loud rendition of 'Ungeduld'. Instead of toiling all day in the heat, I reached Larisa at 11.30. A group of Italian cyclists was just checking out of my hotel as I was checking in. They had planned to leave at 10, but two of their party had overslept and the others were angry. How restful it was to be alone! No one to hold me up, no one to apologise to if I was late, no one to whinge if I changed my plans. Just perfect freedom. It was the Feast of the Virgin and Larisa had closed down completely, so I rested my leg, had a siesta and did a puzzle until it was time for my dinner of delicious spit-roasted lamb, the local speciality.

The next day was even better, as I cycled through the spectacular Vale of Tempe. I saw the sun rise over Ossa, then I was in the shade of the unbelievably lush chasm, which the Ancient Greeks said Poseidon cut with a blow of his trident. In fact, it is the Pinios River which has gouged its way in a tangle of plane trees and evergreens through that narrow cleft in the mountains. Like other sites in Greece, Delphi for instance, which are so awesome they make the skin tingle, the Vale of Tempe was sacred to Apollo. His dark, gleaming laurel bushes still clothe the almost vertical slopes. It made me nervous to see the road being upgraded to motorway standard at both ends of the pass. Will this beautiful vale be allowed to continue as a bottle-neck? The existing road and railway occupy all the available space within it, so any road-widening scheme would involve the barbarism of felling ancient trees. I hope I am not one of the last cyclists to see the Vale of Tempe in its wild, archaic glory.

When I emerged from its shadows, I had passed from Thessaly into Macedonia, where Greece meets the Balkans. The change hit me in the eye as I cruised into my overnight stop at Leptokaria. I was in Little Poland! Huge bottle-blondes in miniskirts crowded into fur shops, where all the signs were in Polish, and gold was being snapped up as fast as ice cream. When I went out in search of dinner, I found that all the restaurant menus were written in Polish. Even the food was Polish. I managed to identify some chicken, but it came with a mountain of chips and sauerkraut, with a side salad of sauerkraut, russian salad and onion. A slimy mess! I sent it back and it was replaced with a normal green salad, but sitting in a hot dish with a sweet dressing. The next night, I took rooms in a house in Methone, next door to a Polish family with a toddler, who was fascinated by my orange bike. It had been another glorious day's cycling, across rolling farmland with long views from the ridges, like the Cotswolds in high summer. Methone was not a beach resort, as the sea in the bay was too shallow. It was just a salt marsh with wading birds. There was a row of fish restaurants, but I could tell from the low prices that they were serving farmed fish from the bay – with Thessaloniki and all its effluent just round the corner! I played safe with chicken again, then had a chat with a group of old ladies who invited me to join them on the seafront. They were very kind, but hard work, and my Greek was pushed to its limits answering all the usual questions. People in the north of Greece seemed more welcoming, but there was still the language barrier.

I cycled into Thessaloniki along the Roman Via Egnatia and saw a sight which gladdened my eyes. It was a hotel called simply Hotel Bill. Every hotel I had stayed in throughout Greece had been named after some classical god or hero – the Hotels Hermes, Diana, Jason, Hera, Medusa, Achilles, Miltiades, Pegasus. There were even Demeter greengrocers, Alexander farm machines, Apollo discos and Hercules cement. And every town hall, library and museum in every town was built in the classical style. It was as if we in England had decided that our most magnificent age was the age of Elizabeth I and had ever afterwards named all our hotels and companies Drake, Raleigh, Leicester or Shakespeare and designed all our public buildings in Tudor style. The Greeks are a mongrel race, like the rest of us in Europe, but they constantly hark back to classical times and claim direct descent. 'Welcome to Greece, the land of heroes!' The intervening centuries are lost in collective amnesia. It is all part of a rampant nationalism, which would be ridiculous, were it not a provocation.

While public buildings were all neoclassical, churches were Byzantine, to reflect the glory days of Constantinople. Splendid new churches, mini Saint Sophias, were springing up by the dozen, and old churches were being repainted and refurbished – all this at a time when society was increasingly secular. Except in Western Roumeli, the little wayside shrines, which used to be so lovingly tended, were neglected, often vandalised, their icons smashed. Faith was dying while the Church prospered. The Orthodox faith was Greek and the Orthodox Church was a nationalist symbol. Priests paraded with civic dignitaries and marching soldiers on feast days, and spoke out in favour of the Serbs, another Orthodox people. 'Long live Serbia!' 'NATO murderous pigs!' 'USA Fascists!' Graffiti said it all.

That is why the modestly named Hotel Bill was so attractive. I checked in immediately and went out to buy some new socks in the street market. They were 'Nile Brand', with a pyramid on the label, which I thought was very suitable. I was so fed up with the Greeks and their Orthodoxy that I revisited none of the great churches in Thessaloniki. Instead, I made a pilgrimage to Vergina, the ancient capital of Macedonia and the burial place of its kings.

Any other tourist country would have organised day-trips from Thessaloniki to this important tourist site. Not so the Greeks. I had to take a taxi to the out-of-town bus station, a bus to Veria, another bus to Vergina; and on the return journey, a taxi to Veria, a bus to Thessaloniki and another taxi back to the Hotel Bill. Seven hours door-to-door and £15 in fares (a fortune in Greek terms) for a one-hour visit. But it was worth it.

The tomb of Philip II of Macedon, the father of Alexander the Great, has been excavated, along with a number of subsidiary tombs. Then the tumulus was restored and an underground passageway constructed down to the tombs, which are displayed as they would have been when the royal corpses were first interred. The effect is magical. I walked down the covered way and it took my eyes some time to adjust to the underground gloom. Then the exhibits appeared in pools of subtle light, with dark spaces between one display and the next. It was a stunning collection. The tombs had marble doorways like the entrances to Doric temples and they were decorated with frescos of outstanding vitality. I was particularly struck by one of Pluto and Persephone. He has seized her in his chariot to take her down to his Kingdom of the Dead and she leans back with outstretched arms, her mouth wide open in an agonised shriek. There are reconstructed tomb couches, with their original ivory decorations, including small portrait heads of Philip and Alexander. Because ivory outlasts wood, the battle friezes on display have lost all the barbarians' bodies. Ivory was used for flesh and the Greeks fought naked, so their little figures survive in their entirety, while the wood used for the clothed barbarians has rotted, leaving only their ivory hands and faces. Careful reconstruction has fitted all the pieces together again and they make a fine display. But the glory of the collection is its gold. Philip's touchingly small gold sarcophagus, emblazoned with the Star of Macedon, his golden crown of oak leaves, complete with gold acorns, and case upon case of gold jewellery are wonders of Hellenistic craftsmanship.

An interesting minor tomb contains a silver urn with a golden oak-leaf crown around its rim. This may possibly hold the remains of Alexander IV, the son of Alexander the Great, said to have been born to his Persian wife Roxane after his death. The boy was born King of Macedonia, so Roxane brought him to Greece to claim his throne, but they were both assassinated when Alexander was a teenager.

Beyond Thessaloniki, the Via Egnatia is now a six-lane highway, where I cowered from the roaring, speeding traffic up a long steep, shadeless climb. I crossed the ring road, perched high on a mountain shelf, and struggled on up to Laguna, where the road to Bulgaria branched off. Soon we were down to two lanes, but that was even more frightening. When I cycled that way in 1987, it was a peaceful road leading nowhere but Turkey, with whom the Greeks were on bad terms, so traffic was light. In 2001, post Iron Curtain, it was flooded with East European trucks. And because the direct route to Greece from Germany was blocked by the fighting in the former Yugoslavia, the Bulgarian and Hungarian monsters were joined by convoys of speeding German juggernauts. It was hair-raising cycling.

I like to stick to my objectives, but I am no masochist. One look at the three great rocky prongs of Halkidiki, with their crowded holiday resorts and yacht marinas, and I decided to cut across the northern edge of the peninsula. It was not quite such a watery route as the littoral, but with two large lakes, Koronia and Volvi, a river and irrigation canals, it was good enough. Despite the traffic, I enjoyed the ride past stubble fields with flocks of sheep and the long swoop down through a wooded valley to the sea at Asprovalta. The air was noticeably cooler up here and the oleanders, which had gone over in Athens, were still in luxuriant bloom.

In Kavala, after a hard, mountainous ride, I made a happy discovery. I was wandering through the old Turkish quarter, climbing up the steep, cobbled lanes to the citadel, when I reached a kind of belvedere with a stunning sea view. In its centre a spirited bronze horse was pawing the ground, mounted by a sabre-brandishing warrior in a turban. I read the inscription and realised, with a shock of delight, that the warrior was none other than Mohammed Ali, the Pasha of Egypt who gave us Cleopatra's Needle. The Turkish mansion, where he was born in 1769, occupied a corner of the small square and I was able to wander through its wood-panelled rooms and get a flavour of life in a prosperous farming family.

Mehmet Ali (to give him his Turkish name) had an extraordinary career, of the kind which is only possible when a large chunk of the world is united under one rule – in this case, the Ottoman Empire. He was born in Greece of Albanian parents at a time when both those countries were ruled by the Turks and, being an ambitious lad, he enlisted in the Albanian Corps of the Sultan's army and was posted to Egypt. Although the Ottomans had conquered Egypt in 1517, their power was constantly challenged by the Mamelukes, who had ruled there for the previous three centuries and still had considerable influence. Mehmet Ali broke their power the easy way. Created Pasha of Egypt by the Sultan in 1805, he invited the 470 top Mamelukes to a grand dinner at his palace in Cairo and slaughtered them all. That gave him absolute power. Though the Ottoman Sultan was still nominally in charge, Mehmet Ali went his own way, modernising Egypt with technical help from the West. He built factories, railways and canals, introduced cotton-growing from the Sudan and eventually grew so powerful that the Sultan had to recognise his independence. Mehmet Ali became Mohammed Ali Pasha, founder of the dynasty of Egyptian kings which ended with King Farouk's abdication in 1952.

His house and the elegant almshouses which he built near his birthplace are maintained by the Egyptian Government. Left to the Greeks, these painful reminders of their Turkish past would probably be in ruins now, because Kavala is wildly nationalistic. Churches fly the Greek flag on one side of the gate and the gold flag with the black double-headed eagle of Byzantium on the other.

The black Byzantine eagle glares out from yellow road signs, which give the distance to Constantinople, not Istanbul. And inflammatory 'Remember Cyprus!' notices are plastered on walls, with Northern Cyprus shown in red, dripping blood.

The Greeks of Kavala perhaps feel that they are the final outpost of Greece proper. Once I crossed into Western (Greek) Thrace, I saw Muslim women in headscarves and long coats shopping in the shadow of minarets. In the exchange of peoples agreed in the Treaty of Lausanne (1923), whole villages of Greeks living in Turkey and Turks living in Greece were resettled within their national boundaries. But the Turks were allowed to maintain their foothold in Western Thrace in return for a continued Greek presence in Istanbul which, as Constantinople, is the senior patriarchate of the Orthodox Church.

Greeks and Turks used to live amicably together in Thrace. The Turks even fought side by side with their Greek compatriots in World War II. But over the last decade, there has been inter-communal violence. Turkish political leaders have been prosecuted and the Greeks have interfered in Muslim religious appointments. The Turks now feel discriminated against, and the Greeks are on the defensive, trapped in a claustrophobically narrow corridor between the sea and Bulgaria. Yet I saw glimmers of light. The Hotel Orpheus in Komotini was filled with coachloads of Greeks on their way to Istanbul for a holiday, and there seemed to be fewer Greek armoured cars on the roads than there were when I cycled through in 1987.

If I were a birdwatcher, which I'm not, I should have been very happy in Thrace, cycling along beside salt-pans and lagoons where herons fished – when they could stand up in the wind! Great gales blasted down from the Rhodopi Mountains in the north. They were against me on the climb up to Komotini from the salt flats of Lagos and I got so exhausted that I felt sick. I had twinges in my knee and my spirits, which had risen in Macedonia, plummeted again. 'Is it time I gave up cycling?' I wrote in my diary. 'It all seems so relentless. The wind and the heat and the early rising.' The days were shortening and I had been looking forward to the luxury of a 5.45, or even 6 a.m. alarm call, but I was travelling east and my progress was cancelling out the later sunrise. I still had to get up at 5.30. My stomach felt too wobbly to cope with the greasy fast food, which was often all I could find, but the evening brought me one piece of luck. I found a restaurant serving fresh grilled sardines. With a squeeze of lemon juice and a green salad, it was exactly the supper I needed.

After Komotini, it was tobacco and cotton fields all the way, a boring landscape where the only living creatures were a few sheep grazing in the corn stubble. I wanted to follow the old road from Sapes, but I got lost and found myself on the new motorway. I turned for help to an old man working in his garden, but he took my map and squinted at it upside down. The highway police were no better. They had no idea how I could get down to the old road, which I could see in the valley below, and advised me to stick to the mountainous motorway, because the surface was better.

On my last day, Greece gave me a final poke in the eye. I followed the road signs to Turkey, but they totally ignored the old road to the border, so I found myself on the motorway again, going a dreadfully long way round. All the trucks branched off towards Edirne and I was left alone, the only vehicle on a six-lane highway. It was quite eerie, cycling for miles on a perfect new surface, with no traffic whatsoever in either direction. The landscape was hidden from view by high embankments on both sides; there were no trees, no birds, nothing to break the stillness. There were no distance markers to tell me where I was, and I started to wonder if I was dreaming. Was I on an imaginary road that led nowhere? By the time I reached the frontier, where the perfectly adequate old road joined up with my white elephant, I had worked myself up to a state of high indignation at the waste of EU money. When there were so many worthwhile projects crying out for funding, so many problems to be addressed, who on earth had decided to pour millions into the construction of a totally unnecessary motorway?

I crossed the broad Evros River, where the Greek and Turkish flags were flying side by side and there was only one sentry box for each nation – a great improvement on the large numbers of troops who had lined the long bridge when I crossed it in 1987. It seemed that Kevin and Roula were right and that relations between Greece and Turkey were gradually getting better.

Above left
Cleopatra's
Needle, London.
Thutmose III

Above right
Setting out from
Cleopatra's
Needle

Left My stately
B & B at Cobham
Hall

My tranquil road
along the Seine

The Burgundy
Canal enters its
two-mile tunnel
under Pouilly-en-
Auxois

It always rains in
the Jura!

The rainy Lake at
Geneva

Cycle Path near
St. Maurice

Terraced vineyards,
Le Valais

Climbing the
Nufenen Pass
over the Alps

The Ticino rushes
through the Valle
Bedretto

Ascona, Lake
Maggiore

The Corinth Canal

Mustoe's wine!

Dinner in Istanbul
(clockwise:
Canteke, Shirley,
Anne, Pinar)

The Library,
Ephesus

The misery of
The Green Line,
Nicosia

Crac des
Chevaliers, Syria

The Cedars of Lebanon
under snow

Right Ommayad
Mosque, Damascus

Below left My favourite
hotel, The Palace,
Ismaelia

Below right Damietta.
The Nile at last!

Andalucia in Egypt.
Modern Heliopolis

Left Ancient Heliopolis
(On). Modern El
Matariyya

Below left My cycling
companions, Ismaelia

Below right Journey's
end at the obelisk of
Senusret I

Above left Cleopatra's Needle, New York. Thutmose III

Above centre Luxor Obelisk, Paris. Ramses II

Above right Karnak Obelisk, Istanbul. Thutmose III

Left The one remaining obelisk in Heliopolis (ancient On). Senusret I

Right English Egyptiana, Highgate Cemetery.

11. AEGEAN TURKEY

Does the road wind up-hill all the way?
Yes, to the very end.

Christina Rossetti, 'Up-hill'

The tide of humanity was still sweeping west at the Kipi border post. For every traveller moving eastwards, there were at least a hundred struggling in the opposite direction. I bought my entry visa, got my passport stamped at an empty counter and cycled off within minutes. I was lucky. The westbound women in their hot headscarves and long gabardine macs had to hang around for hours in the sun-baked compound, harrassed out of their minds, bribing their fractious children with sweets while their husbands trudged wearily from one paperwork queue to the next.

I escaped on to an empty road, but this was no bleak motorway. It was the ancient Via Egnatia, with trees, peaceful fields and marshes of heron. The only other traffic in view was a horse and cart. The horse was ambling home, while his two teenaged drivers kicked a football to each other across the road. They asked me for cigarettes, but I told them I didn't smoke, and they shrugged and smiled. It was all so rural, so innocent, that I felt I had travelled back at least a hundred years. I stopped at a roadside fruit stall to buy four juicy tomatoes. The boy in charge thought I wanted to buy four kilos and reached happily for a big paper sack to put them in. When I got it across to him that I meant four single tomatoes, not four kilos, he picked the best four out of his box and insisted on giving them to me; and as I was stowing them away in my panniers, he came over shyly with a gift of an apple and two pears. I was in Turkey again, where generosity is as natural as breathing.

Once away from the Ebros delta, the road became bleaker, with long shadeless climbs across a steppe-like landscape. The east wind was still against me and it grew stronger as the day warmed up, until I even had to pedal hard to go downhill. I had intended to cycle the E84 all the way to Istanbul, but I knew the road, and knew that it was desolate right up to the city outskirts, with long stretches between towns and hotels. I turned off to spend the night in Keşan. If the next day's forecast was for equally windy weather, I would cut out the ride to Istanbul round the sea of Marmara, and cross the Dardanelles directly into Asia.

Keşan had gone downhill since my last visit. In contrast to Greece, which was obviously prospering on EU money, Turkey's economic problems were plain to see. The town used to be smart, but now it was decidedly down-at-heel. There were more horses and carts in the centre than cars and I saw children scavenging in the refuse. The only grand vehicle was a gleaming new German-registered Mercedes convertible. Four young men, all in designer casuals and shades, were driving it grandly round the square, top down, radio blasting away. Such mindless showing off in the middle of poverty made my toes curl. Young men can be so appalling.

The Turkish lira was in free-fall. I got over two million to the pound at the frontier and the teller said, 'Just change enough for today. You'll get more tomorrow.' The exchange rate was a disaster for the Turks, but for me Turkey was a cheapskate's paradise. I couldn't believe how cheap everything was. I pulled up at the best hotel in town. I was a tourist! A gift from heaven! The delighted desk clerk rushed out to carry my bike up the steps, then produced a complimentary glass of tea, the first of hundreds I should be offered all the way across Turkey. The manager himself carried my panniers up to my room and invited me to join him in the lounge for more tea, whenever I felt like it. I was made so welcome, not only for my money, but for myself. They were really interested in my travels and wanted to hear about them. I bathed in the warm glow of all this attention. It was such a contrast to the indifference of the Greeks. It felt like coming home.

Breakfast was included in the room rate and it started at 5.30. I tucked into fresh bread, butter, cherry jam, cheese, olives, tomatoes, cucumber, boiled eggs and börek, those delicious deep-fried filo pastry fingers, stuffed with cheese, and sizzling straight from the pan. The TV weathergirl was predicting strong east winds for the next three to four days, so that decided me. I would cycle to Gelibolu (Gallipoli) and take the ferry across to Çanakkale.

Memory is kind to us. It obliterates pain. Whenever I looked back on my 1987 ride from Keşan to Gelibolu, I remembered the heady scent of pines, the carpet of tiny blue flowers, the stork which flapped lazily across the road just in front of my handlebars, and the stunning view of the deep blue Gulf of Saros from a hilltop. What I forgot was Kurudaği, the peak which soars nearly 2,000 feet (645 m) into that baby-blue sky, and the gruelling ten-mile climb up to the pass. This time, the pine-covered slopes of the mountain were just as lovely, but there was mist over the gulf. I swooped down to the narrow peninsula which divides it from the Dardanelles. From the crest of its spine, I saw first one stretch of water, then the other, but never quite managed to see both together. I stopped at a petrol station for a cold drink and the attendant presented me with a nice new yellow duster when he heard that I'd come all the way from London on my bike.

The cobbled waterfront at Gelibolu was as picturesque as I remembered it, though the holidaymakers there were more up to date. A rash of new holiday villages along the gulf had drawn families from Istanbul for the summer and these more sophisticated people paraded along the quayside in shorts and skimpy sun-tops, along with the young Anzacs on pilgrimage to the battlefields and cemeteries of Gallipoli.

As I sat on the harbour wall, a stout old lady plumped herself down beside me and produced two ripe plums from her shopping bag.

'Erik?' she asked.

She was not asking me if my name was Erik. She was offering me a plum, which in Turkish is an *erik*. But she did go on to ask my name.

'Rose,' I said. 'Turkish Gül.'

'Mine's Yildiz (Star).'

I always change my name in Turkey. Names there *mean* something and Anne is an embarrassment. It means 'mother'. So conversations in the past tended to go:

'What's your name?'

'Anne.'

'O lovely! How many children have you got?'

We then had to go through the drill of our respective families – children, husbands, brothers, sisters, aunts, uncles, and at the end of all that, they would say, 'Well, that's very nice. What a lovely family. Now what's your name?'

The only way to avoid this confusion was to rechristen myself. I picked Rose, not because I have any illusions about being a perfect English rose, but because Rose is a name in English that translates into a popular girl's name in Turkish. The change makes all the difference in chance encounters, such as the one with Yildiz on the harbour wall. My friend Shirley had a similar problem when she first went to live in Turkey, because her name means nothing at all. But it sounds almost the same as the Turkish word for a banquet, so the Turks have come to terms with it.

When we finished our plums, the old lady tried to sell me the whole bag of them for 25p. It was a bargain but, on a bicycle, I didn't have room to carry so much squashy fruit. So she turned and offered them to a local man for half the price, still not quite believing that I could follow her financial dealings. Turkish is a phonetic language, so the pronunciation is simple. What you see is what you say. My Turkish is basic, but Turks can understand me and I can understand them, more or less, which is a terrific asset. They realise that their language is unrelated to any other, except possibly Finnish, and they never expect foreigners to cope with such a strange tongue. A little effort brings huge rewards.

My ride down the Gallipoli Peninsula was a ride made in heaven. Great ships steamed up the Dardanelles, so close to my road on the edge of the rocks that I felt I could reach out and touch them. The sun glimmered through the pines of a National Forest and, best of all, the powerful east wind was behind me.

'Why don't you buy a house in Çanakkale?' asked the night porter at my hotel. 'It's the bridge between East and West. Very handy for a traveller. It's the starting point for every journey.'

He was an affable young man, a final-year English student at the University of Ankara, doing a vac. job in the hotel.

'When I graduate,' he said, 'I hope to get a job in England as an au pair.'

That took me a bit by surprise, but he said it was quite common for Turkish male graduates to do that. 'We love children. I can't think of anything nicer than living in a family, improving my English and caring for little children. There's an agency at the university which fixes it up.' When I recovered from my surprise, I thought how lucky any family would be to find such a serious, well-mannered boy to look after their children.

I arranged for Condor to spend a few days in the hotel baggage room, while I took the bus to Istanbul to meet Shirley, my Ankara friend. She was due to arrive there with her bicycle to join me for part of the ride and I knew that we could travel back together to Çanakkale on the bus, bicycle and all. In Turkey, everyone and everything goes by bus, and bicycles are accepted without fuss, free of charge. The hotel manager was obviously delighted that I was going to Istanbul to meet a friend. Like all gregarious Turks, he felt sorry for me, travelling alone. He just couldn't see the pleasure in it. I always enjoy it, though a bit of company from time to time, especially Turkish-speaking company in Turkey, makes a change.

I arrived in Istanbul two days ahead of Shirley, as I had a few practical jobs to do, like picking up my post from American Express and buying the latest edition of the *Lonely Planet: Turkey*. As far as I know, Cleopatra never went to Istanbul, but there is one tenuous link. An obelisk of Thutmose III, the Pharaoh responsible for Cleopatra's Needle, stands in the Hippodrome. It is roughly the same height as the Needle and hewn from the same red granite. The Emperor Theodosius transported it from Egypt in AD 390 and an engineer called Proclos erected it on the *spina*, the low wall running down the centre of the chariot-racing track. I wandered along there from my hotel in Sultan Ahmet and took some photographs. What I specially like about that obelisk is its marble base, which shows Theodosius watching the races and crowning the victors. Compared with classical sculpture of the great age, the figures are static and stolid, but Theodosius is surrounded by his family in the royal box and there is a kind of cozy domesticity about the scenes.

Shirley is well known to readers of my earlier books. A ballerina, she went over to Ankara with Dame Ninette de Valois, to help start up the Turkish National Ballet, married a Turkish tenor and has lived in Turkey ever since. We went to stay with friends of hers in Suadiye, a suburb of Istanbul on the Asiatic shore. They were a delightful family, who made us both extremely welcome.

'I think you're terribly brave,' said Canteke, 'going off to Egypt on a bicycle. I can't even ride one. I never had time to learn. I was too busy playing with my Barbie dolls.'

He was a flamboyant character. On their wedding photographs, he preened himself in a long coat of scarlet velvet, with white frills at the neck and cuffs. As it was a special occasion, he was wearing discreet make-up. Yet Canteke was not the least bit effeminate. He was just warm, funny and sociable. His working hours were tremendously long, as he was the start-up manager of a lavish new hotel, which was due to open shortly in Istanbul. It was to be furnished with antiques and chandeliers and have a French chef. It was the perfect job for him. He would dress up and manage his hotel with great style and panache, loving every sociable moment of it. His wife, Pinar, was the calming influence in the household. She had a steady career in a bank and looked on Canteke with fond amusement. Sonia, a Moldavian nursery teacher, worked as nanny to Yunuscan (Dolphin-life), who was quite the sunniest eighteen-month-old I have ever met.

On Sunday morning, Canteke took us all out for brunch at the local yacht club. There, among the weekend sailors with their smart boats and BMWs, there was little sign of Turkey's economic problems. Some people were obviously doing quite well for themselves. We had a wonderful spread, though the service was slow, because the child-dotty waiters were too busy playing with Yunuscan to bother with a dull job like organising our breakfasts.

In the afternoon, Shirley and I took the ferry across the Bosphorus to have tea in the Marmara Hotel with my friend Gülden. I met Gülden some years ago in Marmaris, when I was laid up with the most dreadful cold. Gülden happened to be managing the hotel for a friend that week, and she really took care of me, bringing me hot drinks, soup and tempting little snacks. We had kept in touch and now she was planning to join Shirley and me on our cycle tour round the Turkish coast as far as Antakya, though she was not a cyclist. She had not met Shirley before and I was slightly apprehensive as to how our international threesome would get along. But it became clear, over the tea and baklava, that I had nothing to worry about. Gülden is a person with a wide circle of friends and relations, and it turned out that she and Shirley knew a lot of the same people, so they had plenty to talk to each other about – and Gülden's English is perfect, as she was educated partly in the States. I relaxed. There would be no problems.

We had quite a complicated journey to Çanakkale. Shirley cycled to the Bostanci Ferry Station on the Asiatic side, while I took a taxi with all our gear. We crossed over to Yenikapi, on the European side, where Gülden met us, an unusual vision for a Turkish lady, in flouncy navy shorts with large white spots. She said she would be travelling light, but her luggage consisted of a giant suitcase, heavy enough to hold a few bodies, a large leaden shoulder-bag and three plastic bags. Not a cyclist's idea of limited luggage! We hauled our combined effects, plus Shirley's bike, on to a catamaran, and two hours later we were in Bandirma, where we all boarded a bus to Çanakkale.

'Here are your friends! I'm so glad you found them,' said the hotel manager, with genuine feeling. 'You're not on your own now.'

Shirley and I checked into our room and Gülden came up to change into an elegant skirt and jacket. She came from a distinguished family. Her father had been Governor of the Dardanelles under Ataturk, a key strategic appointment, and she was off to pay a formal call on the current governor. As she expected, he arranged for her to stay in official accommodation. She was excited to be back in Çanakkale, as she had started school there. She took Shirley out to show her the town and reconnoitre the harbourside restaurants for our dinner. That suited me very well. It gave me some time on my own to catch up on my notes, the daily task which is always more difficult when I travel in company.

Afterwards, Shirley and I turned our attention to the new bicycle saddle she had just bought in England. In the shop, she had been concentrating on her comfort and had taken no notice of the brand name. When she got back to Turkey, she realised that her saddle was a 'Trans Am' and she was horrified. *Am* in Turkish is a very rude word. It is the common man's term for that part of the female anatomy which sits closest to a cycle saddle. 'I can't possibly go around with that printed across my saddle,' said Shirley. 'I shall be a laughing stock!' We tried scraping off the print with a penknife. Then we tried obliterating it with a black marker-pen. All to no avail. In the end, she covered up the offending word with a plaster from her first-aid kit.

Over our seafront fish dinner, we worked out our plans for the next day. Shirley and I would go off early on our bicycles, keeping as near to the sea as the roads allowed, while Gülden went south by minibus to Odunluk and found a suitable hotel. Shirley was carrying a mobile, so we could keep in touch.

It was not a good day. We tried to follow the shore and came to the end of the asphalt. A goatherd told us there was only 1 km of unpaved track, but when we had soldiered on for at least 10 km over rocks and sand, we realised that we were going in the wrong direction anyway. We were heading for the point at Kumkale, the very tip of the Dardanelles, which was a dead end and not at all where we wanted to be. There were no signposts, so I got out my compass and we set off down another stony track, to try to find the road past Troy. We got lost again and again, and went round in circles before we finally got on to asphalt near Geikli. I was worried all morning about my tyres, and the tight suspension on my tourer gave me a very uncomfortable ride. I did a lot of walking. Shirley was on a mountain bike, which was better adapted to the stony paths, but she was not in training, as I was, so she suffered in a different way.

We struggled wearily into Odunluk. No Gülden. As we sat dejected on the beach, Gülden phoned. We were in New Odunluk, but there was evidently an Old Odunluk, 3 miles (about 5 km) further down the shore, along another stony, sandy path, and that was where Gülden was waiting for us. We found her, fresh and merry, sitting in a café by the sea with a glass of beer, waiting to take us to the charming pension she had found. It was only when a girl arrived in a car to drive her there that we discovered we had yet another 3 miles to ride, up and down hills, panting behind Gülden's car. What should have been an easy 29-mile (47 km) run-in for Shirley turned out to be 48 miles (77 km) of rough terrain under a blazing sun. We were like two zombies that evening, while Gülden, who had been on her own all day, looking forward to our arrival, was ready for a nice social time. She was not a cyclist. She had whizzed past us in her tooting *dolmuş* shortly after we left Çanakkale, and she had no idea how exhausting it had been to get to Odunluk on bicycles. Was the arrangement going to work? Shirley and I were too tired even to enjoy our dinner or admire the sea view. We collapsed into bed early and fell asleep to the drone of Gülden's voice, as she chatted away to the other guests under the lemon trees.

Gülden had the luxury of a late departure and sped past us mid-morning in a cloud of dust. She rang us shortly afterwards from Babakale to give us the name of the hotel. Meanwhile, Shirley and I cycled through the rich countryside of the Troad, past the olive-shaded ruins of Alexandria Troas, once a great city, to Tuzli

(Salty), where iron-red springs ran down to a grim, rusty lake, scabby with salt, like an infected moon. Then there were orchards and market gardens, and it was a pleasant enough ride till we came to the outskirts of Gülpinar and saw the village towering above us at the top of the steepest cobbled street I have ever had to climb. It was more than we could manage to push our laden bicycles up there, but two kind men saw us struggling and took over. The older man told us that it was at least another 5 miles (9 km) to Babakale, along a terribly mountainous, deserted road. He wanted us to rest in his house and wait for the cool of the evening, but we felt we should persevere and cycled along the hilltop to the road junction. The tarmac on the Babakale road was no more than a narrow, broken strip and we could see the mountains looming ahead. According to a group of old men on the corner, there was no road from Babakale onwards; it was a dead end and we should have to come back the next morning to Gülpinar. We might have steeled ourselves to make one journey down that horrendously difficult road, but two journeys were more than we could face. We arranged for the man at a local café to look after our bikes for the night and caught a *dolmuş* to Babakale, congratulating ourselves on our cleverness all the way along the winding mountain road. Gülden, who was strolling along the beach looking as elegant as Grace Kelly in Monte Carlo, was surprised to see us climb out of the *dolmuş*. 'Oh, you didn't cycle from Gülpinar. Why ever not?' Again, we must have been a disappointment to Gülden, as we were both too tired to be entrancing company.

The next day was fabulous, the sort of day when I know exactly why I cycle. We collected our bicycles from the Gülpinar café and climbed up to a scrubby plateau, where we sat on windy hilltops, eating grapes and apricots, while the pine trees creaked overhead and the mist in the valleys cleared to give us stunning views of the sea and mountains. We were on top of the world in every sense. The west wind was so strong that it pushed us up the great basalt cone of Behramkale's acropolis before noon. This was ancient Assos, where Aristotle lived for three years, doing the ground-breaking research into the organisation of the natural world, which was to lead to the establishment of the life sciences, the disciplines of biology, zoology and botany. The ruins of the ancient city dotted the mountainside down to the small harbour, but they were too exposed to the sun for us to explore them at that time of day. We left our bicycles with Genghis at his café and climbed up through cobbled alleyways, shaded with the awnings of tourist stalls, to the castle walls. Shirley was on her way to visit a friend. She opened a rickety doorway into what I thought was a derelict building, but it turned out to be a simple, rather broken-down little pension, run by an engaging young man called Timur.

Genghis and Timur (Marlowe's Tamburlaine), two terrifying names in one morning! As a change from names which mean something, ambitious Turkish parents sometimes name their sons after historical characters. The problem is that they never know in advance how those sons will turn out. I once had the most gentle friend called Attila, and Shirley's friend Timur would have found it hard to kill a cockroach, let alone massacre and pillage his way to Great Khandom. Conversely, I have met really nasty men who rejoice in names like 'Steadfast', or even 'Gates of Heaven'.

Timur, whose miserable little pension was obviously tottering on the brink of collapse, was still the generous host. He offered chilled mango juice all round and enquired about our travels. When he heard we were on our way to Egypt, he tipped his baseball cap over his eyes in amazement. Every so often, he would come back to it. 'Egypt!' he would gasp and tip his cap again. He told us of a brand new tarmac road, too recently opened to be on the maps, which ran along the seashore from Behramkale. That was welcome news, as it cut out a great mountainous inland detour.

Gülden was staying for a day or two with a poet friend in Behramkale. She said she had no wish to stay along the coast beyond Behramkale, as it was full of fundamentalists, so she would join us again when we turned south. Shirley and I were invited to stay with friends too. First, there was Haldun. He was an artist, living a hermit-like existence high up on the slopes of Mount Ida, with no car or telephone. While his tycoon wife stayed in Ankara, building hotels and tourist villages, Haldun, in his thick pebble spectacles, planted vegetables, built stone walls and painted his strange little animals, always a bit blurred round the edges, with big eyes. To get to him, we had to leave our bicycles with the blacksmith in Zeytinli, at the foot of the mountains, and take a taxi from there. We searched high and low for this blacksmith and were eventually directed to a house in a back street. A dear little old man answered our knock, but he was an ironmonger, not a blacksmith. He told us he had retired when his shop fell down! He had no idea who Haldun was, and his house was too small for our bikes, but by this time a crowd had gathered and the local carpenter volunteered to keep them in his shed. When we finally got there, Haldun's house was more comfortable than I had feared. There were three proper bedrooms with low divans and a stone terrace, where we dined under the stars. The only strange feature was the lavatory. It was plumbed into the outhouse, which Haldun used as his studio, and it had no door, so that Haldun could sit there and contemplate the painting on his easel. Our next visit was more normal. We stayed for two nights with our friend Christine, a retired Professor of English from Ankara University. She was spending the summer in her beautiful seaside house, where she cooked and gardened to perfection. After weeks on the road, it was such a treat to be with an English friend in a proper home, where we could swing on the garden seats over drinks and good conversation, while our clothes spun round in the washing machine.

Somewhere along this stretch of coast, Shirley was surprised to receive a call on her mobile, welcoming her to Greece. We had obviously come within telephone range of Lesbos, whose olive-clad mountains were clearly visible across a narrow channel. It seemed a bit ridiculous that an island so close to Turkey should be part of Greece – but I suppose it's no more ridiculous than a rock on the end of Spain being British.

My next Cleopatra connection was in Bergama, ancient Pergamum. In Hellenistic times, it was the glittering capital of the Attalids, the greatest city of fertile Aeolia, rivalling Athens and Alexandria in wealth and sophistication. Later, it retained its power as the capital of the Roman province of Asia, but by then its cultural ascendancy had waned. Most of the existing ruins are Roman, but I wanted to see the Hellenistic rubble which was once its library.

The greatest library in the ancient world was the library at Alexandria. When Cleopatra reigned there, it held 532,800 scrolls, all catalogued by the Head Librarian, Callimachus. The library at Pergamum, with more than 200,000 scrolls, was its only rival. On one of his visits to the city, Mark Antony robbed it of many of its rarest volumes and took them to Alexandria, as a gift to the love of his life.

It was a hard ride into the wind from Christine's house near Ayvalik to Bergama, punctuated by Shirley's third flat tyre in three days' cycling. The knobbly tyres on a mountain bike may look indestructible, but they are only as tough as the interstices between the knobs. My smooth Kevlar touring tyres were holding up much better. We walked to the next service station, where the *lastikci* (the tyre man) could change tyres, but didn't sell them. Shirley obviously needed a replacement, so she took him in a taxi to the nearest town, where he found a new tyre of the right size and brought it back to fit it. Like me, Shirley is not into cycle repairs – and even if she had been, she was not carrying a spare. Throughout this lengthy performance, I was kicking my heels in the service station, drinking Pepsi and seething at the delay. We were now into September, but the sun was still far too strong for comfort in the afternoons. Despite our good intentions, what with punctures, shopping, long, elaborate breakfasts and lots of cold-drink stops, we never seemed to reach our destination before late afternoon, by which time we were too hot and exhausted to see anything of the town. We just flopped down on our beds.

In Bergama, I was determined to get to the Acropolis, so we lay down at 3.30 and I set the alarm for 4.30. We had to take a taxi up the mountain, as it rises sheer from the plain to a height of almost 1,000 feet (300 m). Its most spectacular building is its Hellenistic theatre, carved out of a dizzyingly steep slope. Standing at the top of its eighty rows of seats, we looked straight down, beyond the stage, to the valley below, and it seemed as if one false step would see us tumbling head over heels all the way. My vertigo was not amused. We found the patch of weedy stones which was once Pergamum's great library and Shirley took a photograph of me, reading in the midst of the ruins. We spent our last tranquil evening in a *lokanta*, surrounded by at least twenty photographs of Ataturk – Ataturk the soldier, Ataturk the politician, Ataturk the sophisticate in evening dress and an opera cloak, Ataturk the huntsman, Ataturk the international statesman, Ataturk at every stage of his life and in every one of his roles. Dictators in other countries come and go. Their photographs are plastered over every wall, their statues dominate every public place. Then they die and, like Stalin, Lenin, General Galtieri and Chairman Mao, they either fade away or are brutally dismantled. Only Ataturk survives untarnished, the Father of Turkey, the man who in one lifetime dragged a backward, defeated Ottoman people to universal suffrage in a secular state, persuading them even to change their dress and their script. He was one of the real giants of the twentieth century.

It was our last peaceful evening, because the next day was September 11th. We arrived at a hotel to find everyone glued to the television, watching slow-motion replays of planes crashing into skyscrapers and frantic people jumping out of windows to escape the flames. At first, we thought it was a film. Then Shirley picked up the commentary. 'It's real! It's the World Trade Center in New York!' Everyone started to talk at once. 'It's Iraq. Will Bush retaliate? Will we be caught in the bombing? It's the Afghans. It's Japan. It's Israel. It's an Israeli plot to throw suspicion on the Arabs.' The Israeli conspiracy theory was not widely held in Turkey, but I was to hear it put forward quite often as I continued my ride into the Middle East.

Gülden, who had friends in New York, phoned to say that she was too upset to continue with her travels. She was going home to Marmaris, where she had CNN and could keep abreast with events. Shirley and I were bewildered. The world was suddenly in turmoil and it seemed selfish to be thinking about our own petty concerns. Yet we had decisions to make. What should we do? Could we go on? Would the Middle East be safe? By the end of the evening, it was clear that the Turks were keeping their heads. A few were murmuring that the Americans had it coming to them, but the official line, which seemed to be gaining popular support, was that Turkey would stand by the West. In their economic crisis, the last thing they needed was some costly, controversial involvement, but they offered the use of their air bases, then sat tight, hoping the situation would just go away. As two Western non-Muslims, we were as courteously treated as ever and Shirley, whose Turkish is fluent, was included in the general discussions going on in the hotel. We decided there would be no problems as long as we were cycling in Turkey, though there was still a big question mark over what would happen beyond.

Christine had told us of a brilliant way to avoid downtown Izmir. There was a ferry from Bostanli, on the north side of the Bay of Izmir, to Üçkuyu on the south side. Over sesame buns and coffee, we sat on deck as the boat cruised past the serried ranks of tower blocks. Izmir is a traffic-ridden hell-hole. We watched a million windscreens glinting through the distant smog and gloated. We had avoided a terrible ride.

By the evening of 13 September, Osama Bin Laden had become the chief suspect for the terrorist attacks in America and world attention was shifting east, from Turkey's immediate neighbour, Iraq, towards Afghanistan. The Turks began to breathe a collective sigh of relief. On one stretch of coast, owned by the army, troops were practising landing from frigates in rubber dinghies and some poor sweating recruits were struggling to take their entire kit for a run in the midday heat. They were all training hard, but they were relaxed enough to smile and some of them gave us a wave. Their clouds were lifting.

The mountainous region between Izmir and Kuşadasi was a great trial in the heat, though we had sweet-smelling pine woods on the Kuşadasi road. I am always a bit wary of popular package-holiday resorts, but I liked this one more than I thought I would. Our hotel room had a balcony overlooking the wide, breezy promenade and because there were swarms of British tourists, I got English newspapers for the first time since September 11th. At last, I had background information I could understand, with comment from a Western perspective. I also found a good bike shop, where I had a new odometer fitted to replace the one which had just been stolen. The idiot thief had used a screwdriver to detach the meter from the handlebars, not realising that it was useless without the sensor, which was still securely fixed to the wheel!

We were now in more of a hurry than ever. The Syrian deadline was always there and was always a nagging concern. But in addition, two friends of mine, Diana and Francis, were on a Swan Hellenic cruise, which was due to put in for the night in Fethiye, where Shirley has her holiday home. It would be a wonderful surprise for them, if we could get there in time to meet them off their ship. After that, my classical friend Heather was flying out to Izmir to join me for a week's tour of the Ionian Greek cities. So Shirley and I had to get ourselves to Fethiye to meet Diana and Francis, then I had to leave my bike at Shirley's and take the bus back to Izmir to meet Heather's plane. My social life was getting complicated.

Our race to Fethiye started well. There was a great climb out of Kuşadasi, but after that we bowled at speed across the wide valley of the Great Menderes River. The land here is so fertile that it produces two different crops every year – either wheat followed by sunflowers, or maize followed by cotton. The cotton had just been picked and it was an anxious time for the farmers, who were sitting around in the cafés waiting for the Government to announce the price it would pay. The Government bought the entire crop at a fixed price. One farmer told us that the Government paid 4 million liras a kilo in 2000; but in 2001, inflation had been running so high that his cotton crop had cost him 7.5 million to produce. Like farmers the world over, he was enjoying a good moan. When we took to the road again and cycled through his rich, well-tended land, we didn't feel too sorry for him.

After the Menderes Valley, we had to turn inland. We had entered ancient Caria, a region so mountainous that its ports were once accessible only from the sea. Even today, despite modern roads, its coastline is still more or less cut off from the rest of Turkey. We spent a night in a campsite bungalow on the southern shore of Lake Bafa, a sky-blue sheet of water mirroring the surrounding peaks. It used to be part of a great bay formed by the Menderes River, but the stream has changed course over the centuries and silted up, leaving Lake Bafa to fend for itself. The cook in the campsite restaurant took us into her kitchen to show us the freshwater fish, which are the lake's speciality. They were salmon-sized, but black in colour with ugly teeth. 'They look as if they would need a lot of mayonnaise – or something!' said Shirley. We opted for the chicken.

To get over the next lot of mountains early, I persuaded Shirley to skip her beloved breakfast and manage with an early croissant and Nescafé in our bungalow. Half an hour later, we passed a restaurant advertising lentil soup, which was too great a temptation. What with the bowls of soup and the chat, we lost the hour we had gained. I couldn't win!

I shall draw a veil over the next few days. The mountains were so horrendous to climb and the sun was so hot that we sometimes flopped down in the shade of a pine tree for five minutes' rest and slept like two logs for an hour. There were rich, fertile valleys, where horses and cows grazed in orchards of nut trees. Then more mountains, more terrible climbs and the occasional scary black tunnel through a mountain peak, with no alternative path for cyclists, just a narrow pavement between roaring trucks and the tunnel wall.

Milas, the main city of Caria, gave us a welcome break. We strolled in the cool of the evening over an elegant Ottoman bridge, through streets of Ottoman houses to the Ulu Cami, its most ancient mosque, constructed of Roman bricks and marble. An old gardener was dozing on a bench in the shade of a plane tree. As soon as he heard us, he hobbled over to greet us and show us his pride and joy. 'I started the garden myself fourteen years ago, when they cleaned the mosque – and look at it now! It's God's gift. Praise be to Allah!' The small, walled enclosure was a profusion of mature vines, roses, figs and pomegranates. He gave us two pomegranates. They were not quite ripe, but the thought was there. He was a Muslim of the old school, devout enough to dedicate his retirement to the garden of his mosque and to invoke the name of Allah at every turn. Yet he greeted two Western women with grace and generosity. We need not have worried about September 11th. We walked back to the hotel along avenues of magnificent neoclassical houses, all yellow and white stucco, which our waiter told us had solid gold taps in the bathrooms.

After dinner we sat on the hotel balcony and watched a circumcision party. The boy, about twelve years old, was dressed up in a splendid white and silver general's outfit, with a dashing white satin cloak, trimmed with fur, and a silver turban with a cockade. He led the dancing, the Turkish and Greek kind, where all the men line up and hop around in a circle, waving their arms in the air. In the old days, the boy would be led off for his circumcision in the middle of the party, then carried back in a bed to have his mind taken off his discomfort with a shower of presents and good wishes. Today, as I understand it, things are more humane. The operation is usually performed in a hospital a week or so before the party, so that the boy can enjoy the celebrations. That was probably the case in Milas, because the little general looked remarkably carefree. He was rushing round in the thick of his party, dancing, stuffing himself with cakes and generally having a wonderful time. There were about three hundred guests, who had arrived in convoy, sounding their horns and waving balloons out of their car windows. I thought of a very different circumcision party I had seen in Istanbul. The boy there was wearing the same expensive general's costume, but his parents were shabbily dressed and his party was a trip to McDonald's for a burger and coke with two little friends.

My left knee had been holding up well since its crisis in Dieppe, but the mountains of Caria were too much for it. It was an old problem with the patella, which had been knocked slightly out of place during a hockey match at school. I hated hockey, but children were obedient in those days and it never occurred to me to bunk off. I turned up for every lesson in my little aertex blouse and shorts, even in the frost and snow. And my reward for all this docility was a skid on the frozen turf and a damaged knee! In Caria, I did my exercises dutifully and concentrated on the correct pedal action advised by my physio, but I still had twinges which developed into real pain as the days went by. I started to hobble like an old crock. How I hated those endless mountains with their pine trees and goats! There was one fantastic morning, when we hurtled from the summit above Muğla right down to the sea, almost twenty miles of vertiginous, hair-raising descent. That morning, we finished with gruelling Caria and reached the shimmering turquoise waters of the Mediterranean. I hoped my knee would improve.

Not that the mountains were over. The Lycian shore is gorgeous, but its necklace of ancient cities and sandy coves has only recently been threaded through with a road. As in neighbouring Caria, a boat was needed in the old days to journey from place to place – and it's still the best way to travel there. Fleets of wooden caiques ply the waters throughout the season, dropping their passengers ashore for a picnic in some deserted crystal bay, then sailing on to drop anchor by the ruins of an ancient city, before sunset drinks and dinner are served on deck. Shirley and I had no such blissful life. We toiled by our own leg-power along rocky shelves with the sea glittering like scattered sequins below us. The sun blazed to our right and the heat bounced off the burning cliffs to our left. We baked like loaves in an oven. But there were pleasant resorts from time to time, a flat run around Dalaman and a series of pine-covered mountain passes towards Fethiye. They were hard work, but at least they were shady.

We arrived in Fethiye just in time. We parked our bikes, showered and changed, then sped down to the docks in Shirley's car. Post September 11th, security on the SS *Minerva* was tight and we were not allowed on board. We had to stand at the top of the gangplank, while Diana and Francis were paged – most unimaginatively. The voice over the ship's loudspeaker simply told them to report immediately to the purser's office. Consternation all round the bar. Had someone died? We took them out for a restorative raki in a harbourside restaurant. It turned out to be the 36th anniversary of the day Diana and Francis got engaged, so once they were over their fright, and the astonishment of seeing Shirley and me on the gangplank, we had a delicious celebration dinner of mezes, sea bass, salads and crisp Turkish wine, perfect food for a velvet evening under the stars.

I found a *Sunday Telegraph* in Fethiye bus station and read it from cover to cover on the bus to Selçuk. America seemed poised for reprisals. Against whom? And with the world's attention focused elsewhere, Israel seemed about to intensify its actions against the Palestinians. It was probably not a good time to be cycling in the Middle East. Heather and I spent a week touring classical sites – Ephesus, Miletus, Priene, Didyma, Halicarnassus and, best of all, Aphrodisias – chewing over my problems. Was I wise to continue in the current political uncertainty? And would my knee hold out? Scrambling over stony classical sites was hardly a rest cure and I was developing a serious limp.

I was glad to be able to practise my Turkish that week. When I was with Shirley, and even more so when Gülden was there as well, I was a silent passenger, while they booked the hotels, ordered the food in restaurants and did the shopping. I felt a bit cut off from the Turks, even though I was meeting more of them. Now it was Heather's turn to be the silent party. In our Selçuk hotel, she never had a name. She was simply my friend, my *arkadaş*. 'Does your *arkadaş* take tea or coffee? Would your *arkadaş* like an egg? Does your *arkadaş* eat olives?' It was the kind of hotel we like, at the top end of the local market, used by Turks rather than tourists. But there were plenty of British and Australian holidaymakers in town, as Selçuk was handy for Ephesus and the coast, so the waiters in the restaurants spoke English. One of them challenged Heather and me. 'What funny English you speak! I can hardly understand you.'

Sounds of Yorkshire, Lancashire, Essex and Oz were rising from the neighbouring tables and the waiter was quite happy with all of those. But we puzzled him. 'What's *your* accent?' he asked. 'Standard. We speak what's known as the Queen's English.' It sounded prissy and I regretted the words as soon as they were out of my mouth. The waiter thought it was a great joke and ever after, when we passed his restaurant, he would wave and shout, 'Good morning, Princesses!'

After a couple of social days back in Fethiye with Shirley and her friends, I strapped up my knee in a support bandage and off we went again. In Esenköy, Shirley pulled off the road into a yard, where there were donkeys in a stable, a couple of horses and three silky angora goats, who stared at us with great interest. The house belonged to one of Shirley's 'donkey men'. She sometimes leads walks into the Lycian mountains for British travel firms, accompanied by men with pack-donkeys. This particular 'donkey man' offered us Coca-Colas and complained about the economic situation.

'There's no money at all round here. I'm riding a bicycle now, because someone's stolen my scooter. People are so desperate, they even took my animals. These are all new ones and I have to keep the poor things locked up in this shed. I can't let them wander around the place to find grazing as I used to.'

His daughter, who was a very pretty girl, needed an operation to rectify a hormonal imbalance, which was causing her to grow a beard. Shirley asked if she could help, but Ali was proud. He told her that it was all being taken care of. Despite the hard times, people in the village were being wonderfully generous and they had almost collected enough money for the operation.

The Turks look after one another. They look after their animals too. We stopped at a service station for a cold drink later that day and heard the most pitiful mewing. A tiny white kitten had been dumped there in the night. We asked if they were going to keep it. 'Of course we'll keep it. What else can we do with it?' It was obviously hungry and they were worried because they had no milk there, only bread and tea. It would have to wait till the next morning, when they could bring some milk into work.

We called in at Xanthos, not to visit the classical site, which we both knew well, but to chat to the custodian, who was another friend of Shirley's from her donkey-walking tours. He led us on his scooter down the mountainside to the village on the river below and showed us the way to a small hotel over a hardware store. Usually these days, the call to prayer in mosques is played on a tape, with a mellifluous professional singer. In Kinik the muezzin was obviously live and local, judging from his flat, tuneless smoker's croak.

Despite the support bandage, the vertical road from Patara was the last straw for my knee. When we reached the summit, there was a fantastic view of Patara's long, white beach stretching out behind us, while the clear sea of Kalkan's bay beckoned us on. But I was past caring about views, however magnificent. We zoomed down the hairpin bends to Kalkan and I took to my bed. The town was too steep for comfortable walking, and the sight of the zigzag road ahead made me even more gloomy. There was no way I could struggle on over those mountains to Kaş. We took a minibus the next day, buying the whole row of seats along the back for our bikes, as there was no baggage compartment, and it was as well that we did. We should have needed a tent and provisions to cycle that road, particularly the stretch from Kaş to Kale, where there was an absolute monster of a climb, followed by an eternity of steep, desolate, scrubby mountains. That 24-mile (39 km) stretch alone would have taken all day, with nothing and nobody along the road.

When we reached Antalya with its international airport, I decided to fly home to London for a few weeks. I could get proper medical attention for my knee, while I waited to see how the situation in the Middle East evolved. If the Arabs all remained calm and bombers Bush and Blair kept their aircraft out of Iraq, I could fly back to Antalya and continue the ride from there.

Shirley told me she got a reduction on Turkish Airlines, because she was a retired person.

'Why don't you ask for one,' she said. 'You're retired. I don't know if it applies just to Turkish citizens, or if other retired people qualify. But it's worth a try.' I wheeled my bike into the ticket office. 'Emeklim (I'm retired),' I announced. The ticket clerk laughed so much he nearly fell off his chair. 'Emekli bisikletli,' he said gaily – a nice rhyming phrase for a retired person on a bicycle. He consulted his computer, which said nothing about retired persons having to be Turkish, so he sold me a ticket at a substantially reduced price and Condor and I boarded the aircraft for Heathrow.

12. MEDITERRANEAN TURKEY

And the windows of heaven were opened
And the rain was upon the earth forty days and forty nights.

Genesis 8.11–12

Heathrow was sunny. There was fog in Vienna. Istanbul was awash with rain. I had booked a cheap flight to Istanbul, then spent sleepless nights wondering how I would manage when I got there in the December dark. I knew that the airport was miles away from the city centre and coach station. There were no airport hotels and I would be lumbered with a bicycle. Now, to top it all, it was raining cats and dogs. Of course, I need never have worried. There was a service bus from the airport to the coach station and it took bikes. A kind official wheeled Condor to the right queue and I was off in a matter of moments. As we swished through the lakes of rainwater on the interminable ring roads and overpasses of outer Istanbul, I thought how excellent it was to be sitting in a warm, dry bus. In the coach station, I was helped across from the *servis* to the correct ticket counter and I just had time for a quick snack before my coach left for Antalya. What had seemed a nightmare at 2 a.m. in London had turned out to be simplicity itself in Istanbul. Why are we always such chickens in the night? We never learn.

In one of his books, Paul Theroux (who can usually, on his own admission, find something to grumble about) describes a night journey in a fuggy, smoke-filled Turkish coach as a near-hallucinogenic experience. That was a few years ago. Now smoking is banned and coaches are air-conditioned. My only problem was that the heating was set at a slightly too warm 24° throughout the night, just the right cozy temperature for the cold germs of the sneezing woman next to me to multiply. We stopped a few times for tea and snacks. *'Affiyet olsun!'* said the waiters. 'May it do you good!' That conventional Turkish phrase is so much more sensible than *'Bon appetit!'* or 'Enjoy your meal!' You can enjoy all sorts of things and eat them with good appetite, and they can all be thoroughly bad for you!

It pelted with rain throughout the night, until we reached the Taurus Mountains, where the driving rain turned to blizzard. As dawn broke, we passed hundreds of stranded drivers up on the high passes. The snow had arrived unusually early that winter and they had been caught out without their snow chains. We had no chains either, but somehow the relay of skilful Kamil Koç drivers managed to inch our coach over the top and down again into the pouring rain of Antalya. I would normally have cycled from the coach station into the city centre, but there were lakes where there should have been roads. Everyone felt sorry for me. A security guard took me out to a local bus and persuaded the driver to take my bike, even though it was strictly against the rules. The bus filled up and the other passengers cheerfully strap-hung, while Condor occupied the entire rear end of the bus, blocking off two rows of seats.

I spent the winter of 1988/89 in Antalya, when I was writing *A Bike Ride*. The city stands in a most dramatic situation at the head of a sweeping bay, with the sheltering Taurus Mountains as its backdrop. Its ancient heart still beats steadily in the middle of its concrete sprawl. The gracious Ottoman mansions, which line the steep cobbled streets down to the harbour, have been sensitively restored and turned into pensions, while the old Roman harbour itself has become the yacht marina. In 2001 I was startled to find Benetton, Burger King and KFC, but the Turkish restaurants were still there and were as good as I remembered. I got off the bus by the Seljuk mosque with its unusual fluted minaret and sheltered under the awning of a car-hire firm, trying to get my bearings. A man came zipping out to offer me a hire car.

'I don't need a car,' I said. 'As you see, I'm on my bicycle. I'm cycling to Antakya.'

'On your own?'

'Yes.'

'How horrible! You should be with a friend.'

As soon as he disappeared, another man came up and offered to escort me under his umbrella, bike, rain-soaked panniers and all, to a nearby carpet shop, while yet another tried to sell me an umbrella. The next day, when the sun came out briefly, the same street-corner opportunist tried to sell me sunglasses! September 11th had killed the tourist trade and everyone was desperate. When I spent the winter in Antalya, the tradesmen got to know me and stopped pestering, but that rainy morning I was just an unknown tourist, ripe for the plucking. I dripped into the best city-centre hotel, where I got a double room with central heating, TV, a minibar and a proper bath in my large bathroom for £10 a night, including breakfast.

The *Turkish Daily News* reported serious flooding in Mersin, further along the coast in the direction I was heading. Highways and bridges had been washed away and there were many fatalities. Rain was forecast for the next nine days. When I strolled down to the harbour in Antalya during a break in the clouds, there were rivers of rainwater pouring down the cliffs and I had to step over a wall of sandbags to get into a café. More rain had fallen in a week than they normally get all winter. I seemed to be carrying rain, floods and general disaster with me, wherever I went on this ill-starred ride.

Antalya's best tourist beaches are out to the east of the city, in Lara. It would have been lovely to cycle all the way along the coast to Side, but I was told that Lara was a dead end. I always take what motorists tell me with a pinch of salt, so I took advantage of a glimmer of sun to go for a bus ride out there. We drove through lakes of water and crossed a stream which had grown to a turbulent little river. Then, sure enough, we came to the wire fence of a campsite, where the road and the bus both terminated. That was a disappointment, but my walk up from the beach to the main road was magnificent, as the first dazzling white snowfall of the winter, the one we drove through on our way to Antalya, was glittering on the peaks of the Lycian mountains.

I didn't want to spend another whole winter in Antalya, so I defied the forecast and set off for Side. I rode along the cliff tops through Muratpaşa, then joined the six-lane highway. The old road had been left to run alongside, so I was able to cycle in safety with only a few tractors for company. Between the orange and tangerine orchards were rows and rows of vehicles for sale, everything from luxury coaches to motor scooters – another sign of hard times. I was racing the rain. The morning had started sunny, but the sky soon darkened, and its grey became black and menacing. Fields were waterlogged and streams swollen. A woman in traditional Turkish dress was standing guard over a flock of sheep, with big yellow wellies at the end of her baggy trousers. The shepherds of poetic idyll sang lovelorn laments and played their rustic pipes to fair, disdainful shepherdesses. These days, according to a headline in the *Turkish Daily News*, 'Mobiles are a *Must* for Shepherds', not Pan pipes. Theft of flocks has become so rife that shepherds are not hired unless they come equipped with the latest Nokia. The old lady in the yellow wellies was not of the mobile generation, but her dozen sheep were presumably her own, so she could manage without. After an easy morning's ride, I cruised down the Side peninsula, past the city's majestic Roman monuments, just before the heavens opened again. It might be very wet out there, but at least ancient Pamphylia was flat.

Side is one of the many places along the Turkish coast where Cleopatra is said to have bathed. Asses' milk, mineral springs and sea water, all seem to have been equally attractive to this bathing queen. Now tourists crowd the beaches in the season and the ancient port turns into a cross between a funfair and an Oriental bazaar. In December, the local people turn in on themselves. I expected to be able to stroll down the main harbour road, studying the menus and choosing my restaurant. But there was no choice. A few fast-food eateries were open at lunchtime for the visitors, mostly German, who were staying in the five-star beach complexes on long winter packages, but most of the small hotels were closed and the town was tightly shuttered in the evenings.

The first night, I was paddling around in the rain, desperately searching for food – any food – when I caught a glimmer of light through the cracks in a sheet of green tarpaulin. It was closing off the open front of a restaurant. I splashed over to peek through it and saw a large wooden table in front of a cheerful wood stove. A woman sat in front of the blaze holding a skein of knitting wool, from which a man was winding a ball, watched by a little girl and a cat. The man was probably in his sixties, plump, with a round cherubic face behind large spectacles. He was wearing a Pringle golf sweater, patterned in pink and blue diamonds, and a plaid wool scarf. I heard him talking to the woman and her daughter in correct, but very deliberate Turkish. They were replying in what was obviously their own language. I guessed that he was a foreigner, married to a younger Turkish woman.

I burst in on this charming domestic scene and asked if they served dinners. They did. A space was cleared for me at the table and the woman went to her stove at the back of the one big room and grilled me chicken breasts, which she served with salad and a soft round loaf, sprinkled with poppy seeds. I had never been offered this kind of bread before. The Turks usually eat French bread or flat, unleavened *pide*. This new variety was baked only in Ramadan for the daily *iftar*, the sunset breaking of the fast, and it was delicious.

While the chicken was being grilled, I took over the holding of the skein and got into conversation with the winder. I found that nothing was as it seemed. Jan was not the husband, but a Dutchman wintering in Side, and it was he who was the knitter.

Switching to perfect English, he told me that he had been a theatrical producer and had worked for a time at the Royal Court in Sloane Square. When he went back to Holland, three of the people closest to him had died in quick succession and nobody seemed to care. He got very depressed and finally cracked. He now spent his winters in Turkey, because he felt safe there. It was a country where people still cared about one another.

'But why Side?' I asked. 'It's such a small place. Is there enough to do here, to fill up a whole winter?'

'I like a small place. Antalya's nice, but I feel safer in Side. Every year, I tell myself that *this* winter is the one when I shall travel round Turkey and see some more of the country. But then my courage fails me and I never get further than Alanya, where I've got friends. I'm settled here. I take a room every year in the same empty pension and do my own catering, except for dinner, when I come across here. And I always have something to do. I was put on to craft work when I had my nervous breakdown and I keep myself busy with that. I've been doing my embroidery today and I've just designed a jersey for Gizem, for Christmas, which is why I'm winding this wool.'

He was a great find. He had studied Turkish for four years and was able to act as interpreter. Gizem went off to bed and I watched the disasters on television with Jan and Seher – people being rescued from the floods in Mersin, cars being washed away in Istanbul, swirling waters where I had walked the previous day in Antalya, and Edirne cut off by snowdrifts. Seher's husband, Musa, a slim, bearded man, ran in from the rain and there were mugs of coffee all round.

'It's the worst year anyone can remember,' said Musa. 'Blazing heat until mid-November. Then no proper autumn, just this endless torrential rain on the coasts and piles of snow in the mountains, a month before it should have fallen. The simple people are blaming the American bombing of Afghanistan. They say it's disturbed the atmosphere.'

All night I heard the rain crashing down on a corrugated iron roof. In the morning, the square outside my hotel was a lake, and still it rained. I sat by the window in my warm room and watched men wading in yellow wellies and oilskins to buy bread at the corner shop. It was no day for cycling. When the torrents turned to drizzle, I made a dash for the museum. I bought my ticket at the entrance gate and the ticket-seller shouted, 'Mehmet! A friend is coming!' He said it in Turkish, not knowing that I could understand, so 'friend' was not intended to flatter. I heard a key turn in a lock and a very sleepy Mehmet peered at me from inside the museum door. He shook hands with his new 'friend' and switched on the lights, not holding it against me that I had disturbed his slumbers.

Museums are fascinating places. Ancient sites are usually little more than groundplans of cities, carefully labelled. Archaeologists have guessed the identity and function of each pile of rubble, and they may or may not be right. But either way, these sad, ankle-breaking relics of former glories tell us so little about the lives, hopes and affections of the people who moved among them. We can only get a feel for those in the site museums, by looking at their everyday items – their cooking pots, jewellery and lovingly carved children's toys. These simple things never lie and their interpretation is not subject to the whims of academic fashion. In the Side museum, the exhibits were mostly late Roman, and they told me something about those successful, prosperous citizens that I would never have learned from the ruins. They were animal-lovers. One marble sarcophagus was carved with dogs, their snouts pointing intently at a group of dancing cherubs. A fragment of another was engraved with a pair of monumental doors; they were slightly ajar and a dog's head was peering through the crack. A young woman in flowing draperies lay relaxed on top of a third sarcophagus, her right hand caressing a tiny lamb.

On the way back to my hotel, I ran the gauntlet of desperate traders. They tried me in German, then switched their patter to English. 'Cheaper than Tesco! Asda prices!' I went into a small general store for batteries and a supply of snacks. 'English mad people!' said the storekeeper. 'Mad shopping! These boxes of 200 cigarettes. The Germans buy one. The English buy thirty, forty boxes. One man bought 180! 180 boxes of 200 cigarettes! I think your customs people must be less strict than the Germans.'

I bumped into Jan outside the shop, looking very jaunty in a red tartan cap. He greeted me with 'See how the place has emptied! All those tourists scuttle off to their beach hotels at sunset, away from the dangerous streets of Side. They're scared to be out in the dark – and in any case, they've paid for their dinners in their packages. So poor Seher and Musa get no customers. Four of them, rich Germans, did come to Seher's at lunchtime. They were showing off to one another about all the wonderful places they'd travelled to and their expensive cruises. They took no notice of me. I was knitting quietly in the corner, so they thought I was some sort of a simpleton. When they left, they queried the bill and got into an argument about the cost of their snacks. How I hate those people!'

The wind blew up a gale that evening, but I had my sanctuary behind the tarpaulin, where Gizem was dressed up as a fairy, in a white shawl and a white tissue-paper crown, waving a stick with tinsel on the end. Emir, the teenage son, was in a sulk because he wanted to go out and play video games at the internet café and was not being allowed. Jan arrived, and he and Seher resumed work on the tangled skein of extremely fine wool, like a spider's web; it was so fine, it would have to be knitted up in at least treble thickness. Jan told me that he often ate with the family and I thought it might save Seher work if I did the same. 'No. She likes cooking for you. There's not much trade at the moment and you're regular income. Anyway, I doubt if you would like it during Ramadan. She's fasting, so they have their evening meal at five, as soon as the sun sets.'

I had expected to stay one night in Side, but the rain was relentless and I was imprisoned there for six. The summer Mediterranean seems a tame sea, but the December gales were rousing it into huge ocean rollers. The deciduous trees lost the last of their leaves and the palms tossed their heads in anger. I read and solved puzzles, relieved that I had been able to renew my Syrian visa in London. All through the summer, I had felt under pressure, as I had to enter the country before the end of October. Now, with a November renewal, I had until May to get there, so I could take a relaxed view of the delay. And being alone helped. There was no one I had to discuss my plans with, no one I had to meet, no one else's agenda to consider. I just woke up in the morning, looked at the weather and made up my mind on the spot. No explanations, no compromises. There were two days when I might have ventured forth in, say, France. But in Turkey, distances are great and empty. If I set out for Alanya and the heavens opened, I doubted if I should find any intermediate stopping-place. It was 50 miles (80 km) or nothing.

I was the only guest in my hotel. There seemed to be two young men and two older men running it, none of whom spoke a word of anything but Turkish. They watched television in the lobby all day and the young ones hooted with laughter whenever I used the Turkish word for my room key. Jan said they were probably not paid. They were just minding the empty hotel and doing odd jobs in return for somewhere to live. They would have been poor company for six days and nights. I was lucky to have found Jan, and Seher's welcoming little restaurant.

I finally awoke one morning to a slightly calmer sea. Shreds of blue slit the uniform charcoal of the sky. I had an on-off breakfast. Shall I? Shan't I? At 8.45, I suddenly decided to go. I packed my bags in a rush, paid my bill and left.

The seaside highway to Alanya was raised above the scrubby, waterlogged fields, where disconsolate sheep and goats paddled round the bushes. Men were scavenging on the beach for planks of wood and branches washed up by the storms. There were slabs of collapsed masonry and disused huts. Half-built hotels and apartment blocks stared out with empty eyes, their concrete grey with rain. I asked a man in a roadside tea shop why there were so many abandoned buildings.

'With the inflation we've got here, there's no point in saving money in the bank. It's better to put it into the foundations of a building, even if you can't afford to finish it. Then you wait till the next bit of money comes along and build the next storey. It's not ideal, and it looks a mess, but at least bricks and concrete keep their value. And you're providing employment for a few months, for men who would otherwise be out of work.'

I flew along with the wind behind me, racing the gathering storm. After 25 miles (40 km), I began to relax a little, as I always do after the halfway mark. I had launched myself into the unknown, but from now on, every turn of the pedals was bringing me closer to shelter. In fact, shelter came sooner than I expected. Alanya's overspill of hotels and holiday villages began a good 20 miles before I reached the town. Apartment blocks in a hideous shade of yellow, like cheap rancid butter, mingled with the smart hotels. Apart from stalls selling leather goods and postcards, there seemed to be no shops, no cafés – just miles of highway, where elderly tourists in anoraks plodded along, looking despairingly for something to do. Alanya itself was hardly livelier. The estate agents were open late, their windows full of seaside properties described in Dutch and German. The other shops closed at five o'clock, if they had opened at all. I was on the verge of a cold and hurried through my evening meal, afraid of shocking my fellow diners by having to wipe my nose in the restaurant. It is far politer in Turkey to let one's nose drip.

My cold matured in Gazipaşa, which I reached after a hesitant eleven o'clock start. I was leaving the flat beaches of ancient Pamphylia and returning to a landscape of daunting vertical cliffs and rocky headlands. The gentler south-facing slopes were perfect for growing bananas, the main crop of the region. The higher peaks were crowned with sweet-smelling pines, their needles gleaming dark green against the ferrous rock faces, which were blood red after the rain. Until the twisting rollercoaster of a road was hacked out of the mountains in the 1960s, the settlements in the bays could be reached only by sea. They were plagued throughout history by pirates and the ruins of ancient fortifications litter the inlets.

This rugged area was ancient Cilicia, coveted for its wealth of ships' timber. The Romans brought it to heel when Pompey was given extraordinary powers to clear the Mediterranean of pirates. With a fleet of 270 warships and 100,000 legionaries, he established a cordon across the Straits of Gibraltar, then moved eastwards, systematically sweeping the sea. The pirates who had terrorised the eastern Mediterranean were rounded up by Pompey's special flying squadron and herded into their last refuge in Cilicia, where the Roman infantry demolished their strongholds and took them prisoner. With remarkable leniency, Pompey spared them and set them up as respectable farmers and tradesmen.

Thirty years later, Antony bestowed this hard-won Roman province of Cilicia on Cleopatra. Egypt is a desolate, sandy, rocky waste, habitable only along the narrow snake of green beside the life-giving Nile. It has always been short of timber, and Cleopatra needed timber for her fleet, so Antony obliged. His gift incensed the Romans and contributed to his fall from grace.

To gain a full appreciation of gloom and boredom, you need to spend a cold, rainy December evening in a small Turkish town. The locals were miserable. They were in the middle of an economic depression, they were worried stiff about American intentions in Afghanistan and Iraq, and the weather was appalling. I braved the rain to buy a bottle of raki and had a quick medicinal snifter in my bedroom before I went out to my alcohol-free restaurant (no alcohol was served in Gazipaşa during Ramadan). Then I watched the TV news in the bleak hotel lobby, crouching over the one-bar electric fire with ten workmen and shuffling my feet on the concrete floor in an effort to keep them warm. Two people had died in a snowstorm in Thrace and the floods in Mersin were rising higher. I took my streaming cold early to bed.

My bedroom had no heating. The floor was tiled and rugless, the green emulsion on the walls was mottled with damp, and the window rattled in its unseasoned pine frame. In the bathroom, the pipe from the cistern to the toilet bowl was a plastic snake, which had to be held firmly in place, otherwise it jumped out and a cisternful of water gushed over my feet and flooded the floor. I learned this the hard way! At least the bed was clean and comfortable. There was no top sheet, but I slid into the luxury of my silk sleeping bag under the warm blankets.

Flashes of lightning woke me early. Thunder rolled and rain oozed through the cracks in the crooked window frame. I resigned myself to a day and another night in Gazipaşa. My next stop, Anamur, was fifty miles along a tortuous, mountainous coast road, where the exposed cliff top fell vertically into the sea. I had passed that way once in a bus and I knew there was absolutely nowhere to stay, or even to shelter from the rain. I turned over and went to sleep again. Later that morning, I bought a newspaper for the weather forecast. It was dire. I seemed to have no prospect of cycling to Anamur in tolerable conditions so, after a great deal of soul-searching, I crept guiltily into the bus office and bought myself a ticket for the following morning. Pouring rain and a bad cold were a terrible combination for an arduous, exposed ride. Had I been staying anywhere else, I would have waited for my cold or the weather, or both, to improve. But a long stay in Gazipaşa would have sent my marbles scattering. I had to get away.

When it seemed that things couldn't possibly get worse, they did. The next night, to add to the misery of my cough and streaming nose, my stomach began to heave. I rushed into the bathroom. When I flushed the lavatory, I held the plastic pipe from the cistern tightly in place to keep my feet dry, and the entire cistern came crashing down from the wall. Water poured everywhere. I struggled to reattach the cistern and was copiously sick again, all down the front of my one and only nightdress. It seems comic now, but at the time it felt like death.

Cleopatra was Queen of Cyprus as well as Pharaoh of Egypt, and Cyprus was enjoying better weather than mainland Turkey. I had always wanted to visit the island, particularly the unspoilt northern part, and there was a ferry nearby. As I mouldered in my cheerless Gazipaşa bed, I decided to treat myself to Christmas in a comfortable hotel on Cyprus, where I could explore Cleopatra's realm until the Turkish rain abated and the flood-damaged roads and bridges around Mersin were repaired.

Still too wobbly to cycle, I rode the bus through Anamur, past the 36 towers of its splendid mediaeval fortress, straight to Silifke. In season, the ride would have been very demanding but possible, as there were one or two modest pensions tucked away in tiny bays between the formidable headlands. Out of season everything looked closed. I realised how far east I had travelled when the bus filled up. The only vacant seat was next to mine, and the passengers boarding at the next stop were men. Rather than place one of them next to me, the conductor split up the married couple in the seats in front. He asked the wife to sit with me, so that one of the men could be seated next to her husband.

The Silifke bus station (*otogar*) was way out of town. The highway was unlit and there were potholes and long stretches of mud, where the floods had swept away the tarmac. I was the only guest in the sizeable best hotel and the only customer in the echoing restaurant. The four waiters were watching television.

'Where are you from?' one of them asked.

'From England.'

'I thought so. You look just like your Queen. You've got the same face.'

I decided to take this as a compliment.

'What's your football team? We're all Liverpool supporters and there's a big match on tonight – Liverpool v. Chelsea.'

Football is not my favourite game, but I have a god-daughter called Chelsea. I didn't know the Turkish word for god-daughter, or even if such a relationship existed in Turkey, so I simplified my answer.

'I live in London, so I'm a Chelsea fan.'

That decided, we got down to the less important matter of my dinner. I was still not feeling too well, so they produced a bowl of lentil soup, scrambled eggs and a Pepsi, which is always good for an unsettled stomach. Then we all concentrated on the match. They cared passionately about the result, puffing desperately on their cigarettes and slurping endless glasses of tea in their anguish. Chelsea kept scoring and I was supposed to be feeling triumphant. Instead, I felt so sorry for the waiters that I wished I had never picked the winning team. When Chelsea won 4–0, they were dejected, but they brought me a victory saucer of Turkish delight, to show there were no hard feelings.

It was my winter for being marooned. I discovered that there were no ferries to Cyprus for the next three days. This time, the problem was not the weather, but the public holiday for Şeker (Sugar) Bayram, the end of Ramadan. In Turkey, they celebrate the end of the month-long fast not with alcohol or slain sheep, but with the innocent pleasure of giving one another sweets. There were colourful displays of sweets and chocolates in the shops, and every counter in every bank, post office, shop and hotel had its dish of sweets to offer to clients. A cheerful *'Iyi Bayram!'* (Happy Bayram) would produce a handful of assorted toffees and boiled sweets. But there was sadness too that Bayram. Women who had lost everything in the floods were weeping on the television news. Sweets for Bayram? Their homes were destroyed. They didn't even have beds for their children to sleep in, never mind sweets!

Silifke had a Middle Eastern look and feel. The Migros supermarket attracted some younger women and married couples, but the older men were still following tradition and doing the household shopping themselves in little neighbourhood stores. Most of the men wore Turkish trousers, tight round the ankles and shins, ballooning out above the knees. One passed me on his bicycle, looking from behind exactly like an Edwardian lady cyclist in bloomers. The younger men dressed in jeans and bright jerseys, but if older men wore Western dress, it was invariably a flat tweed cap and a grey jacket, with dreary dun trousers and black shoes. The townswomen were in Western dress, while their country cousins, in Silifke for Bayram, waddled through the streets like exotic birds in baggy velvet harem trousers, cardigans and shawls, layer upon layer of hectic, clashing colours. Headscarves were almost universal. I discussed this with an English-speaking woman I met in a café. She was wearing a scarf herself, but she told me that she was discouraging her daughter from following suit.

'It's like this,' she said. 'If you don't cover your hair as a young woman, no one except the religious fanatics thinks any the worse of you. But once you cover, you have to stay covered. I began to wear a scarf when I got married, not because my husband insisted – he couldn't care less – but because I thought it would be a nice, respectable thing for a married woman to do. It was a great mistake. I'm fed up with wearing a scarf now, but if I were to go out one day without it, it would cause a scandal. "What's she up to, walking down the street with her hair flying in the wind? She must be on the look-out for another man!" I would lose my reputation. I'm not letting my daughter cover. I don't want her to fall into the same trap.'

Silifke has a Roman bridge, which still carries the town-centre traffic. Angry floods from the Taurus Mountains were hurling themselves against its sturdy piers, and its bordering trees and oleander bushes were fighting for their lives in the swirling waters. It was a dangerous scene, but it had obviously been much worse. I could see from the shreds of detritus hanging from the topmost branches that the waters had subsided at least six feet from their peak. It was easy to imagine the Emperor Frederick Barbarossa drowning here, while leading the Third Crusade.

I strolled from the bridge to Silifke's oldest mosque, built by the Seljuk Sultan, Alaeddin Keykubat I. I swathed myself in a large cotton square, uncertain of my reception as an infidel on a holy day, post September 11th. Old men in Turkish trousers and woolly hats were hobbling in on their walking sticks for the noon prayers. It was perishingly cold in the courtyard, but they all washed their feet in icy water and dried them on their handkerchiefs before entering the mosque. I followed them inside. 'Iyi Bayram!' I said. 'Iyi Bayram!' they chorused, beaming at me. I obviously need not have worried. A young man stopped sweeping the carpet and rushed over to shake hands with me. 'Alaeddin Keykubat, 900 years old,' he glowed. Like all Seljuk mosques, it was an elegantly simple structure. The interior walls were whitewashed and the carpet was plain red, divided into prayer-rows by green stripes. There was a simple mini-dome over the *mihrab*, the prayer-niche pointing to Mecca. The only showy items were two brass chandeliers. The young man walked outside with me to point out the Seljuk pastry-frill above the doorway and the indented leaf pattern. A piece of flowing Arabic calligraphy, with a discreet frieze of green leaves and arabesques, was protected from the weather by a glass cover.

The Bayram weather was too stormy for me to venture up the mountain to Silifke's Byzantine fortress. More depressingly, when Bayram ended, it was too stormy for the ferries. I was marooned again. Night after night, the waiters plied me with gifts of baklava, Turkish delight and chocolate blancmange. When there was no football, we watched interminable concerts in the arabesque style. The singers choked with strangulated passion. They were either solo males, wailing falsetto to a female chorus, or desperately lovelorn solo women with a gasping male-voice choir in the background. The usual accompaniment was a group of six or seven violins, with zither, mandolin, clarinet and percussion. The waiters were entranced.

I finally sailed from Silifke's port of Taşucu, wading to the gangway in driving rain through a lake of mud. The sea was so rough that the express ferry took twice as long as usual to make the 40-mile (64 km) crossing and the Turks were seasick. I managed well, because I offended my neighbours slightly by turning down all their offers of Pepsi, Fanta and tea. They indulged themselves in the early stages of the crossing and regretted it later.

We landed in Girne, formerly Kyrenia, in the shadow of its formidable Crusader castle. As the British had once controlled Cyprus, I expected to see notices in English, but I was disappointed. I suppose we left too long ago. None of the harbour officials spoke anything but Turkish and without my own smattering, I should have been lost in the crush and confusion of the docks. I had no guidebook and no map, so I cycled after the taxis – along the left-hand side of the road. That was one legacy at least of the island's British past. The sun was shining and the air was balmy. I even heard crickets singing. It was hard to believe that the glacial rain of Silifke was only a short ferry-crossing away.

I arrived on 17 December and found the seafront hotels fully booked. Turkish holidaymakers, attracted by the casinos at the Dome and the Grand Rocks, had come over from the mainland for Bayram, and were mingling with the influx of Europeans, mostly British, who had come for Christmas and the New Year. I negotiated a long-term stay at the Socrates Hotel, which was built round a courtyard with a swimming pool and tables under the lemon trees, just one road back from the sea. Even in Cyprus, it was too cold for swimming, but I imagined myself sipping coffee outside, enjoying the sunshine.

It was not to be. The rain pursued me from the mainland. On the evening I arrived, the jagged crests of the Five Finger mountain range above Girne were clearly defined, like a row of shark's teeth against the sky. In the night, the clouds descended and I rarely saw the mountains again. On 18 December it rained and then, on the day after, there was hail.

The exhibits in Girne Castle occupied one rainy morning. A wrecked ship, raised from the harbour with its cargo of amphorae and almonds still intact after five thousand years, watercolours of Cyprus, a Chamber of Horrors in the dungeons and, in one of the towers, models of soldiers from all the garrisons who had occupied the castle throughout its history, starting with its Byzantine builders and running through Crusaders, Venetians and Ottomans to a British Army officer. A crowd of young men was milling around. Judging from their haircuts, which were the nearest thing to shaven skulls, I guessed they were Turkish National Service boys on a day off. Their manners were impeccable. They stood aside and opened doors for me. There was a bit of clowning in the Chamber of Horrors, where they took photographs of one another, pretending to turn the rack or standing with their arms round the shoulders of a friar, but it was all quietly good humoured, even decorous. Seventy or so young men, out for a day on the town, and not a sign of alcohol-churned testosterone.

There were English newspapers in Girne and The Green Jacket, an English bookshop run by a former officer of that regiment, so I was able to replenish my stock of reading matter. I also had Horace's *Odes* with me, in Latin, which I had to reread in preparation for a speech about Horace on a Bicycle, which I had rashly agreed to give at the annual dinner of the Horatian Society. When there was a break in the rain, I went on short excursions to explore Byzantine abbeys and Gothic churches, clinging dizzyingly to crags. Sometimes I cycled, but more often I braved the mountains in a *dolmuş*, one of the minibuses or eight-seater Mercedes which supplied the island's transport. Most days, I was a prisoner in the hotel. There was even a sprinkling of snow one morning, only the second fall since records began. It was the worst winter anyone could remember and the hoteliers were worried. Christmas was one of their busiest seasons. They were fully booked, as usual, but what about next year? It would be a disaster if all those disappointed tourists went home and said, 'Don't go to Cyprus. The weather there's terrible.'

One piece of good luck was that I happened to have chanced on the hotel used by the Ramblers. Their leader, Alan, arrived a few days after I did, to be followed by groups over the Christmas and New Year period.

'Is his name really Alan?' one of the waiters asked me. 'What a name to give a child!' As Turkish names mean something, and *alan* in Turkish means 'an open space', the staff were naturally mystified!

The Ramblers were my salvation. They went out on rain-sodden walks in the daytime, but in the evenings I could count on meeting them in the bar for English conversations. Mehmet, the hotel's owner, went to school in London while his father was reading for the Bar, and he and his mother both had good English. Then there was a Turkish Army colonel, who had been Military Attaché in Washington, and was now running a computer hardware company in Ankara, and a rather mysterious, elegantly suited Iranian businessman. They were both on holiday in the Socrates and were both good breakfast companions.

The Iranian was the first I had met in recent years and he was refreshingly outspoken.

'As long as young men think the suicide bomb is the key to paradise, there will be no shortage of recruits. But change is possible. We shouldn't lose hope. We just have to work at it. Look how Iran has changed in the last 25 years.'

I told him that I went to Iran the year before the Shah fell and thought the Iranians were just about the most liberal people in the Middle East. I was really surprised when they got into the grip of the Ayatollahs.

'So was I!' he said. 'Of course, Ayatollah Khomeini was a liar. We were sick of the Shah and his secret police, and the Ayatollah in Paris was promising us all sorts of wonderful reforms. But when we put him in power, he cheated us. We are an educated family, all of us, boys and girls. My father was one of the first pupils when the American School opened in Teheran and he went on to the American University in Beirut. He was appalled at Ayatollah Khomeini's mediaeval mindset and determined to outlive him. He was a sick man, but he said, "When that monster is gone, I can die in peace." And he did. He held on until the month after the Ayatollah's death, then he died too. Now everything in Iran has changed. The nightmare is over and we are leading more or less normal lives again. We have changed. The Americans have changed too. Fifty years ago, a world-famous blues singer was knocked down in the road and the ambulance men refused to pick her up because she was black. Now Colin Powell is Secretary of State. The most important man in America, after the President, is coloured. If the rest of the world can change so radically in fifty years, we have to hope that the Muslim fundamentalists can move on too. They'll get nowhere by harking back to the Middle Ages. When a Saudi man is run over, there is a fine of 2,000 US dollars. The fine for a woman is just 500 dollars. Women don't have identity cards there, so they have no legal status. What a country! Iran is a hundred times better.'

There were Turkish garrisons on North Cyprus and the people there spoke Turkish, but they had a strong sense of their Cypriot identity. 'Greek men bad. Turkish men bad. Cyprus men good.' The taxi driver was just one of many who expressed the same view. Preliminary talks about reunification of the island were taking place between Raoul Denktaş, the Turkish Cypriot leader, and Glafcos Clerides, the leader of the Greeks. Some sort of a rapprochement had become urgent, as Greek Cyprus had applied for membership of the EU. If the application were successful, the Greek half of the island would become even more prosperous, while the internationally unrecognised Turkish Republic of Cyprus would slide further into economic decay. After the weather, the talks were the main topic of conversation among educated Cypriots and I was interested to hear the North Cyprus viewpoint.

'We can't understand why the Greek-speakers cling on to Greece,' said Mehmet. 'They're no more Greek than we are. Just look at the map. See how far away we are from the Greek mainland. We're all the same people, and we're all Cypriots. We've had Myceneans here, Egyptians, Phoenicians, Romans, Byzantines, Crusaders, Venetians, Ottomans, British – everyone you can think of has settled on this island and racially we're a mixed bag. It just happened that some of us stayed with the Byzantine faith, while others converted to Islam under the Ottomans.'

'I blame the Orthodox priests for the troubles,' said his mother darkly. 'They colluded with the Greek Government after independence and tried to force Enosis on us and we refused to be ruled by Greece.'

The family lived in Limassol before the civil war, and had to move north when Cyprus was divided. Like all such refugees, both Greek and Turkish Cypriot, they lost everything and had to start their lives again from scratch. Mehmet's father built up a new legal practice in Girne and bought the Socrates Hotel. I expressed surprise that they had retained the Greek name in Turkish Cyprus.

'Why should we change it? Just because Socrates was born in Greece? He was one of the world's great philosophers. He belongs to mankind, not just to Greece. It's a good name for a hotel.'

On Christmas Eve and at the New Year's party, I sat with the family at their table. I commented that the music and dancing seemed Greek. There was a cry of protest. 'They're not Greek. They're Cypriot. We all have the same music.' Some of the hotel staff were such brilliant dancers that I asked Mehmet if he gave job applicants a dancing test before he took them on. 'No. I pick them for their kind faces. We've been running these parties for a long time, so they've become skilful.'

The jewellers' shops in Girne had displays of pendants, rings and bracelets incorporating the stylised blue eye, which is a charm in the eastern Mediterranean against the Evil Eye. As my cycle ride from London had been so thoroughly jinxed, I decided to protect myself. I bought a very slender white gold bracelet, as fine as wire, inset with a proportionately small and understated Evil Eye charm. I wore it for the first time on New Year's Day, to try to improve my luck. I was anxious to move on, but the storms still raged. Rain came down in torrents, and the turbulent sea smashed the harbour wall and destabilised the lighthouse. Istanbul was snowbound, and the army and civil defence had been mobilised. Anatolia had 285 roads closed and more snow was expected. Further west, a state of emergency had been declared in Athens. What none of the news bulletins mentioned was that all this precipitation was falling as rain on the mild Mediterranean shores. I found an internet café near the hotel and sent emails to my friends, as a change from reading. Time hung very heavy.

Cyprus has two mountain ranges, the narrow strip of the Five Finger Mountains running parallel to the north coast and the more substantial Troodos Mountains in the south. Between the two, the island's capital, Nicosia (Lefkoşa to the Turks), lies on the broad central plain. My plan was to cycle from Girne across to Gazimağusa (formerly Famagusta) at the eastern end of Cyprus and take the ferry from there to Mersin, as an alternative to returning to Silifke and taking my chance on the flood-damaged mainland highway. I wanted to stay beside the sea, cycling along the north coast road and taking one of the eastern passes over the Five Finger Mountains, but that turned out to be impossible. The passes at that end of the island were steep and bleak, with no shelter in the winter. I was forced to leave the sea and cycle to Gazimağusa across the central plain.

On 3 January, the morning finally dawned bright. I was such a fixture in the hotel by that time that the staff kissed me goodbye and the Ramblers came out with their cameras to take my photo as I sped away down the road. It was a steep climb out of Girne. On the topmost mountain crag stood a huge silhouette of Ataturk in military uniform, dominating the landscape like the great Osborne bulls in Spain. A pair of traffic police got out of their car for a chat, and some soldiers crawling muddily on their stomachs over waste ground gave me a cheery wave with their rifles. A strong south-westerly wind arose and by the time I reached Lefkoşa it was raining again.

What used to be the flourishing city of Nicosia is now divided down the middle by the Green Line, which no one may cross. The Turkish half is a sad place. Towards the Green Line the buildings are derelict. Streets are gated off and the cul-de-sacs are littered with cannibalised cars and vans without wheels. Workshops have been abandoned. The dividing fence has observation posts, but even these are empty. I passed only two old men in the deserted streets, both in ragged clothes, pushing a recalcitrant cart through the potholes with a few kilos of oranges. Over the top of the fence, Greek flags were painted provocatively on house walls and Greek graffiti annouced 'Cyprus is Greek'. From the roof terrace of my hotel I could look out on the prosperity of Greek Nicosia. They told me in the hotel that Cyprus Greeks are very rich, richer than the Greeks in Greece. At night the Turkish side was dark, except for a few bravely flickering Christmas decorations in the main square, while the Greek side was ablaze with light. My kebab take-away, the only restaurant I could find open in the shadowy streets, was offering reduced prices for teachers and soldiers.

I had bought a new odometer in Girne, but it had not been accurately calibrated. The tourist office directed me to a cycle repairer on the outskirts. They said he was a teacher, who would be smart enough to adjust an electronic gadget. In this city of dusty, ill-stocked shops, I was convinced that I should find some aged mathematician in pebble spectacles repairing punctures in his front room. Instead, I found a glittering bicycle emporium, owned by a gorgeous young film star of a man in expensive designer casuals. He was into mountain bikes and trained his own racing team. 'My wife is a mountain biker too,' he told me proudly. 'At the International Mountain Bike Races in Alanya, she came in third. The first of the English competitors was placed eleventh.' He calibrated my odometer in seconds, gave me tea and charged me nothing.

It was drizzly when I set out for Gazimağusa. In other circumstances, I might have waited, but I had managed only four days' cycling in over a month and I was desperate to make some progress. So I set out on what should have been a beautiful ride across the fertile central plain, with the Five Finger Mountains to my left and the Troodos to my right. But the mountains were completely shrouded in rain clouds and all I saw were waterlogged, sodden fields. The rain intensified when I was already too far along the road to turn back. Fortunately, one of the two carriageways was closed off for resurfacing and I was able to cycle along it in solitary splendour, free of the spray from passing traffic. That was one redeeming feature of the ride. The other was the hospitality of the Turkish Cypriots, who turned it into a continuous party. When I stopped at a petrol station for a bottle of lemon Fanta, the boys immediately invited me into a little room with a paraffin heater and plied me with tea and *simits,* delicious bread rings sprinkled with sesame seeds. At my next stop, my host told me over the teapot that he had worked in Australia for fourteen years to save the money for his house and garage. 'The Cyprus economy's in a shocking state,' he said, 'but I'm better off than most. I can always go back to Australia, and my children are Australian citizens. They went to school and university there, so their English is excellent and they've managed to find good jobs, even in Cyprus.' I asked if he was born in the village where his garage stood and he roared with scornful laughter at the very idea, nearly losing his false teeth in the process. I thought he was going to tell me that he was a sophisticate, born in Istanbul, or Nicosia at the very least. 'No. I was born in a village 15 miles away from here!' I was offered more lifts along the road than I could count, one by a van driver with a red carnation behind his ear. 'You're cycling for sport? How brave in this weather!' and he jumped out of his van to fix the carnation to my handlebars. When I finally dripped into my hotel in Gazimağusa, I found that rain had trickled down the neck of my totally waterproof Helly Hansen and soaked me to the skin. I was wearing a new purple shirt I had bought in Girne and it was evidently not colourfast. I looked like an Ancient Briton, painted with woad.

The port of Famagusta (Gazimağusa) was once one of the richest cities in the Mediterranean. When Cleopatra ruled the island, it was called Arsinoe, one of the royal women's names used by the Ptolemies. Later, it had a church for every day of the year and St Nicholas Cathedral, the finest Gothic building on the island. The Lusignan rulers were crowned Kings of Cyprus in Nicosia, but their more sumptuous crowning, as Kings of Jerusalem, used to take place in the cathedral in Famagusta (1192–1489). Frustratingly, when there was so much I wanted to see in the city, I was imprisoned in my outskirts hotel by roads knee-deep in flood water. My balcony was a marble paddling pool, and still it rained, the fat drops bouncing up from the surface like rubber balls. The city's power failed, but fortunately my hotel had its own generator. I lay on my bed for two days, watching BBC World and eating sesame seed brittle with honey: 'Gives the skin beauty and gives sex power.'

For the hundredth time, I was on the verge of giving up. Then, on Sunday, the miracle occurred. The sun shone from a clear blue sky and honey-coloured Gazimağusa was at its best. I walked over the moat between its perfect double ring of Venetian fortifications and was stunned by the nobility of the city's ruins. The stupendous cathedral (now the Lala Mustafa Pasha Mosque) had been white-washed inside, so there were no tawdry distractions from the majesty of its soaring Gothic nave. It seemed closer to heaven in its unfurnished simplicity than a church tricked out with candles and gruesome paintings. When I left, I was touched to find that my shoes had been moved from the porch to the very edge of the mosque carpet, so that I could step straight into them without getting my feet cold.

As I walked along a street just inside the city's fortifications, I passed a family eating their leisurely Sunday breakfast from a groaning table out on the pavement. There were parents, grand-parents and two little boys, all in their bedroom slippers. '*Affiyet olsun!*' I called ('May it do you good!') and was immediately invited to join them. There was still no electricity in the city and they were eating outside because it was so dark indoors. Neighbours appeared, drawn by curiosity, and soon we were a large crowd, all drinking tea and chatting in the street. The younger boy, an engaging eleven-year-old in a cheerful multicoloured jumper, showed his Crusader ancestry in his blue eyes and blond hair. He spoke a few words of English and the whole family beamed when I praised his accuracy. They kept offering me more tea, buns, fruit and boiled eggs, but I made my excuses and left to continue my tour of the town. The fire brigade was much in evidence, struggling to pump out cellars. By the Victory Monument just outside the city walls I found a strange collection of bronze statues streaked with blood-red paint, recording atrocities perpetrated by the Greeks in 1964. The most sickening exhibit was a real bath-tub with a beaten-up bronze woman and two blood-soaked children huddled together inside it. They were the family of a Turkish Cypriot army officer. A noticeboard nearby displayed cuttings from the *Daily Express* and *Le Figaro*, describing the carnage of civilians found by the Turkish troops when they entered Nicosia. With the two communities accusing each other of civilian massacres, the path to reconciliation will be stony.

Just along the coast from Gazimağusa lie the ruins of the much more ancient Greek port of Salamis. Under the Ptolemies and the Romans, its strategic situation in the heart of the Mediterranean made it almost as important as Alexandria, Antioch and Ephesus. It was a safe haven on the crossings between Europe, Africa and the Middle East, but a series of earthquakes smashed its elegant buildings and sent them toppling into the sea. When I was a teenager, a friend told me how he had dived there and swum in crystal waters between the columns of the ancient city. That vision had enchanted me. Would I be disappointed when I finally got there? I put on my thermal gloves and woolly hat and cycled to its vast, deserted site, overgrown with wild olives, myrtle and maidenhair fern. Apart from the gymnasium with its marble floor-tiles and the shell of the Emperor Augustus's theatre, the city was unexcavated. The ruins which poked through were Roman, overlaid on Hellenistic Greek. They were mostly marble, as Salamis was a wealthy port. On such an extensive site, I was glad to have my bicycle. I cruised around, alone except for an earnest young Turkish couple, both in black leather jackets and spectacles, who walked solemnly hand in hand over the stones.

I have seen so many wonders over the last fourteen years; so many that sights in the second league of excellence now seem scarcely worth the effort involved in visiting them. Bellapais, for example, said by many to be the finest monastic ruin on Cyprus, seemed nothing architecturally when I compared it with Fountains Abbey or Jumièges. I feared I was becoming blasée. But in Gazimağusa and Salamis, I was bowled over by the romantic ruins and the magic of the atmosphere. I was relieved to find that I could still be stirred by beauty.

My bracelet against the Evil Eye may have stopped the rain, but in other respects the jinx was still upon me. When I cycled to the Gazimağusa shipping office, I was told that the ferries to Mersin ran only on Tuesdays and Thursdays. The Tuesday one was cancelled because the sea was too rough, and the next two ferries after that had been requisitioned by the Turkish army for the transfer of a regiment. I could not face another ten days of BBC World and sesame brittle, so I gave up the struggle and took the bus back to Girne. This time I took the slower car ferry, owned by the splendidly named Ufuk Ship Management Ltd, and spent the rough seven-hour crossing glued to the television with rows of unshaven Turkish truckies. We watched an interview with the Girne Chief of Police, who turned out to be a glamorous woman. We watched children's television, football, and the daily episode of a popular Turkish soap, in which a young photographer husband is constantly outwitted by his much smarter wife. But what really riveted the drivers were the newsreels of snow. The number of cut-off villages in Anatolia had risen to 9,000. Istanbul Airport and the Bosphorus Bridge were closed and there was even snow in Alanya and Mersin.

Our ferry nosed up to the bitterly cold, black dock in a sprinkling of snow. It was dark in the town and the streets were deserted. I hesitated at the approach to a dark alley, where a Swiss traveller on the ferry had recommended a hotel, and a lone passer-by rushed up to reassure me. He pushed my bike up the alley, then ran with it, panniers and all, up a flight of stone steps like Jack's beanstalk to a surprisingly modern hotel. My room had a fine view of Ataturk's statue and the ships in the harbour, but it was glacial. I stripped the blankets off the second bed and crawled under the pile into my silk sleeping bag. It was not a particularly comfortable night, but I was happy to have progressed back to the mainland. I was out of my Cyprus gaol!

After 38 days of rain, almost enough for the Biblical flood, the weather seemed finally to have cleared. I cycled into Silifke, where the Göksu River was still sweeping high and turbulent under its Roman bridge, then took the bus along the coast to Mersin, the port I would have reached had I been able to sail from Gazimağusa. The next day I cycled on to Tarsus, to my first undisputed encounter with Cleopatra since Athens.

Tarsus, famous as the birthplace of St Paul, has had its ups and downs in history, but has always retained a degree of importance because of its strategic situation. It stands at the southern end of one of the few passes over the formidable Taurus range, the

Cilician Gates. In 41 BC Mark Antony was in Tarsus, preparing for a war of revenge against the Parthians, who had defeated the Roman legions under Crassus at the Battle of Carrhae (53 BC) and disgraced them by capturing their standards, their usually invincible Roman eagles. Antony's recent victory at the Battle of Philippi had given him the edge over his chief rival, Octavian, so Cleopatra decided it was time to accept his invitation to a meeting. There were political advantages on both sides. Antony hoped to draw on Egypt's untapped riches to finance his Parthian war. Cleopatra was looking for another patron. Since the assassination of Julius Caesar in Rome on the Ides of March, 44 BC, she had been without influence in Rome. She had borne a son, Caesarion, to Caesar and she had his future to protect, as well as the integrity of her kingdom. An ambitious politician, she was determined that Egypt should not slide into the position of a vassal state in Rome's eastward expansion. She set out to captivate Antony.

Drawing on Plutarch's account of her arrival, Shakespeare wrote some of his most mellifluous lines:

The barge she sat in, like a burnish'd throne,
Burn'd on the water. The poop was beaten gold;
Purple the sails, and so perfumed that
The winds were love-sick with them; the oars were silver,
Which to the tune of flutes kept stroke . . .

Cleopatra herself, dressed as Aphrodite, the goddess of love, lay on a couch of gold brocade, fanned by dimpled boys. They were dressed as Cupids, and her gentlewomen attendants were sea nymphs, making a charming pretence of steering the boat and pulling on the silken rigging. We can see from the few surviving portrait heads of Cleopatra that she was not a particularly beautiful woman, but she certainly knew how to capitalise on her assets.

Antony could not fail to be impressed. Lured by this ostentatious display of wealth, he spent the winter as her guest in Alexandria. He tracked down and executed Cleopatra's only remaining rival to the throne of Egypt, her sister Arsinoe. In return, Cleopatra agreed to subsidise Antony's war against Parthia.

There is a gate in Tarsus, once one of the Roman gates into the city, which is now called Cleopatra's Gate – though, like

Cleopatra's Needle, it has no connection whatsoever with Cleopatra. On the morning I cycled there, it was so abnormally cold for southern Turkey that I wore my woolly hat pulled right down over my ears with my silk balaclava underneath it. The wind had swung from the west to the north east, bringing icy blasts from Siberia across the frozen snows of central Anatolia. In Kayseri, at the northern end of the Cilician Gates, they had to improvise chains on their shoes, and Istanbul was an ice rink, where vehicles spun round like dodgem cars. The Taurus Mountains were clothed, head, shoulders and knees, in dazzling white snow, which turned iridescent pink at sunset.

On the way to Adana I seemed to take endless detours round the flood damage. The road was not so much washed away as buried under heaps of rock and concrete, swept down the mountainsides by swollen streams. There were mechanical scoops and towering machines that looked like cranes, but were in fact giant hoovers, sucking up mud and stones. In the autumn of 1987 the Tarsus River (ancient Cnidus), where Cleopatra sailed in her golden barge, was no more than a miserable trickle, shallow enough for goats to graze in its bed. In January 2002, I cycled over a roaring torrent, which had burst its banks and spread over neighbouring fields. Justinian's stone bridge, a little further up-stream, stood with both ends submerged in the river's depths. Cleopatra must have chosen her sailing time very judiciously.

Since my last cycle ride along that road, the Cilician Gates had been widened to a motorway, which continued far beyond Adana, and factories had sprung up everywhere. I have never liked Adana, and I liked it even less as a prosperous industrial mushroom. The unobliging staff in my flashy hotel snatched my money the minute I walked in the door and relegated Condor to a shed at the far end of the car park. It was in sad contrast to our reception the previous night in Tarsus. There I was given tea on arrival; there was no thought of cash in advance; and the dear, doddery old proprietor had been proud to put Condor on display in the lobby, under his personal supervision.

The land around Adana, the Cilician delta, is prodigiously fertile. Nurtured by the rich silt of the Seyhan and Ceyhan Rivers, orange and tangerine groves stretch to the horizon, their golden globes gleaming through glossy leaves. And no land is wasted. There are even seas of lettuce between the roots of the trees. Eastern Turks and Kurds are usually economic migrants. But this bountiful corner of eastern Turkey has become a magnet for those who are even poorer than the poorest Turks. Itinerant Middle Eastern orange-pickers brave the chilly nights under sheets of plastic, and gypsy women cross the roads in a swirl of skirts, a baby on the hip and a toddler in tow, startling the Turkish drivers with their flashing eyes, naked legs and provocative smiles. Out east, away from the tourist zones, Turkish women are modestly covered and very self-contained.

Turning the corner beyond the delta and Ceyhan, I started to move south through Alexander the Great country. On the Plain of Issus, he won a brilliant victory over 600,000 Persians and put King Darius to flight. Then he continued south and founded the port of Alexandretta, modern Iskenderun (Iskender is Alexander's Turkish name), before marching on to Egypt. I followed him down to the sea, looking for the promenade, but all I found were high walls and soldiers. The once great port was a dreary naval base, so I decided to take a siesta rather than a walk. With a big climb ahead of me, I needed to conserve my energy. I entered my hotel lift with a handsome young smart-suited businessman.

'Do you want a friend?' he asked, in a flash of pearly teeth. 'I am only.'

I was now in the corner of Turkey known as the Hatay, which was part of France's Syrian Mandate until the Turks annexed it in 1939 after a referendum. Arabic was widely spoken and *'Salaam aleikum!'* was as common as the Turkish greetings.

Fortified with two sticky buns and two large mugs of Nescafé, I set out early to cross the mountains to Antakya (Antioch). I was pleased to find that the rough road of my 1987 ride had been replaced by a smooth double carriageway, but the steep 11-mile (18 km) climb to Belen was as tough as ever. The sea at Alexandretta soon fell away below me and I mostly plodded up to the village through forests of young pines. Just above it, walls of shale enclosed the 2,430-foot (740 m) Belen Pass, once known as the Syrian Gates. I cycled cautiously round a bend, where the road ran along a ledge over a head-spinning, stomach-churning drop. A view from the edge, like life on the edge, is always sharp, terrifying, but strangely alluring. At the Belen Pass, the reward for danger was one of the greatest spectacles on Earth, the vast sweep of Antakya's fertile plain, melting into the distance under a sprinkling of snow. It was breathtaking – one of those magic, skin-tingling moments when I know that climbing a mountain on a bicycle is worth all the pain and toil. The road down the other side was as bumpy as before, and Condor and I were nearly jolted to death on our descent to Antakya. The weather deteriorated too. Once over the top, we left the sunnier skies of the Mediterranean coast and ran first into a mountain blizzard, then a rainstorm on the flat.

Antakya was once the third greatest city in the Western world, after Rome and Alexandria. A relative latecomer to power, it soon gained ground. It was founded in 300 BC by Seleucus I Nicator. When Alexander the Great died of a fever in Babylon in June 323, he was a young man of 33 without an heir. He took to his bed and continued to make plans with his Admiral Nearchus for an expedition to Arabia. It occurred to no one that he would be dead within two days. There was no obvious successor, no one with the power or vision to hold such a vast empire together. After a few turbulent years, three of his generals emerged from the pack of contenders and divided the empire between them. Antigonus took Macedonia and Greece, Seleucus Syria and Persia, and Ptolemy Egypt. Alexander's conquests in the Punjab were won back for the Indians by the brilliant young Chandragupta Maurya. Seleucus was the only one of the three generals who had no capital city. He selected the site of Antioch, near the sea on the River Orontes, where silks and spices passed along the caravan routes from Arabia, Africa and the East. It was an inspired choice. Magnificent under the Seleucids, it expanded even further under Roman rule, and retained its status as the Middle Eastern capital of both the Byzantines and the Frankish knights. But Baibur and his Mamelukes razed it to the ground in 1268 and it degenerated into a handful of hovels in the midst of its noble ruins.

There are no surviving monuments, but to wander through its streets and bazaars is to fall under the spell of its past splendours. One of its main roads, Kurtulus Caddesi, follows the same course as the vanished Roman thoroughfare, once a magnificent colonnaded street with triumphal arches at both ends and a nymphaeum in the central forum. It was built by King Herod of Judaea to honour Augustus, when he paid a triumphal visit to Antioch after his victory over Antony and Cleopatra at the Battle of Actium. To walk along Kurtulus Caddesi is to tread in the footsteps of Augustus himself. There are even traces in the air of our friendly Egyptian Pasha, Mohammed Ali, who seized the city from the Ottomans in 1831 and would have held on to it, had not the European powers helped the Sultan to drive him out.

I have spent many happy days in Antakya. My friend Meridel once taught English here and I stayed twice in her flat overlooking the Orontes River. She kept two rabbits, Kedi and Blossom, on her front balcony. Every evening around eight o'clock they came to the French windows and peered through at us, waiting to be let inside. It was their evening treat. They bounded into the flat, jumped over the furniture and rested on our laps to have their silky little bodies stroked. I found it quite amazing, as I had no idea that rabbits could be house-trained. These two were impeccably mannered and there were never any accidents. Meridel's only problem with them was finding a suitable home when she left. The Turks are not unkind to their animals, but they are essentially practical people. Dogs are for guarding houses and rounding up sheep, cats are for catching mice, and rabbits are for stew-pots. A loving family, who would give Kedi and Blossom the pampering they were used to, took a lot of tracking down, but Meridel succeeded in the end. When she checked up on them a year later, they were still alive, sleek and glossy.

My hotel room looked out over the same River Orontes and I could see the Amanos Mountains on clear days. I was in the old town, across the river from the smart shops and soulless apartment blocks of modern Antakya. Behind my hotel lay the maze of a real Middle Eastern bazaar, where stalls were lined up according to their wares. A walk down a whole street of cloth merchants would lead to a glittering alley of shops selling nothing but gold, then a hundred shops with a thousand piles of Turkish delight in every flavour imaginable, followed by mountains of identical socks and underpants. Even the schoolboys and little old men who weighed passers-by for a pittance, stood their machines along the pavement in rows. Some were wearing bundles of shoelaces round their necks. They were the only double-traders in town, as everyone else was a specialist. Shoppers for shoes or digital clocks had to travel the breadth of Antakya to buy them down one particular street. But the good news was that prices were low and identical. There's no control so effective as close competition.

The market traders were bilingual, switching from their guttural border Turkish to Arabic and back again with shaming facility. How can a stallholder be fluent in two notoriously difficult languages, when I toil for years over grammar books and can scarcely say 'Thank you' correctly? Not that *teşekkurederim* falls trippingly off the tongue. I spent hours memorising it, then discovered that *merci* was just as acceptable! The receptionist in my hotel spoke to me in Turkish, but chatted to his friends on the phone in Arabic. And there were Saudi merchants staying in the hotel to buy vegetables wholesale, who spoke Arabic, Turkish and a little English. They huddled muttering in corners, wheeling and dealing and twiddling their worry-beads. They were feeling the cold. Even at breakfast in the perfectly comfortable dining room, they wore grey gabardine raincoats, which fell to their ankles over long black winter-weight robes and were buckled tightly at the waist and wrists to keep out the chill. Their faces looked pinched and peevish under their red and white *keffiyehs*. Along with the Turks, they kept warm by drinking *salgam*, sold off carts by itinerant traders. I ordered it one evening with my kebab dinner. The waiters told me it was made of turnip water, violets, salt and chilli pepper, and was probably an acquired taste. They were quite right. They laughed gleefully at my screwed-up face and streaming eyes. 'Perhaps you would like a beer instead?'

As you would expect of ancient Antioch, where St Peter once preached, there are functioning churches in the city, Orthodox, Protestant and Catholic, as well as mosques. When I went out to dinner on my first evening, there was a large party, mostly American, occupying two long tables in the restaurant. They puzzled me, because some of the women were wearing gold crosses, while many of the men were in Jewish yarmulkes. An American Jew stood up and led them through the Sabbath Eve prayers and the taking of bread and wine. Being by nature nosy, I went over for a chat after dinner. As I guessed, they were a mixed group of Jews and Christians, who were open to other faiths. They all worked in Israel and had come to Antioch on a week's study tour. With the escalating violence in occupied Palestine and the anti-Jewish feeling throughout the Middle East, it might have seemed rash to make such an open display of infidel status in Turkey. But the Israelis and Turks are good trading partners, and the Turks are tolerant people. The Muslim waiters obligingly served dinner, as if groups of people flaunting crosses and yarmulkes were normal, everyday clients.

In the hills above Antakya lies the modern suburb of Harbiye. This is ancient Daphne, the place where Antony and Cleopatra are said to have gone through a form of marriage in 37 BC. The ceremony was never recognised in Rome, because Antony had just taken Octavian's sister, Octavia, as his wife. The two men had struck a deal at Brundisium, giving Octavian control over the western Roman provinces, while Antony governed the east. Antony's marriage to Octavia was intended to cement this partner-ship. Octavia was a dutiful wife, who bore Antony two daughters, but she was no match for the wily, seductive Cleopatra. When Antony sent Octavia back to her brother in 35 BC and divorced her three years later, the strained relations between the two rivals for power turned to animosity, at least on Octavian's part. He began to gnaw insidiously at Antony's standing in Rome. 'Spin' is not a modern invention.

As the road was all uphill, I caught a minibus to Daphne, to visit the famous waterfalls in their groves of cypress and laurel. Like so many mysterious, nymph-haunted woods, it was sacred to Apollo, who had an oracle beside the Castalian spring. It was here that Apollo fell in love with a beautiful naiad. She turned herself into a laurel (Greek *daphne*) to escape his advances, which I always thought was a silly thing to do. If I were pursued by the most handsome of all the gods, who was a sublime musician, patron of the Arts, the god of healing and justice, as well as god of the sun and intellectual illumination, I should think myself extremely lucky. I should certainly not prefer life as a tree.

Under the Seleucids, the glorious shrine of Apollo at Daphne rivalled the temple of Diana at Ephesus, but its splendours have gone the way of ancient Antioch, rocked by earthquakes, besieged, captured and sacked by every invader in history. The celebrated cascades still chatter down over the rocks of Harbiye, but they chatter behind rusty barbed-wire fences. A few dark cypresses pierce the sky, reminders of another tree-person, Cypressus, who mourned himself into a cypress tree when he killed his pet stag by accident; and there are a few green descendants of Daphne's laurel. Otherwise, the branches were bare that winter morning and the paths were lined with ugly toilet blocks and rickety shut-down cafés. It was difficult to imagine Harbiye in the summer, when it is a favourite picnic spot, thronged with Antakyans sipping tea in the shade.

I spent my last evening in Antakya wrestling with a Turkish computer keyboard in an internet café. Ataturk persuaded his people to give up Persian script and adopt Roman, but Turkish looks like Roman script with a bad attack of measles. There are so many diacritical marks – cedillas under c's and s's, umlauts on o's and u's, the letter i with a dot and without a dot, and g's with breve signs, like little inverted hats – all of which have to be accommodated on the normal 'querty' keyboard. Until Mehmet on the next computer came to my aid, I couldn't even find the full stop. It was masquerading as a c with a cedilla, upper case! But I eventually managed to send an email to my family and friends: 'I'm crossing into Syria tomorrow, so you may not hear from me for a while.'

13. THE EASTERN MEDITERRANEAN

*To awaken quite alone in a strange town is one of the pleasantest
sensations in the world. You are surrounded by adventure. You have no idea
what is in store . . .*

Freya Stark

At last, I was entering unknown territory. Since I started cycling
fourteen years ago, I have been to so many places that the world
has shrunk to a familiar comfort zone, like a well-worn slipper.
There are countries I feel I know intimately and others where I
have just skimmed the surface, but I have visited every continent
and know roughly what to expect. The coast of Syria was one of
my gaps and I was excited about breaking new ground.

I had been to Syria before. One evening in November 1992 I
went to Victoria Coach Station with a small suitcase, to see how far
I could travel on ordinary inter-city coaches. I got to Bosra in the
south of Syria – and I could have got further, had my time not run
out. Nothing could have been easier. I took a coach to Dover, slept
on the night ferry to Ostend, then took a bus from there to
Brussels, and another from Brussels to Cologne. Munich, Linz,
Vienna, Budapest, Belgrade, Sofia, Edirne, Istanbul, Ankara, Konya,
Antakya, Aleppo, Damascus, Palmyra, Bosra. Bus after bus. I got
off in the evening, wherever I happened to be, and checked into
a hotel near the bus station. I spent four days sightseeing in
Vienna, passed through Serbia, despite the fighting there, and was
pleased to leave my dirty hotel in Sofia on a sparkling clean
Turkish coach. But the highlight of the trip was undoubtedly
Syria. The people were welcoming, I made friends with lecturers
from Aleppo University and British archaeologists, I toured
magnificent mosques, cathedrals, castles and Roman ruins, and ate
and drank remarkably well. It was one of the most delightful weeks
of my life.

But I had followed the Syrian tourist trail inland, through the
heart of the country. I had not crossed the western mountains. The
coast was unknown to me, and so was the situation after September
11th. I don't pretend to understand the complexities of Middle
Eastern politics, but I do know that Syria's hard-line government

has been out of favour at various times with the West, accused of harbouring terrorist groups such as Hamas. President Bush and Prime Minister Blair were making menacing speeches and I was not sure what kind of reception I would get on this visit, or even if I would be safe.

The first hurdle was the mountain range between Antakya and Lattakia. The Turks in the hotel told me I was mad even to think of crossing it on a bicycle in winter. There was snow up there, the border post was on top of a mountain, it was a steep 30-mile (48 km) climb, the days were short, the Syrian border formalities long, and there were no hotels. I checked with the police and got the same answer, so I capitulated.

For a traveller, the bus station in Antakya is a wildly romantic place. The buses there are lined up like magic carpets to whisk you straight to Aleppo, Teheran, Baghdad or even Mecca. I boarded the daily bus to Lattakia at some ungodly hour in the morning, followed by a huge bundle of wobbling fat, scarves, shawls and long socks, which turned out to be a Syrian granny. She deposited her bags on the seat beside me and disappeared. The time for departure came and went. 'Where is that stupid woman?' asked the conductor. 'What does she think she's playing at? Come on! We'd better go and look for her.' He summoned me off the bus and divided the station between us. 'You take that side, and I'll take this.' I found her in a shop, haggling over the price of various bottles of cheap scent. 'The bus is leaving,' I said in Turkish. She took no notice, so I fetched the conductor, who grabbed her by the arm and yanked her out of the shop. We were the only two passengers in the 42-seater coach. I nipped in ahead of her and transferred my hand luggage to another seat. She looked dismayed. She sat down in the seat in front of me and patted the empty space beside her. It was probably Middle Eastern courtesy, some idea that it was rude and unfriendly to leave a visitor sitting alone. But when there was a whole empty coach available, I had no intention of being squashed by a fat lady all the way to Lattakia. We went through the civilities in our halting Turkish – birthplace, destination, number of children and grandchildren – then she mercifully fell asleep and I was left in peace to look at the scenery.

The bus went first to Samandağ on the coast, to pick up a few more passengers, then we climbed up a dizzy, corkscrew mountain road to the *yağla*, the high summer pastures on a spreading, open plain. The surrounding hills were perfectly terraced and sown with winter wheat. Then we climbed again through a thick forest of firs and plane trees, deep in snow. I had some anxious moments. The driver was obviously a popular fellow; his mobile kept ringing and he chatted gaily, negotiating icy bends with one hand on the steering wheel and the other clapped to his ear. When the conversation got really exciting, he waved his driving hand in the air, and the coach skidded along like a learner on skates. It was a relief when we came to villages and he had to slow down in the narrow lanes and concentrate. They were poor little hamlets of rickety, broken-down peasant houses, where the people lived above their animals for warmth. Women were struggling through the frozen mud with bundles of firewood and pails of chicken-feed. Perhaps life was pleasant enough up there in the summer, but there was desolation and hardship on that cold winter's morning. I looked out of my warm coach and, not for the first time in my travels, thanked my lucky stars that I wasn't born in such a place.

We reached the summit and the border at Yağladağ. The Syrian granny took my arm to lead me to the right offices. I was soon stamped out of Turkey, but the border formalities to enter Syria took forever. The police said 'Welcome to Syria' and invited me to sit by their paraffin stove while they scrutinised my passport. And what a scrutiny it was! They were checking my visa and I knew they were making sure that I had never visited Israel. The Syrians are virulently anti-Israel and will admit no foreigner who has been there. They know that the Israelis will sometimes stamp a piece of paper, rather than the passport itself, but that never fools them. If they see an exit stamp from Egypt or Jordan and no corresponding entry stamp, they know that the traveller must have passed through Israel. I had many Middle Eastern stamps and visas in my passport, so they had a lot of checking to do. I watched them for a while, then I said 'Israel *yok*!' The emphatic Turkish negative broke the ice. They started to laugh, and 'Israel *yok*!' was repeated round the guard room. When the sergeant took my passport into the station commander's office, I heard him say 'Israel *yok*!' and the commander laughed too. I was such a success with my 'Israel *yok*!' that

I was offered tea and the treat which had had my mouth watering from the moment I sat down. On top of the paraffin stove lay two flat unleavened loaves, sprinkled with sesame seeds and honey. The aroma as the bread warmed was overwhelmingly delicious, and it was a long time since breakfast. I gobbled half a loaf with my tea and it was every bit as ambrosial as I had imagined. The police sat round the fire with me, chatting amicably in a mixture of Turkish and French, until the sergeant was summoned to collect my passport. There was just one more short delay – I had to confirm the date of birth I had put on my entry forms. They had seen my bicycle when they searched the coach and couldn't believe that someone so advanced in years, and a woman too, was intending to cycle through Syria. In Syria, only young men ride bicycles. Formalities over, we all shook hands and I was finally allowed back to the coach, where the Syrian granny and two young Syrian arrivals had been patiently waiting for the best part of an hour. There was a spring in my step and I hummed as I crossed the snowy yard. If the border guards were anything to go by, Syria's welcome would be as warm as ever. I was in for a good time.

The descent from Yağladağ was less terrifying and we were soon down among citrus and olive groves. It had turned into a beautiful morning, so I stopped the coach and asked to be let out. I wanted to get a taste of the Syrian countryside. By this time, there were quite a few passengers on the coach, and there was general horror and consternation. 'You can't cycle to Lattakia! It's too far! It's at least 30 kilometres!' When I insisted and set off down the road, they all waved and shouted '*Mashallah!*' (What wonders God has willed!) There were *Mashallahs!* too from people working in the fields, who brandished their scythes and hoes in greeting as I cruised by. The road surface was reasonable, it was all downhill, and traffic was sparse, right up to the outskirts of Lattakia. It was the perfect start to my Syrian journey.

I don't know quite what I was expecting of Lattakia, but it was certainly not the bustling, free and easy city I found. With its rush-hour traffic, plate-glass windows and trendy bars, it felt more Mediterranean than Middle Eastern. It was a bit dilapidated, like the rest of Syria, but it was a port, a window wide open to all the breezes of the world. The only utterly predictable feature was the giant statue of the late President Hafez al-Assad, which towered over the end of the city's main thoroughfare, Sharia 14 Ramadan. I cycled down to the Corniche, looking for a seaside hotel.

An enthusiastic proprietor spotted me from his upstairs balcony. 'Welcome!' he shouted. 'Welcome to Lattakia!' Before I had time to decide whether I fancied his hotel or not, he had hurtled down to the street in a swirl of white robes, hauled my bike up the entrance steps and rushed me up to a bedroom. 'See the beds. Clean. Clean,' he cried, stroking the bottom sheet and sniffing the pillowcase in ecstasy. 'Hot water all time,' running the tap. 'Television. CNN. English,' pressing buttons and switching channels. 'Balcony,' running out and waving his arms at the sea view. 'Bootiful sea!' It was in fact a very nice, clean room, with a private bathroom and a splendid view of the habour, and it was only £4 a night for the double. I said I would take it. Ten minutes later, he dashed upstairs again to see if I was all right. I needed a towel, so he dashed off and dashed back with one. 'How many nights you stay? Two, three nights? You go Ugarit. Saladin's Castle.' When I left to explore the town, 'Where you go? Wait!' and he brought along an English-speaking neighbour to ask if I needed any help. He introduced me to his wife, two small children and his mother, and offered me tea. It was all kindly meant, but a little overwhelming. The only solution was to dash around as he did, so I dashed out of the front door like a greyhound out of its trap. I was free! I could pause for breath.

There was not much to see in Lattakia, considering that it had existed as a port since Phoenician times. The Seleucids had built it up into a major Hellenistic city and it had for a while been the capital of Roman Syria, but it had suffered the same string of invasions, sackings and earthquakes as its neighbour, Antakya. There were no significant ruins. Modern Lattakia was faring better. Dictators generally shower favours on the friends and familiar places of their childhood. Hafez al-Assad grew up, a poor farmer's son, in a mountain village near Lattakia, and showed his attachment to the region by developing the city into a major container port. It stretched the whole length of the Corniche. Crickets were singing in the palm trees, but the broad pavement was disturbingly empty. No families were strolling out there enjoying the sea breezes; there were no lovers, no children on bicycles. There were no seafront cafés with gay umbrellas and no restaurants. It was serious industrial space. It even took on a sinister air as evening fell and the great black harbour cranes towered before the backdrop of a blood-red sky. I hurried up a deserted street towards the lights of the city centre. There I was spoilt for choice. My delicious dinner of hummus, grilled chicken, chips, carrots, salad and some strange-looking bright-pink cauliflower was washed down with a very palatable Syrian wine. I reached my hotel just fifteen minutes before a 9.30 power cut. An early night. I fumbled into bed by the light of my torch and fell into a deep, peaceful sleep after my long day.

Panic! I woke with a start to the rattle of machine-gun fire. Terrorists in the hotel! Murderers! An Israeli invasion! I was suddenly blinded by a brilliant light. When I came to, I remembered that I had not switched off the switches. Power was restored at 2.00 a.m. and it was my own fluorescent light that was flooding the room, along with the CNN hourly news bulletin.

'You stay another night. Sleep. See Ugarit. See Saladin. Wait!' The proprietor got his English-speaking nephew on the phone to entice me with the wonders of Ugarit and Saladin's Castle.

'Please explain to your uncle that I should love to stay here and visit Ugarit and Saladin's Castle, but I am running short of time and have to move on. I have to be back in London soon.' It was true. We were already in the middle of January and I had February talks booked in England, which gave me only three weeks to get myself to Egypt. Ugarit and Saladin would have to wait for another visit.

'Have tea! No? Have coffee! Cakes? Bootiful cakes.' I extricated myself and began to load up my bike. My host looked utterly forlorn. Syria had few tourists at the best of times and post September 11th, I think I was the one and only foreigner in Lattakia. His prize, and perhaps his livelihood, was slipping from his grasp.

When they cause so much trouble in the world and take up so much media space with their squabbles, it comes as a surprise to realise what mini-states these Middle Eastern countries really are. I cycled almost the entire length of the Syrian coast in one easy day. And what a wonderful day it was! It was just about my best day's cycling ever. When I rode out of Lattakia, I had the perfect surface of the main Damascus highway virtually to myself. There were two or three lanes on either side of the central reservation and a wide hard shoulder – and an amount of traffic which would make a sleepy English village on a winter's night seem busy. It was a cyclist's dream. I cruised along within sight of the sea. Then I joined the old road, which actually ran along the shore. The sun was comfortably warm and the countryside smiled. There were orange and olive groves, and more plastic tunnels of tomatoes and lettuce than I had ever seen in my life. I bought bananas, biscuits and a cold drink in Baniyas and took them down to the fishing harbour. Passers-by beamed at me, and anyone who had a smattering of anything but Arabic came over for a chat. I felt like a queen, holding court on the harbour wall beside the brilliant turquoise-blue sea.

My quiet old road rejoined the highway just before Tartus, a large port of high-rise concrete apartment blocks. I passed a gypsy encampment on the outskirts, sited on a stinking rubbish tip. They lived in tents of old plastic tomato tunnels and sat on orange boxes. As I cycled past, they crowded up to the wall, waving and shrieking with excitement. However poor a country, there's always someone even poorer, scratching a living on the fringe. Nearer in, there was a row of opulent palaces with verandahs overlooking the sea. They had high walls and wrought-iron gates enclosing paradise gardens of emerald grass, rose beds and ornate fountains. In one garden a small child was zooming round in a miniature electric Mercedes. These ostentatious homes, gleaming with fresh white and pastel stucco, were completely out of scale with the crumbling concrete boxes most of the people of Tartus lived in. Syria spends about half of its national income on arms, and the neglect of its civilian needs is all too evident. Life for the man in the street is said to have improved under Assad's rule, but there are still broken roads, run-down housing, schools with smashed windows, and uncollected refuse in the streets. The blue Mediterranean off Syria looks wonderfully inviting, but only from a distance. Raw, untreated sewage bobs in the sea, and it would be madness to bathe there. Turkey may have its economic problems, but its general appearance is prosperous compared with Syria's, and its beaches are clean. Travelling from Turkey to Syria is still a journey to the frayed edges of the Third World.

Hafez al-Assad died in 2000, after almost thirty years as President, but his portrait was still all over the place, in duplicate, triplicate, even decuplicate. He was a strange-looking, top-heavy man. He had an overlarge square head, with a few strands of hair carefully positioned across a bald pate, then broad shoulders and a barrel torso, all tapering down to a pair of ridiculously spindly legs. Even when he was a statue miles away on a hilltop, his peculiar shape was instantly recognisable. His jet-setting son Basal was destined to succeed him as President, but Basal loved fast cars and lost control of his Mercedes at 100 mph (160 kph), when he was rushing to Damascus Airport one night in 1994 for a Swiss skiing holiday. So the studious younger son Bashir, who was training to be an ophthalmologist in London, was hastily summoned home. He was sent to an army college, where he quickly rose to the rank of colonel. Then his father began the political grooming process, to ensure Bashir's hold on power.

The official photographs which adorn every shop, office and public place tell the whole dramatic story. There is Daddy Assad in a suit, looking benign as Father of the Nation, and Daddy Assad in uniform, looking stern as Defender of his People against Israel, Iraq, America, or whoever happens to be the villain at the time. Then there is Daddy Assad in a suit, standing proudly beside Son Basal in uniform. All three types now have a black line across the top left-hand corner, but they are still prominently displayed. The ones of Bashir al-Assad show a different character. President at 34, he has a faraway, wistful look in his blue eyes, as if he rather wished he were doing something else, like treating patients. He wears a neat moustache and usually a neat suit, though occasionally he tries to look macho in his colonel's outfit and dark glasses. Some portraits show a rosy-cheeked Son Bashir with a ghostly Daddy Assad looming just behind his shoulder. One portrait of Bashir even has his father's head and shoulders in the background, floating on a bank of white clouds in a blue sky. Bashir is playing a cautious game. He has assumed the role expected of him and is careful to remind the Syrians that he is his father's son, President with his father's blessing. Change will come, but it will come gradually and will be cleverly orchestrated.

I needed cash for an excursion to Crac des Chevaliers and Syria is still not strong on ATMs. I had to brave the intricacies of the Syrian banking system. I walked into a looking-glass world. A bank employee beckoned me into a private office. He had a German lottery ticket and wanted my advice on the mechanics of having the money remitted to Syria, should he win a prize. Another teller joined us. He showed me a scrap of paper, which purported to be a *Reader's Digest* cheque for $1,500,000. He said he had won the prize for 'human help'. How could he claim it? We all know these *Reader's Digest* gimmicks, but they were obviously new to Syria. The poor man really thought he had won this great fortune. I showed him the address to write to, and helped him fill in the coupon, pointing out as gently as I could that *Reader's Digest* often sent out such things to boost their circulation. The 'cheque' was not actually a proper cheque and his chance of receiving $1,500,000 was about 10 million to 1. Neither of these bank employees had the foggiest idea of international finance. It was a completely topsy-turvy situation, where I, the customer, was acting as financial adviser to two bankers! When I asked them about changing a few dollar bills, they said, 'You mustn't do it here. The rates are terrible. There are little secret shops.' They gave me directions. To my relief, the 'little secret shop' turned out to be a perfectly legal money-exchange bureau.

It was misty the next morning as my minibus climbed into the foothills of the Jebel Ansariya. I feared I should get nothing but fleeting glimpses through wisps of cloud, but the sun broke through and there, in all its sharply defined glory, towered the world's most romantic castle. Crac des Chevaliers was a dream of knightly chivalry. Commanding the Homs Gap between the coast and Syria's central plain, its mighty bastions, glacis, moat and machicolated towers were so formidable under the Hospitallers that even the great Saladin was discouraged.

The driver dropped me off in the village of Al Qalaa, at the bottom of the long road which curved up the crag to the castle's main entrance. I was standing below, feeling small and daunted, when I heard someone calling. An old man was pruning his fruit trees, high up the terraced hillside. He pointed to a path through a farmyard. I dodged the cow pats, then scrambled up to his level. He started to lead me even higher. 'Ten minutes,' he said. 'Road one hour. Problem.' It was a steep climb and I panted to keep up with my small, stout, but surprisingly nimble guide. Suddenly, he stopped and looked me in the eye. 'Cretin!' he said. *Cretin*? I thought. *What have I done to deserve that?* He smiled, his eyes crinkling over his bushy grey moustache. 'You Cretin. Me Muslim.' He crossed all eight of his fingers. 'Here, Cretin, Muslim – friend, friend.' We continued our climb. It was often difficult to get a foothold and I gave my right ankle a painful little wrench, but we reached the gate in ten minutes, as he had promised.

Once inside the outer defences, I climbed the broad entry ramp, designed for a garrison of 2,000 knights on horseback. It was vaulted to protect them from the weather, with apertures to let in light on friends and boiling oil on foes. Then I wandered through the great expanse of the inner courtyard and explored the warren of halls, cisterns, storage rooms, refectory and chapel. The style was Norman on the cusp of Gothic – massive octagonal pillars supporting round arches, with just a promise here and there of a point – except for the loggia, where thirteenth-century Gothic soared in lacy elegance. But it is not so much the detail of the Crac as its sheer size, power and impregnable situation which takes the breath away. Even T.E. Lawrence was lost for words, describing it simply as 'the finest castle in the world . . . quite marvellous'. The present stonework goes back no further than the Crusaders, but much older fortresses have stood on that commanding crag. The Ancient Egyptians are said to have occupied it as early as the thirteenth century BC, in their war against the Hittites.

There were no other visitors, which added to the romance of the windswept battlements. Strangely, Crac des Chevaliers is not perched on the highest peak. It is built on the spur of a higher mountain to the south west, its one vulnerable and most heavily fortified direction. Elsewhere, the land falls away so steeply to the valley, 1,000 feet (308 m) below, that the castle is impregnable. I climbed to that south-west peak, to get an overview of the whole complex, then made my way down to the road in the valley floor. The mountainside was lovingly terraced and planted with fruit trees. Every village house seemed to have a cow or two in the basement, the garage or just in a downstairs room. They were the first cows I had seen in Syria, and I wondered what they did with them, as I had never been offered beef there, or milk in my tea. I shared my minibus back to Tartus with two American and three Canadian undergraduates. All earnest Christians, they had just spent a lean night at St George's Monastery. When they got there, they discovered that the monks were fasting, so there was no dinner and no breakfast. They survived for twenty-two hours on ten dates and a bar of chocolate between five.

The cycle ride from Tartus was as horrible as the ride to Tartus had been idyllic. It started badly, when I dropped the rear wheel of my bicycle, heavy panniers and all, from a hotel step on to my big toe. Ouch! South of Tartus, there was an oil refinery and the shore was disgustingly refuse-clogged. I could scarcely see the sand for the mountains of plastic bags, cans, rags and sewage. There was garbage in the fields too, so I cycled down a fetid, stinking corridor. Where there was good land, there were plastic tunnels of tomatoes. Where the land was waterlogged and strewn with rubbish, there were plastic cubes, the makeshift homes of squatters. These were not gypsies, but refugees from Palestine and Beduin, drawn to the coastal cities in search of a livelihood.

I crossed the border into Lebanon, buying my transit visa on the spot. I expected an improvement, but it was worse. The plastic shanty towns were bigger and filthier, generating even more refuse on the beaches. And in Lebanon, there was traffic – huge trucks, hooting as they sped past me. I missed Syria's clear road signs. Once across the border, directions ceased and I had the greatest difficulty finding my way into the centre of Tripoli, Lebanon's second city and great industrial port.

I had noted down the names of a few medium-range hotels near the clock tower, the city's central landmark, but they looked dirty and dilapidated. And the atmosphere in the main square was positively threatening. I pulled up to consult my map and was immediately surrounded by a gang of cheeky young men, who mocked and harassed me. One of them stood astride my front wheel, thrust his nose into my face and tried to snatch my guide-book. Another pulled on the brakes, while a third prodded the buttons on my odometer and sent the meter back to zero. I couldn't imagine staying in such a district and going out on my own at night to find a restaurant. I went to the tourist office for help. The woman in charge was delightful. She spoke English and was most anxious to fix me up with a suitable hotel. 'I will find you a room for $10 a night.' Lebanon is an expensive country and I knew that a $10 hotel would not be to my liking. But no one in prosperous Lebanon rides a bicycle, and she was convinced that I was desperately short of money. She got a colleague to take me round the corner to a respectable hotel, but it was on the top floor of an apartment block and quite unmanageable with a bicycle. Then she suggested some out-of-season beach hotels. With no signposts in the town, I couldn't even find the beach. In the end, I gave up. Worn out, depressed and filthy with exhaust fumes, I staggered into Tripoli's top hotel, the Quality Inn, and treated myself to the most expensive night of my entire trip. I felt I deserved it.

But it was not a peaceful night. The Lebanese mountain chain runs close to the sea, with the main north–south highway at its feet. That means tunnels. There was a long one just south of Tripoli and there was no pavement inside it for pedestrians or bicycles. I asked if there was an alternative, old road. 'There is,' said my helpful friend in the tourist office, 'but it has an even longer tunnel than the one on the highway. There's no hard shoulder and it's curved, so you wouldn't show up against the exit light. It's far too dangerous.' I tossed and turned and magnified the problem all night. How on earth would I manage to get south? Of course, in the morning, it was simplicity itself. I went to the bus station and bought five tickets on a minibus travelling to Byblos – four tickets, the whole back row, for Condor and one seat near the front for me. How stupid to lose a night's sleep over such a trifle! But we never learn. Small problems become monsters in the cowardly early hours.

After the frenzy of Tripoli, Byblos (modern Jbail) was a delight. The minibus dropped me off on the highway above the town and I cruised downhill, first through modern shopping streets, then through the neatly restored souks of the mediaeval city, right down to the dinky little horseshoe harbour with its colourful fishing boats. The beaches were clean. I could actually imagine myself swimming there. I turned my back on the sea and gazed up at a honeycomb, a jumble of stone-built houses, churches and mosques climbing the hillside, white under the noonday sun, with splashes of garden flowers. In the evening, the stone turned golden, with shadows like copper coins on its porous, volcanic surface.

'Why you come Liban in winter? Weather ees 'orrible.' In the 'orrible weather, I was exploring Byblos in a light pullover, feeling rather warm and wondering whether or not to take it off. The sun shone. I had finally left the rain and cold behind. I checked into a room with a sea view and decided to stay an extra day. From now on, my journey would be fraught. I needed to gather strength.

I had skipped the Crusader castles in Tartus and Tripoli. There are strings of them down this Middle Eastern coast, and I am not a castle enthusiast. I would just skim the cream – Crac des Chevaliers in Syria and Sidon in Lebanon. In Byblos I did a cursory canter round the battlements, the Romanesque Church of St John the Baptist and the smallest, neatest little Roman theatre I have ever seen. But what interested me more was Byblos's ancient history, especially its long connection with Egypt.

Some claim that Byblos is the oldest continuously inhabited city in the world. Certainly, the earliest finds are neolithic tools, dating back to around 5000 BC. Two centuries later, Byblos was a wealthy Phoenician port and religious centre, flourishing on the export of the Lebanon's famous cedars. These were highly prized by the Egyptians, who had no wood of their own. They imported Lebanese cedar to build their fleet, and used it in the construction of their palaces and temples. Cedarwood has even been found in the pyramids. In return, the Egyptians sent papyrus to Byblos (*byblos* is Greek for the papyrus plant and the word, by extension and in different spellings, came to be used for paper, books and the Bible). Compared with today's container ports, Byblos is tiny. Yet this ridiculously small dot on the coastline once controlled two of the most lucrative trades in the ancient world. Caravans arrived there from Anatolia and Mesopotamia, bringing ideas as well as goods, so that Byblos became the centre of a cosmopolitan cultural web. The gods of Byblos were Semitic, but Reshef, their god of war, was worshipped in a temple crammed with little obelisks, a fashion obviously imported from Egypt. And not surprisingly, with all that papyrus flowing through their port, the scribes of Byblos are credited with inventing the first proper alphabet, somewhere around 1300 BC. It was the ancestor of all our alphabetical scripts. An earlier alphabet was in use at Ugarit, but it was a sort of Sumerian cuneiform, imprinted on clay tablets. The Byblos alphabet was cursive and well adapted for use on papyrus.

Byblos/Jbail is a peaceful backwater now. It was not important enough to be involved in the recent civil wars, so there are no bullet-riddled buildings or bomb craters. Apart from a bit of fishing, the town's livelihood is tourism and that has virtually dried up. I was the only foreigner enjoying the town. One of the two hotels was closed and I was the only guest of any nationality in the other. When I went down to breakfast, a place had been laid for me at the owner's table. He was 84, in a wheelchair and extremely corpulent. I could see why. He ate steadily throughout our family meal and carried on eating long after the rest of us had finished. He spoke in courteous, rather old-fashioned French, pointing to the wonderful Roman mosaics round the walls and telling me how he had found them when the workmen were excavating the site for the hotel. Later, his son showed me his private museum. There were more exquisite mosaics, oil lamps, pottery and jewellery. Coins of every age were beautifully encased in perspex, as were a variety of fish fossils from the mountains above. It was a private collection of astonishing richness. 'You just dig a hole in Byblos, as we did, and you find layer upon layer of treasure, seven millennia of it, lying there at your feet. You don't have to go looking for it.'

I had Lebanese Arabic television in my room and sat watching cartoons over tea. Tom and Jerry are funny in any language. Suddenly, Jerry was cut off in mid-trick and the muezzin sounded: *Allah akbar* (Allah is great) echoing over mountains, trees swaying in the breeze and old mosques. Then a little boy in Palestinian dress appeared on the screen, shaking his fist and screaming about Israel, between close-ups of a baby's stomach with a gaping gunshot wound, her funeral, and a cluster of Israeli tanks firing on unarmed, stone-throwing Palestinian teenagers. It was highly inflammatory, so I decided to walk round to the mosque, to see if such broadcasts were drawing crowds of irate Muslims. I took off my shoes and crept in at the back. The congregation consisted of one old man and a boy. That evening, I watched *Monarch of the Glen* with Arabic subtitles, before going out to dinner with a Lebanese family. They had migrated to Sydney 27 years ago and were bringing their very Australian daughter on her first visit to Lebanon.

Throughout the Middle East, I was struck by the chasm between the rhetoric of the politicians and media, and the calm reasonableness of the people I met. They lived in the midst of war, threats of war and political turmoil. Their economies were taking a battering. America was often damned in the press, with Britain not far behind on the hate list. Yet no one displayed the least animosity towards me as a person. They seemed quite well able to separate people from politics. I was not held personally to blame for Western arrogance, bias or past misdemeanours. I was simply a guest in their midst and it was their duty, as Arabs, to be hospitable.

The motorway from Byblos to Beirut was hacked out, high in the mountains, and was engineered to be flat. My old coast road followed the contours of the land. Small seaside resorts and commuter suburbs with neighbourhood grocery shops and veg-etable stalls clustered round every inlet, where a small stream fed into a bay. Between, there were leg-breaking climbs over mountain spurs, then a dip down to the next bay. I cycled through quiet prosperity, where it was difficult to imagine there had ever been civil war.

Junieh came as quite a shock. I knew it was Beirut's playground, an extravagant escapist haven where the wealthy could forget the civil war in a high-rolling night at the casino. I knew there were nightclubs with glittering extravaganzas, and restaurants to drain the fattest wallets. But I had not expected anywhere quite so glitzy. The beautiful people were flocking in and out of the designer shops, even out of season, and no car was smaller than a Mercedes, unless it was a Ferrari. Still, it seemed a less complicated option than downtown Beirut, where the layout was bewildering and the traffic a nightmare. Simpler to play safe and base myself in handy Junieh, just 12 miles north of the capital.

I chickened out of cycling in Beirut and took a coach tour of the city. The Green Line, which formerly divided Muslim West Beirut from Christian East Beirut, was dismantled ten years ago, but the buildings on both sides of it were still bullet-ridden and derelict, their shattered windows staring down like empty eye sockets on the bustling rue Damas beneath. Elsewhere, the coach toured totally refurbished quarters, where the old Ottoman houses had been meticulously restored. As for the financial district, what used to be 'the Paris of the East' was rising from the rubble in a burst of skyscraper banks and smart apartment blocks. The Lebanese have always liked banks and known how to profit from them. They are the wheeler-dealers of the Middle East. Not for them the begging bowl and the miserable pleas to the World Bank. Through the *Societé Libanaise pour le Développement et la Reconstruction du Centre-Ville de Beyrouth (Solidère*, for short), they have exploited their financial expertise to raise money on international markets. They are well on the way to rebuilding their shattered city, reclaiming additional building land from the sea for even more banks and hotels. The Corniche is buzzing again with expensive restaurants and cafés. They are such efficient people and they are doing such a wonderful job of reconstruction. They even have the most splendidly laid-out National Museum I have ever visited, a gleaming new pavilion of archaeological delights. I just wished I could like them more.

'Poor Lebanon! All these other people fight their wars in our country, and here we sit in the middle, unable to defend ourselves,' complained our guide. 'We are everybody's battleground.'

There was some truth in this. On top of their own civil wars between Christian militias, Druzes and Muslims, the Lebanese have had to contend with the Shi'ite, Iranian-backed Hezbollah, and incursions by Israel and Syria. Arafat and his PLO settled there at one time, then waged internecine war in Tripoli against another PLO faction. Even now, there are still Syrian troops in the Bekaa Valley, and the Israelis and their proxy army, the SLA, are still menacing the south of the country. Another destabilising factor is the estimated third of a million Palestinian refugees, who are mostly Sunni Muslims. In such a tiny country, they make up about one-tenth of the entire population and upset the delicate balance between religions on which the inter-faith constitution depends. Finally, to add to their melting pot, their revived prosperity has drawn economic migrants from as far away as Sri Lanka. I was amazed to find a man from Colombo sweeping the approach to the Byblos Pizza Hut. The Lebanese have trodden a hard road since independence in 1947. They seem to have settled their internal differences, but they are still living next door to potential conflict. No wonder there has been a brain drain in recent years. The Lebanese, especially the well-educated Christians, have the business and professional skills to make them very attractive settlers.

Once I reached the south of Lebanon, my coastal ride would be over, because the Lebanese–Israeli border was closed. I wondered if it was possible to take a ferry from Beirut to Cyprus and another one from Cyprus to Alexandria. 'We used to run boats to Cyprus,' said the shipping agent. 'When our airport was bombed, it was the only way we could get out of the Lebanon. We flew from Cyprus. Then the Israelis started bombing the boats and we had to abandon the service. There are no passenger ferries now, and none from

Lattakia either. We've lost the use of the sea.' So I had to leave the friendly waterside for the first time and travel overland to Egypt, via Damascus and Amman. It was technically possible for me to enter Israel from Amman, but Israeli tanks had invaded the Gaza Strip, so even if I reached the Israeli coast, my ride would soon come to another dead end – and I might come to a dead end myself, caught up in the *intifada* between a suicide bomber and a trigger-happy Israeli conscript. No cycle ride was worth that risk. And 'Israel *yok!*' would no longer apply. I should have the inconvenience of obtaining a second passport if I wanted to travel to my lovely Syria again.

I toyed with the idea of cycling the 50 miles (80 km) down the coast to Tyre, staying overnight there, then cycling back again to Junieh. I could leave most of my gear in the hotel and travel light, with a few overnight things in my backpack. But I hate retracing my wheel-tracks. I hate going round in .circles, out of the same door and back again. So I took another coach trip to the south of Beirut. I explored the souks of Sidon and crossed the causeway to its romantic Crusader sea castle. Then we drove on to Tyre, where I was pleased not to be staying. There are three large Palestinian refugee camps around the city and despite the UN-controlled security zone, tempers sometimes flare. The odd Molotov cocktail is lobbed across the barbed wire of no-man's land, to answering Israeli fire.

Like Byblos, Sidon and Tyre were wealthy Phoenician ports, with strong Egyptian trading connections. King Hiram of Tyre supplied Solomon with cedarwood to build his temple and joined him in trading expeditions to East Africa and Arabia. But the chief source of income for both Sidon and Tyre was the *murex trunculus*, the mollusc from which the Phoenicians produced purple dye. The process was enormously expensive and laborious, requiring thousands of murex shells to produce just one gramme of dye – which probably explains why purple became the colour of royalty. Cleopatra had purple sails on her ship, Roman Senators had purple edges to their togas, Byzantine Emperors were 'born in the purple' and the Chinese Emperors were so enamoured of it that they sent consignments of silk from Xi'an all the way along the Silk Road to the Mediterranean, to have them dyed purple and returned to China. Now, like Byblos, these once great ports are fishing villages and Tyre, in particular, suffers from being at the end of the Lebanon line.

Beirut's Charles Helou Poulman Station was conveniently sited opposite the port. I cycled along the seashore from Junieh, past nose-to-tail beach complexes with chalets and watersports laid on, until I joined the main road and found myself in the busy commercial dock area. The Poulman Station itself was a concrete labyrinth, an inferno roofed over in concrete to trap the roar of the engines, with their heat, stink and carbon monoxide. I pushed my bike around, looking for the ticket office for Damascus.

'*Americaine*? *Britannique*?'

'*Britannique*,' I said.

'Ha! Visa – no! Arabs no good!'

That exchange was not much help, but I did eventually find the office and managed to buy my $5 ticket for the next coach, which left at noon. Then I had to wander up and down the station looking for the coach, as there were no notices anywhere. I was helped by a French-speaking Armenian woman on her way to Aleppo. She complained loftily about the men at the Poulman Station. 'I speak perfect Arabic,' she said, 'but I can't understand a word they're saying. It's street Arabic. Not at all what I'm used to.' She was an anxious little woman, so small and softly spoken that I had to bend right over to hear what she was saying. In the uproar of the station, I became anxious myself. What if I missed my coach while I was concentrating on her? And what about Condor? The man at the ticket window had not understood my query, so I still didn't know if bicycles were carried on Syrian coaches.

In the event, there were only three other passengers for Damascus, and they were all travelling light. Condor was accepted without a murmur, or even a plea for *baksheesh*, and was laid out in solitary comfort in the luggage compartment. We drove past bomb-damaged buildings on the outskirts of Beirut, in districts where Solidère still had a great deal of work to do. There were sad, abandoned apartment blocks on the hillsides, their plaster crumbling and riddled with bullets, like Gruyère cheese. Then we were in serious mountains. The sea fell sharply beneath us. We made an almost vertical 30-mile ascent to Chtaura and the Bekaa Valley, places whose names are etched on the consciousness of the world. The Bekaa Valley. How often I had heard the name in newsreels, and here it was at last. I was actually driving through it. Once one of Rome's 'bread baskets', its fertile plain was still occupied by Syrian troops. Its orchards were deep in snow. I thought of the old tourist-office claim, in the days when Lebanon still had tourists, that you could ski in the mountains in the morning and sunbathe on the beach in the afternoon. Lebanon is such a skinny little strip of country that you can change climates within an hour, and cross it, into Syria, within two. It's another mini Middle Eastern state, like Israel and Palestine, which has screamed its way to the world's attention like a spoilt child. But unlike its neighbours, the Lebanon does show signs of growing to responsible adulthood.

14. DESERT DETOUR

The Walrus and the Carpenter
Were walking close at hand;
They wept like anything to see
Such quantities of sand:
'If this were only cleared away,'
They said, 'it would be grand!'

Lewis Carroll, 'The Walrus and the Carpenter'

I shook the snow of Lebanon off my feet and marched back into Syria. There was quite a commotion going on at the 'Entry – Foreigners' desk. A Saudi Arabian in full desert attire was shouting at the official. He slammed two passports on the counter. Beside him stood a black wigwam which I took to be a woman. She was totally shrouded, from the black veil covering the tiny eye-slit between her black headdress and yashmak to her black gloves and shiny black lace-up shoes. The official clearly had a problem. How could he check the identity of this mystery woman? How could he compare her face with the photo in her passport? For all he could see, she could be an Israeli tank commander in drag. She stood in silence, while the Saudi raged. There was no way of telling her age. He could have been her husband, father or son. In the end, the officer capitulated. He left his desk and returned with a police-woman, who escorted the lady in black and her passport to a secluded rear office. As soon as she emerged, the Saudi hustled her out of the building and bundled her into the back of a limo with black windows. 'Welcome to Syria!' said the official, with an enigmatic smile.

High up on the frontier, the road was a craggy mountain corridor, absolutely devoid of vegetation. It was Friday, the Muslim day of rest. As soon as we cleared the border zone, we passed hundreds of families, picnicking in the snow. Excited children were squealing and throwing snowballs and everyone, of whatever age, seemed to be building snowmen. The women were dressed in every type of outfit, from sweaters and jeans to black shrouds, but they were all joining in the fun. In one morning, I had made a transition in spirit as well as space, from the world-weariness of Junieh's nightclubs to these innocent domestic pleasures.

Relying on my free map from the Syrian Embassy, I had worked out my route from the bus station to my chosen hotel, but the coach tipped me out I knew not where, on the corner of a teeming, noisy and very scruffy square. In poorer tourist destinations, the arrival of a Westerner is a big event, a real commercial opportunity. I was immediately mobbed by taxi drivers, hotel touts and sellers of everything from postcards and underpants to dancing Minnie Mice on strings. One of the reasons I love my bicycle is the independence it gives me. I don't have to rely on taxis and I can shake off touts in a couple of spins of the pedals. I escaped across the square and cruised along until I rounded a corner and found myself in front of the station for the Hejaz railway, which once carried pilgrims from Damascus to Mecca. T.E. Lawrence famously blew up the line to assist the Arab Revolt of 1916 against the Ottoman Turks, so now there is only a slow and limited service as far as Amman. Once I was outside the fancy late-Ottoman edifice, I had my bearings. I still couldn't find the Sultan Hotel, but I recognised another hotel where I had stayed before and settled for that.

September 11th may have put off Western visitors, but it had not deterred the Iranians. They were coaching round Damascus in droves, the women like flocks of great black ravens. It was the time of year for the Shi'ite pilgrimage to the Tomb of Saida Zeinab, the granddaughter of Mohammed and sister of the martyred Hussein. Like the Mosque of Saida Ruqqiyeh, Hussein's daughter, inside the walls of the Old City, the Mosque of Saida Zeinab was built with Iranian money. Both mosques are modern, as Damascus goes, and lavish in the extreme, Zeinab's with a golden dome and Ruqqiyeh's with a dome of patterned mirror-work. There are slabs of white marble, silver grilles, and flamboyant Persian tiles covering every available inch of wall in a riot of flowers and quotations from the Koran. The Iranian pilgrims stand spellbound. The drearier their own dress, the more they revel in the colour and dazzle of their shrines.

I had two parties of these pilgrims in my hotel. They were mostly women, with one or two uxorious men as escorts. The coach door opened and a huge black cloud of them enveloped the reception desk, where a modern Syrian girl with long black ringlets and plenty of mascara dispensed their keys.

'I hope you don't think these women are Syrians,' said the manager. 'Syrian women don't dress like that. These come from Iran. Pilgrims to the Mosque of Zeinab. Allah be praised! We're having a bad time. No tourists, except you. If we didn't have these pilgrim groups, the hotels would be empty.'

The manager had an open, freckled face, with light-brown hair and grey eyes. Born in Damascus, one of history's major crossroads, he looked Northern European, more of a Crusader than an Arab.

'Can you help me?' he asked. 'Just ten minutes. I need ideas for an essay on friendship, in English. I am writing what is a true friend.'

He provided me with a lemon Fanta, while he dashed off to fetch his essay. When we settled down together on a sofa in the front hall, he told me, rather wistfully, that he was a civil engineer. 'That's what I always wanted to do – to be an engineer. I loved my work. I was involved in so many interesting projects. But my father bought this hotel and wanted me to join the business. I suppose it's a good career and I shall get used to it. My English is bad though, not nearly good enough for a hotel manager, so I'm taking a course at the American Language School.' He reminded me of that other dutiful but slightly sorrowful son, whose portrait decorated the hotel lobby – Bashir Al Assad, the son who would rather have been an ophthalmologist than a president.

Damascus is flat, perfect for bicycles, especially as traffic is thin by capital-city standards. Many of the cars are old American jalopies of the days before petrol shortages. Great Chevrolets and Pontiacs with fins cruise along in clouds of exhaust. Boys on bikes dodge between them and bikes double up as stalls. In the souk, in a lane too narrow for cars, a man was selling chickens. There were about a dozen of them, dangling upside down from a pole across his handlebars, squawking at potential buyers. Another man was using his bicycle as a mobile café. He had thermos flasks of hot water in a crate strapped to his rear carrier, and tea bags, Nescafé, sugar and plastic cups in another crate tied to his handlebars. Others were porters, using their bicycles as carts to transport consignments of shoes, sacks of flour and the occasional sheep. Their bicycles were the first step up the ladder of prosperity. Today, a bicycle. Tomorrow, a donkey. Then a horse and cart. Finally, if their dreams came true, they would reach the magic pinnacle and own a car!

I wandered on foot through the Old City, along the Street Called Straight. The caretaker lent me a black shroud, so that I could visit Saladin's tomb in the green and gold splendour of the Umayyad Mosque, the fourth most holy place in Islam – after Mecca, Medina and Jerusalem's Dome of the Rock. Then out through the spices and jewels of the souk, where the alleys were roofed in corrugated iron, curved into great black arches speckled with tiny holes. The effect was cool and star-like. Down an alley selling women's clothes, a distinguished-looking elderly gentleman in a *keffieh* and long grey mac was buying an outfit for a woman enveloped in black. It was a red fishnet body-stocking, long-sleeved and décolleté, covered in red spangles. The mesh was so wide that the wearer would be virtually, and provocatively, naked. I boggled. What enticements lurked behind those yashmaks! A passing tourist in skintight luminous pink leggings looked positively decorous by comparison.

As I knew Damascus well, I was only staying there long enough to draw breath and book my onward journey. I cycled to the coach station, to the section for coaches to Amman. It seemed they were Turkish, passing through Damascus and Amman on their way to Saudi Arabia. The woman selling the tickets was my first surly Syrian.

'No bicycles!' she said.

'But this is a Turkish company. In Turkey they always carry bicycles.'

'That's Turkey. This is Syria. No bicycles!'

There was a young dwarf loitering at the back of the office. The poor boy was dumb too, but he was obviously extremely bright. He stepped forward and tried to resolve the impasse. He mimed the folding of a bicycle. 'No. It doesn't fold.' He queried the size, miming a big bicycle and a little bicycle. I took him outside to show him Condor, which was chained to the railings. Sadly, he mimed a big bicycle and shook his head. 'What if I pay for the bicycle? I'm quite happy to do that.' He brightened up and led the way back to the ticket counter. He fluttered his hands in the woman's face, then turned to me with a grin, holding up six fingers. 'Six dollars?' He nodded delightedly. That was as much as my own fare to Amman, but it was still cheap at the price. It would have taken me three days to cycle there across the desert, and I didn't have three days to spare on my tightening schedule. My friendly go-between held up more fingers, from which I gathered that I should report to the bus station at 5.30 the next morning, an hour before the scheduled departure time, to pay for the bicycle and see it safely on to the coach.

When I set off for the hotel, I glanced at my odometer. It registered zero. For the hundredth time on my trip, someone had pressed the reset button. Outside Europe, this simple little gadget is irresistible to boys, even to grown men. I try to keep track of my daily distances, my cumulative distance on a long ride, the length of climbs up mountain passes, the distance between cities – all useful for my records. At night, I always remove the little handlebar display, to keep it safe and to enter the figures in my log book. But in the Middle East, the fiddling fingers strike in the daytime, the moment I turn my back to go into a shop. They even strike while I'm astride the bike, stopping to ask the way or consulting a map. For some reason, men and boys feel obliged to test my tyres. Having given them a good squeeze, they then turn their attention to the odometer. 'Kilometres?' 'Yes.' And if I don't move fast enough, the fingers fly out, the buttons are poked – and zero again!

I decided to treat myself to a fine dinner on my last night in Damascus. There was a restaurant a couple of blocks from my hotel, which had white damask tablecloths and wine glasses beside the place-settings. I dressed myself up in my silk suit and walked through the regiment of bowing waiters. There was chicken casserole on the menu, a nice change from the standard kebabs and grills. I asked for the wine list. 'Sorry, madam. No wine. Pepsi? Fanta?' For all its elegance, the restaurant was dry, like most other restaurants in holy Damascus. I was far away from the liberal Mediterranean air of Lattakia and Tartus. The food was beautifully prepared and presented, but it was not enhanced by a wine glass full of Pepsi. I was bitterly disappointed. Had I known, I would have settled for a pizza in a snack bar and saved a considerable amount of money and effort. To cheer myself up, I dropped into a take-away juice stall and bought a fantastic fruit salad for the equivalent of $1 – fresh pineapple, mango, banana, kiwi fruit and sunflower seeds in a mango sorbet. I took it back to my hotel room, where I washed it down with the remainder of my Turkish raki. I had eaten a wineless dinner, but I was still one of the world's fortunate, so lucky to have been born in the right place, at a time of opportunity. Outside my hotel window, two men were scavenging through the rubbish bins, competing for scraps of food with a horde of hungry cats. There was no disguising the fact that Damascus was a poor city, where life for many people was desperate.

The streets were dark and deserted when I cycled to the coach station. Nothing was open, not even the tea stall next to the ticket office. There was no sign of the ticket woman and no friendly dwarf. I grew nervous. Would I be able to get Condor on to the coach without his help? We hung about in the chill before dawn. What finally rolled into the yard was a dusty Syrian Karnak, not the smart Turkish coach I was expecting. I approached the driver. 'No bicycle!' he barked. But a little old man, with a woolly cap pulled right down over his ears, appeared from nowhere and started to load the luggage. He signalled to me to wait until the suitcases were in. Then he opened the spare-wheel compartment. '*Baksheesh*,' he whispered. I gave him a crisp $1 bill, with which he seemed well satisfied. He touched his woolly hat and propped Condor very gently against the spare wheel, steadied by my panniers and backpack. Then he locked the door. Thanks to the absence of the ticket seller, I had saved $5 and made an old man happy.

The coach was full, so I was asked to sit next to the only other Westerner, a man. I would never have been asked to sit next to a Syrian man. That would have been too embarrassing for him. But everyone knows that Westerners are shameless, an opinion confirmed when we actually started to talk to each other. Like almost every American I meet abroad, my seat-mate was named Jim. He was a charming thirty-something computer consultant, self-employed and unmarried, so he was able to take time off. He had spent eighteen months travelling through Africa, China, India and the Middle East, and was booked on a flight home from Amman. His travelling over, his mind was already running ahead. Would he find his former clients waiting for him, or would he have to start up his business again from scratch? He was a Republican, but he disapproved so strongly of Bush's swaggering war-talk that he wondered if he could bear to stay in America. Should he look for work abroad until a less gung-ho, more humane regime got into power? Fortunately, he had the sort of skills which made him employable and useful worldwide. We passed an interesting hour or two discussing his options.

Damascus flourished because it was an oasis in the desert. Its verdant past is hard to imagine in its dusty modern streets, but the desert that surrounds it is all too substantial. Once the early-morning fog cleared, there was nothing to see but sand, sand all around us like a tideless beige ocean, with one black ribbon of tarmac running through it. Part of me was delighted to have a good excuse not to cycle. I could speed along and leave the desolation behind me in hours rather than days. The other part of me was regretful. I knew I was missing so much – small, shy creatures, unexpected wisps of vegetation, subtle changes in the texture of the sand, gradations of colour as the sunlight moved towards its noonday brilliance, and the camaraderie of the tea stalls. Deserts are fascinating places, but only if you move across them slowly.

There was no change in the desert when we crossed the border. Jordan, along with Syria, Iraq and Saudi Arabia, is a segment of the same vast sweep of wilderness. What changed was the feel of the place, like breaking through into fresh air. Jordan has no oil, no industry and no agriculture to speak of. Apart from Petra, Jerash and a few Crusader castles, it has no major tourist attractions. It depends on Western aid to support its own people and its hordes of Palestinian refugees. Yet, thanks to the diplomacy of King Hussein, this impecunious little desert country has become the one beacon of stability in the midst of the terrible conflicts that rage around it. King Hussein walked a tightrope, making enemies of no one. In the course of his long reign, he managed to reach an accommodation with Israel, without losing the respect of his fellow Arabs; and he refused to join the alliance against Saddam Hussein, without losing the confidence of the West. He was quite simply a magician who, against all the odds, brought the gift of peace to his people.

No one could claim that Amman is a beautiful city. It sprawls over steep, rocky hillsides in a rash of ugly concrete cubes, bristling with aerials and satellite dishes. Its main thoroughfares are lined with uninspired high-rise banks and office blocks. But there are little splashes of green everywhere, in every spot where a tree or a few shrubs have the soil to take root. They are really doing their best to make the desert bloom. Amman will never be a garden city, but it may eventually grow into an interesting, arid-environment rockery.

We drove through clean, well-maintained streets. Unlike Syria, Jordan does not spend half its national income on arms, so there is money for infrastructure and public services. Another change I noticed immediately was the switch to English. At the fall of the Ottoman Empire, Palestine and Transjordan came under British influence, while Syria and the Lebanon were mandated to the French. The Lebanon has French as its second official language and Syria still goes in for notices in a charming old-fashioned brand of French: *'Station de Véhicules'* rather than 'Parking'. The Académie Française must be delighted!

When we pulled into the coach station, we stepped into an almost Western world. We were not mobbed by a horde of desperate touts and vendors. A line of taxi drivers stood at the bottom of the coach steps, offering their services. Those who wanted a taxi took the first man in the queue and off they went to retrieve their baggage. Jim sped off in a taxi to look for a hotel. I caused the usual stir by announcing that I didn't need a taxi as I was on my bicycle. Two astonished taxi drivers came to look at it. 'Where can I get a bus to Aqaba?' 'Jett office. Two minutes.' They walked along with me to the corner, to point me in the right direction. There was a clean, well-ordered office. The next coach for Aqaba was standing outside, ready to leave in ten minutes. 'Bicycle no problem,' said the clerk. Condor was stowed away with no whisper of *'baksheesh'* and a smartly uniformed girl, like an air hostess, showed me to my seat. It was all a dream of unhurried efficiency.

Just before the coach left, the hostess came in with a small plastic cup of coffee for the driver. The aroma was exquisite and my mouth watered. 'Where did you get that coffee?' I asked her. 'Do I have time to nip out and buy one?' The driver turned round in his seat. 'Please,' he said, smiling. He insisted that I take his cup. The coffee tasted as delicious as it smelt, strong, black and sweet. I was pleased that the girl had time to rush out and get another cup for the driver before we left.

We took the road along the shore of the Dead Sea. Deserts would not be deserts unless they were dry and empty, but this drab clay-coloured tract was extraordinary. It was arid beyond belief. There was no hint of scrub or cactus, not even a blade of grass. Near the southern end of the sea, we passed a Beduin camp of black goatskin tents. Children were minding the goats on a stretch of shore, where there seemed to be absolutely no grazing at all. What were they eating? Stones? South of the Dead Sea we drove down the Wadi Araba, the border with Israel and Jordan's only strip of anything approaching cultivable land. Here farmers were making valiant attempts to grow a few tomatoes and bananas. I swapped biscuits with a woman in a headscarf and a long grey coat, who lived in Aqaba and travelled to Amman every week, though she offered no explanation. Her English was good and she was very polite, though rather unforthcoming. We were both bothered by the clouds of smoke in our otherwise comfortable coach. If tobacco had been around in Mohammed's day, I'm sure he would have banned it, along with wine. As it is, the Middle East makes up for its lack of alcohol by inordinate chain-smoking.

In my spruce, modern Aqaba hotel, I was given the VIP suite at the single-room rate because I had cycled so far. I brought myself up to date on the news with a copy of the *Weekly Guardian* and a good German news channel on my widescreen television. I did my washing, sent a batch of postcards which never arrived, and bought half a bottle of my favourite J&B whisky. Had I known the difficulties that lay ahead of me in Egypt, I should have bought considerably more! Then I strolled along the seafront in perfect winter sunshine. People in the streets smiled at me and said 'Welcome to Jordan' as if they really meant it. But Jordan was still a lonely place for me, like Syria. In Arab countries, there is no tradition of men talking to women, unless they are members of the same family. Men would greet me pleasantly enough, but they would not enter into conversation with me. Social convention allowed the women to talk to me, but they usually spoke no English, and I spoke no more than a few words of Arabic, so that was a dead end too. I was leading a silent life, with none of the casual chats which establish human contact and open a window on to the spirit of a country. The one exception was the local baker. 'English best!' he beamed, kissing me with more than polite enthusiasm and clasping me to his floury bosom. 'How long you stay? I like to have drink with you, eat with you.' 'I'm leaving this afternoon,' I lied. 'Next time then. You come back to Aqaba?' 'Yes. Next time,' I agreed, clutching my currant buns and beating a swift retreat from the shop.

Without any direct contact with the people, I could only guess at their lives by silent observation. I watched them over giant tankards of fruit juice at pavement cafés. And I tried to draw conclusions from their official portraits. King Hussein was still much in evidence, bearded and dressed in full Arab rig or military uniform. Young King Abdullah favoured a business suit and a clean-shaven Western look. There was one very popular portrait which would have been unthinkable in any other Middle Eastern country. It showed the two men together, dressed in casual open-necked shirts. King Hussein had his arm on his son's shoulder and they were smiling affectionately at each other, sharing a joke. It was any family's happy holiday snap. These were not hard men who needed to glower at their subjects to keep them in order.

It remains to be seen whether King Abdullah will acquire his father's stature in the world. He is moving cautiously and he seems to be doing all the right things within Jordan. Interestingly, he is building bridges with Syria, the one country which had cool relations with King Hussein. He and Hafez al-Assad never really hit it off. They were two very different men. But their sons have struck up a friendship. King Abdullah is half English, and he and Bashir al-Assad were both educated in England, so they have a shared background. They are the same sort of age; they both have energetic, well-educated wives; and they are both technology buffs. There may be changes for the better, even in the strife-torn Middle East.

I was surprised to find 8 miles (13 km) of mountainous road between downtown Aqaba and the docks. It was a hot morning and I puffed along on my bicycle, looking across the gulf at Eilat in Israel. I had seen no foreigners at all in Aqaba, so I was delighted when Georg ran over to greet me. He was a blond hunk of a German cyclist, shiny-black-knickered and psychedelic-shirted, and we were both crossing over to Nuweiba on Sinai. Hans, a German motorcyclist who happened to be staying in the same hotel as Georg, had come down to the docks to wave him off. I joined them in the only patch of shade, under the corrugated-iron roof of a cargo shed. Georg was booked on the slow ferry, because bikes were not allowed on the catamaran. I was booked on the catamaran, because the travel agent I used told me that bikes were allowed. 'That's typical,' said Hans. 'The Arabs wake up in the morning and it's a new day, so they invent the rules all over again! New rules for a new day. One day bikes are allowed. The next day, they're not.'

The catamaran came in first and Georg cycled down with me to the quay. 'No bicycles!' said the sailor in charge of loading.

I waved my ticket. 'They told me I could bring my bicycle.'

'OK then.'

'Can I bring my bicycle too?' asked Georg.

'Why not?' But Georg didn't have the right ticket and the catamaran was due to leave in ten minutes. He hared off, like a cyclist on a Tour de France time trial, just panting back as the catamaran was casting off. I was lucky to have him there, because there was no proper gangplank and the bikes had to be heaved up over the side. Georg lifted them, panniers and all, without so much as a grunt.

We sped down the Gulf of Aqaba, making pigs of ourselves on amazingly cheap Jordanian almonds and cashew nuts. Saudi Arabia was to our left and the Sinai Peninsula to our right. Everyone assumed that Georg and I were together and addressed their remarks to him. No one so much as looked at me. I followed along behind like the little woman, letting him organise the visas and make all the enquiries about our onward journeys. It was quite restful for a change. Georg was particularly efficient in his dealings with passport officials, as he was a Berlin travel agent. He told me that business had plummeted after September 11th and there was not enough work in his small agency for two people. His assistant, who was a single parent with a small son, really needed the money. So, rather than lay her off, Georg had decided to leave her in charge and go away himself for a few months, travelling cheaply on his bicycle.

'My girlfriend thinks I'm nuts, but she's used to me. I'm either zooming down rivers in my kayak or speeding along on my bicycle. She's got a good career in banking and would rather stay at home. Last year, I cycled from Berlin to Istanbul. It was a fantastic ride. I averaged 30 kph over the whole distance! This year, I started in Istanbul. Perhaps I shall manage to go round the world in stages.

I'll cycle now through Egypt and see if I can get a visa for the Sudan. I'll just keep on going until business picks up again.'

In Georg's company, I suddenly became invisible, and so did my bicycle. In the Middle East, my bright orange Condor, with its butterfly handlebars and 21 gears, usually drew crowds of admirers, but it was quite overshadowed by Georg's high-tech machine. It was not his Berlin-to-Istanbul racer, but a silver mountain bike with elaborate suspension and fourteen gears in an enclosed hub. This was a new system, designed to protect the gears throughout the life of the bicycle. They were not expected to develop any mechanical fault, but if they did, Georg had to return the entire rear wheel to the manufacturers, who would replace it. He said the bike was extremely heavy, but it gave him a smooth ride on bad surfaces and he had no worries about sand clogging the gears. I refrained from asking the obvious question: what happens if a fault develops in the middle of Egypt or, even worse, in the Sudan? Those 'What if' questions always irritate me when I'm on the receiving end of them. 'What if your chain breaks? What if you can't find a hotel? What if you run out of water in the desert?' If we worried about all the things that could conceivably go wrong, we would never travel anywhere. We would never cycle across the Middle East, or even walk across the high street at home.

Georg wanted transport to Cairo, where he could lodge his visa application with the Sudanese Embassy. I wanted to rejoin water at Suez, to continue my cycle ride. There was a fleet of Cairo minibuses waiting at Nuweiba docks and these zipped off as soon as they were full. Georg and I, with our two bicycles, needed a proper East Delta coach. We were both shunted straight through Egyptian passport control and customs without query, but the locals had to empty every single item out of their bags. Most of them were Egyptian migrant workers returning from Saudi Arabia and the Gulf States. They were loaded up with consumer goods, the rewards of their exile from their families. The most popular gift seemed to be one of the plush, brightly coloured 'mink' blankets, which had made a cheerful display in the shop windows of Aqaba. I suppose these blankets could have concealed arms or contraband. Whatever the reason, the officials made the passengers take the blankets out of their transparent plastic carrying cases and give them a good shake. There was no surface suitable for refolding them, so the precious new blankets ended up on the ground in the dusty yard, where their harassed owners struggled to get them back neatly into their presentation packs. Georg and I waited almost three hours in the coach, while the mountains of Saudi Arabia turned pink, then purple across the darkening gulf. All this time, a tape was playing at a million decibels, drowning our attempts at conversation. It was a *munshid* intoning the Koran, so we had to tread carefully. Georg solved the problem with great diplomacy, telling the driver that the chanting was absolutely beautiful, but unfortunately our Arabic was not good enough for us to be able to follow the holy words, so could they please be relayed a little more softly.

The last stragglers finally bundled up their blankets and climbed on to the coach. We drove out of Nuweiba, through the long canyon that leads from the coast to the interior of the Sinai Peninsula. In the shadow of the high sandstone mountains, it was already dark and our headlights picked out 'Camels crossing' road signs. Chinese decibels took over from the Koran, as two savage Hong Kong slaughter films poured blood and screams over the coach, with Arabic subtitles. It was too dark to read, so Georg and I peered out of the windows, trying to pick out landmarks in the blackness of the Sinai desert. It seemed a much longer journey than its 200 or so miles (322 km). Interestingly, a succession of male passengers wandered up the coach for a chat with Georg. No one so much as greeted me. Syria, Jordan and now Egypt. It's not very illuminating for a travel writer to be cut off completely from conversation. And it's not very easy for a person to be so isolated. For once in my life, I couldn't wait to reach journey's end and go home.

The boredom turned to nightmare as we neared Suez. We emerged from the Ahmed Hamdi Tunnel under the canal and the conductor approached Georg (not me!) in some embarrassment. He said that the coach was running late, so there was no time for it to go into town. They would be dropping us at a crossroads about twenty minutes' drive from the centre of Suez. Georg was a large, confident man.

'The lady and I are not travelling together,' he boomed. 'I have to go on to Cairo. She's on her own, and you cannot possibly just dump her down at a crossroads, with a bicycle and luggage, in the middle of the night, and drive off. You must either take her into Suez, to the bus station, or you must find her a taxi with a reliable driver and negotiate a fair rate.'

When the coach stopped, he got out with me to supervise the arrangements, towering over the conductor and looking belligerent. The conductor would probably not have listened to me, a mere woman, but when Georg spoke, he did as he was told. He found a minivan with a roof rack and I set out down a long, straight road under the stars. I had never been to Suez before, my Arabic was minimal, I was tired and it was almost midnight. Had I been prone to panic attacks, I should have had one in that minivan. The drive seemed to last for ever, with no sign of habitation. The driver was silent and inscrutable. Was he a fundamentalist? A kidnapper? Where was he taking me? Just as I began to feel really afraid, I saw a distant twinkle of lights.

We entered Suez by the back door, through dark, crowded alleys, swerving round donkeys and climbing up the pavements, missing pedestrians by inches. Suez medina was a chaotic, garbage-strewn muddle. The driver had never heard of the hotel I mentioned, but we eventually emerged from a squalid side street into the brightly lit main thoroughfare and I saw a presentable-looking facade. 'Stop here!' I cried. 'This will do.' It was in fact the hotel I wanted. The minivan fare had mysteriously risen in the course of the journey, but I was so relieved to have arrived safely that I paid up the extra without a murmur. It was a noisy hotel, where I seemed to be the only foreigner and the only woman. The men along my corridor kept their doors open, and shouted and laughed between rooms till the early hours. But I slept well. If I could manage that terrifying arrival in Suez, I could manage anything that Egypt might throw at me.

15. THE SUEZ CANAL

I strongly want to go to Egypt for the next winter as ever is, if so be I can find a sufficiency of tin to allow of my passing 4 or 5 months there. I am quite crazy about Memphis & On & Isis & crocodiles and ophthalmia & nubians, and simooms & sorcerers, & sphingidoe. Seriously the contemplation of Egypt must fill the mind, the artistic mind I mean, with great food for the rumination of long years.

Edward Lear, Letter to Chichester Fortescue

The Suez Canal is not the picturesque Egypt of Edward Lear's dreams. Even at the best of times, when Egyptian tourism is booming, the region is hardly a magnet for Western visitors. And 2002 was far from a boom year.

Tourism came to a halt in Egypt when an Islamic terrorist organisation went on the rampage in 1996. They gunned down a group of 17 Greeks in Cairo and in 1997 perpetrated the notorious massacre of 58 tourists at the Temple of Hatshepsut near Luxor. President Mubarak cracked down on terrorism and a ceasefire was negotiated in 1999. By 2001, the travel trade had just begun to regain confidence and the tourists were just beginning to trickle back to Egypt. Then the World Trade Center was destroyed on September 11th. Western fears of militant Islam resurfaced and the tender shoot of Egyptian tourism withered and died again. After Georg left me in Suez, I saw not a single Western face until I reached Alexandria.

'A new day. A new set of rules,' as Hans would say. In my case, it was a new set of feelings. I woke up full of anticipation, my fears and miseries of the previous night dispelled by the sunshine. I had been to Egypt twice before, but I had been with a group on both occasions and stayed on the well-worn tourist tracks. I had sailed up the Nile from Cairo to Aswan, and climbed Mount Sinai to watch the sun rise from Egypt's highest peak. But the ribbon of land beside the Suez Canal was unexplored territory, much of it desert. I had never even glimpsed it from a ship or a plane, so I had no idea what to expect. I set out into the unknown in a buzz of excitement, with just a touch of nerves.

First of all, I made for Port Tewfiq, the spit of land which curves out so far from Suez City that it almost touches the Sinai Peninsula.

The narrow gap between the two is the Suez Canal. I was intending to cycle the whole length of the canal so, for the sake of completeness, I wanted to begin at its very beginning, the point at which the canal starts its 110-mile (177 km) journey north to the Mediterranean from the Gulf of Suez.

I cycled away from the city centre around the horseshoe Bay of Suez. The long, narrow causeway that linked the city with Port Tewfiq was studded with palm trees. The water glinted in the sunlight on both sides and I soon left the din and confusion of the overcrowded streets behind me. Suez was bombarded in the Anglo-French fiasco of 1956 and virtually razed to the ground in the 1967 war with Israel. People were evacuated, their homes destroyed, and the canal was choked with sunken vessels. The night before, I had seen only patched-up buildings and ugly concrete boxes in the town centre, most of them thrown up hastily to rehouse the population after the 1967 war. Along the Corniche and round the shore of the bay, there were lawns between the road and the white-topped parapets, a few fish restaurants, and hotels which were considerably smarter than the ones in town. It was the place where people came to enjoy a spot of calm, away from the tumult of the Suez streets. The benches under the trees were all occupied by earnest students, reading and testing one another. I went up to a group of girls. They were obviously good friends, despite the fact that two of them were totally enveloped in black, one was in the halfway house of headscarf and long grey gabardine raincoat, while the fourth was casually dressed in a baggy jersey and jeans. She could have been a Western teenager. I found they were all reading Computer Studies at the university.

'Will you be able to find jobs in banks and offices when you graduate?' I asked.

'Yes,' said one of the black wigwams, the only one who understood English.

I tried a number of other conversational openings, without getting any further. I was disappointed, but at least there were plenty of girls sitting around in the park – a great improvement on Syria and Jordan – and they seemed friendly. I might be luckier next time.

I cycled across Port Tewfiq's promontory to Suez Canal Street, where I had my first view of the canal. To my right lay the broader expanse of the Gulf of Suez. There were no ships to be seen, apart from a few local fishing boats. Traffic in the canal is one-way, in alternate directions. The passage through takes about fifteen hours and ships assemble at either end to go through in convoy. That morning, they must have been in transit, or grouping at the northern end, in Port Said.

If downtown Suez is profoundly unattractive, its surroundings are even worse. I had to brave the outpourings of petrochemical refineries and fertiliser plants, then estates of drab prefabricated houses for the workers. Habitation ended abruptly. Suddenly, I broke free of the outskirts and found myself back within sight of the canal, cycling through desolation, which was broken only by large graveyards. Some were Muslim, some Christian, but all had tombs of mud brick built up over the level of the sand. The canal widened into the Bitter Lakes, where the sunlight bounced off the water, piercing my eyes through my Polaroids. Even the grains of sand seemed to glitter like mica. It was a long, hot, shadeless ride, but at least there was a good tarmac road, and it was flat. After Abu Sultan and the end of the Bitter Lakes, the land became fertile, with vast mango orchards and miles of lettuce. I thought of Rudyard Kipling: 'Here is a country which is not a country but a longish strip of market garden.' Cultivation in Egypt was all strips, wherever the Nile or a canal brought water to the parched land.

When I cruised into Ismaelia, I had no expectations at all. Despite reading that it was a favourite honeymoon destination for Egyptian newly-weds, I was convinced that it would be another noisy, chaotic dump, just like Suez. Instead, I found myself in a spacious, gracious, orderly city, where lawns swept down to the tree-shaded Sweetwater Canal, dug to provide fresh drinking water for the navvies excavating the Suez. I made my way to the Palace Hotel, a delightful confection of sugar-pink stucco. With potted palms at the entrance, wrought-iron balconies and French shutters, it could have been the stage-set for a Feydeau farce. I expected saucy French maids in little white caps and comic, overweight businessmen to be chasing one another in and out of the bedroom doors. But it was all very respectable. My balcony looked out over parks and fountains. I had a clean bathroom with really hot water and art deco tiles, a television with a Suisse Romande channel broadcasting in French, and an arrow pointing to Mecca, to make sure that I prayed in the right direction. What more could I want?

Throughout the Middle East, I had become so unused to seeing women around in the evenings that I could scarcely believe my eyes when I went out in search of dinner. There were women everywhere. Women alone, women strolling in pairs, women and children picnicking under the trees, families out shopping, pushing pushchairs and licking ice creams, women arm in arm with their husbands and boyfriends, gaggles of teenage girls eying the boys, mixed groups of teenagers in the Pizza Hut and Kentucky Fried Chicken. It was all so normal. If the women had not been wearing headscarves, I would have imagined myself in Italy, doing the evening *passeggiata*. And Thursday was an absolute ball. As Friday is the Muslim day of prayer, the day when businesses close, Thursday night in Ismaelia was like Saturday night in Hammersmith. The whole town turned into a disco. The windows along the main drag were brightly lit and the doors of the record shops were all open, and all blasting out a mixture of Western and Levantine pop. The garden down the wide central reservation was thronged with people listening to the music. No one was actually dancing, but feet were tapping and heads were bobbing to the beat. There was an amazing party atmosphere, unspoilt by drunkenness or loutish behaviour. I walked through the middle of it all without a qualm. 'Welcome!' 'Hello!' 'Welcome to Egypt!' 'Welcome to Ismaelia!'

I had had doubts about my reception in Egypt, particularly in Ismaelia, the birthplace of a dangerous Islamic terrorist organisation, the Muslim Brotherhood. But my fears were dispelled that Thursday night. There was no sign of anti-Western feeling. In the pharmacy, where I went to buy a new toothbrush, the chemist told me how much he had enjoyed his one visit to London. He was friendly and anxious to establish a link between us, however tenuous. As I left the shop, he called after me, 'Thank you for coming to Ismaelia.'

Ismaelia is a garden city, laid out in 1858 to house the European employees of La Compagnie Universelle du Canal Maritime de Suez. This company, part Egyptian, part French, was set up to excavate the canal and run it for 99 years. Ferdinand de Lesseps, the French engineer responsible, lived in a delightful villa overlooking the Sweetwater Canal. With its cross timbers, fretted wood balconies and high gables, it looks more suited to the French Alps than to sea-level Egypt. It is the grandest of many such villas, which together turn the area into a kind of Chamonix-Outre-Mer. Lawns are simply lawns, and the well-mown grass along the canalside could be anywhere, but the trees along Mohammed Ali Quay are pollarded to within an inch of their lives, and could be nothing but French. They are the cropped and tortured trees of every main square in every town in France.

Unfortunately, de Lesseps's house is closed to the public and only VIPs can inspect his study, where all his plans, papers and photographs are said to be laid out, just as he left them. Given more time, I would have made enquiries about a visitor's permit, but I had to leave for Port Said the next day. I had to content myself with peering through the railings and taking a snap of Condor outside the great man's gates. There was no one around to photograph me. Mohammed Ali Quay was deserted, except for one tattered old man driving a donkey-cart – not a potential photographer, I decided.

The Suez was not the first canal cut to give better access to the Red Sea. Ramses II cut a canal across from Bubastis on the Nile delta to the Bitter Lakes as early as the thirteenth century BC. It had silted up by the time the Persians conquered Egypt, but Darius, who ascended the Persian throne in 522 BC, knew the importance of swift communications. With a vast empire to control, he embarked on a remarkable road-building programme. As part of that project, he cleared Ramses' old canal and dug an extension from the Bitter Lakes to the Gulf of Suez, to give him direct access to Egypt from his Persian heartland. Canals for both navigation and irrigation were well maintained throughout Egypt under the Ptolemies and the Romans, but they fell into disuse in the troubled times between the Roman and Muslim conquests. It seems that the present direct link between the Mediterranean and the Red Sea was first proposed by Napoleon's engineers, but they abandoned the project owing to a miscalculation. They thought there was a 32-foot (10 m) difference between the levels of the two seas. When the error was discovered, Ferdinand de Lesseps presented a new plan to Said Pasha, Mohammed Ali's son, who accepted it and provided one-third of the capital. The French raised the other two-thirds and work began in 1859. Said's successor, Ismael Pasha, saw the project through to completion and the canal opened to shipping in 1869.

It was a profitable enterprise from the start. In 1864 Egypt's total annual revenue was calculated at just under £5 million sterling. By 1875 it had climbed to £145.9 million, thanks partly to the Suez Canal and partly to the American Civil War, which had benefited the export of Egyptian cotton.

The Suez Canal was only one of 112 canals, 8,400 miles of them (13,520 km), dug during Ismael Pasha's reign. Most were irrigation canals, designed to extend the land under cultivation, but he also built the Ismaelia Canal, a major waterway linking the Suez Canal at Ismaelia with a new canal to Cairo. He was also a great social reformer, famously declaring, 'My country is no longer in Africa. It is in Europe.' But major construction work and social reform cost money, and Ismael Pasha overstretched himself. He went bankrupt. This was the chance the British had been waiting for. They had opposed the building of the Suez Canal because it gave their great rivals, the French, control over the strategically important short cut to the Red Sea and India. Disraeli seized his opportunity. Jumping in, he raised a loan from Rothschilds and snapped up the bankrupt Pasha's shares in the Suez Canal Company for £4 million, before the French had time to raise the capital. Overnight, in 1875, the British Government became the largest single shareholder in the company and secured their passage to India.

I had read that the Ismaelia Museum contained an interesting section on the history of Egyptian canals from Ramses II to de Lesseps. My journey to Egypt had taken me along four canals – the Thames-Medway, the Burgundy, the Corinth and now the Suez. They were all very different and all fascinating in their history, as well as providing me with flat and agreeable rides. I was fast becoming a canal anorak, swotting up distances, depths and ladders of locks. So it was a great disappointment when the curator told me that there was no canal exhibition in the museum and never had been. There was nothing there beyond the usual display of unremarkable local finds. I had fun getting there though. I went by bicycle, joining the cycling tradesmen. Ismaelia, like most of inhabited Egypt, is absolutely flat and few but the very rich run cars. It's perfect cycling country. I pedalled along behind a window-cleaner, who carried two long ladders on his head and a bucket on his handlebars. A baker's boy balanced a pyramid of at least a hundred loaves on a head-board and still managed to ride along whistling, as a baker's boy should, with his hands in his pockets.

There were no signs to the museum, but I found the general area in Mallaha Park along the Sweetwater Canal and asked the traffic policeman. He was mystified. I kept repeating the word 'museum'. Then I tried 'musée'. Then I waved my arms around to indicate that the museum must be somewhere in the immediate vicinity. His face cleared. 'Swim!' he said, beaming and miming vigorous breast-stroke. He directed me to Lake Timsah, which was useful, as I planned to ride out there in the afternoon. As for the museum, I finally met a woman who spoke excellent English and knew where it was. There were two guards in sentry boxes on the approach road and no fewer than eight soldiers on duty outside the building itself. Mubarak's crackdown on terrorism. I was the only visitor, so I was quite an event, especially as I arrived on an orange bicycle. The soldiers crowded round me, a cheerful bunch despite their bristling weaponry. I told them they could go for a spin on Condor, if they liked, while I was inside the museum. They laughed, but they were on duty and mimed the difficulty of cycling with a loaded machine-gun. Inside the museum, I had the curator and a bevy of custodians to myself, all following me around.

It was a lovely afternoon, as warm as an English summer's day, when I cycled out of town to Lake Timsah. The name means 'Crocodile Lake', but the reptiles have all disappeared, leaving the lake's sheltered surface to the swimmers and water-skiers. Out of season, the smart beach resorts were deserted and the little lakeside fish restaurants boarded up. Fishermen were casting nets beyond the reeds, and I thought they were the only people around, until I heard a rustling in the bushes. Four eyes peered out at me, somewhere around the level of my waist. Then the bushes parted, and two small boys appeared, thrusting BMX bicycles through the undergrowth. We had no language in common, but we grinned and they decided to clank along behind me on my sightseeing tour, pedalling like mad to keep up. For once, I was the fastest cyclist. When I stopped on a bridge, they grew bored and sped away, blowing kisses and doing wheelies down the road. I stood spellbound. At the far end of the lake, I spotted ships passing through the Suez Canal. There was a sandbank between us, so I could see only their superstructures, but they were a fine sight, like gently gliding house-tops. They were making their way into the stretch of canal that linked Lake Timsah with the Bitter Lakes, and they were the only moving ships I saw in my four days on the canal. I always seemed to miss the convoys.

As I tucked into my delicious baked macaroni and beer that night in the King George Restaurant, I decided that Ismaelia was one of the friendliest, most gracious towns I had ever visited. Egyptian tourist meccas, like Luxor and downtown Cairo, have a reputation for hassle and pushy salesmanship. But people in Ismaelia wouldn't know a postcard, a papyrus painting or a stuffed camel if it jumped up and bit them. They came and chatted out of affability and a measure of nosiness, not as an opening gambit in the selling game. One way and another, my ride from London had been hard, what with rain, snow, mountains, a wonky knee, a robbery, the violence in Israel and the aftermath of September 11th. In Ismaelia, life seemed a bright adventure again and my journey looked set for an agreeable end.

On the way to Port Said, I had my one and only unpleasant encounter of the whole trip. I stopped at a village bus depot for a cold drink. There was a mullah leaning on a pillar, waiting for his bus. He smiled at me, so I smiled back. His robes and turban were beautifully laundered, his beard neatly trimmed, his whole appearance respectable, even distinguished. Still smiling at me, he raised his hand and slowly made the throat-slitting gesture. Then he turned his back on me and strode off. It was not a frightening incident. There were too many friendly people bustling around for me to be afraid. But it left a nasty taste. He was supposed to be a man of God!

I chose my Port Said hotel, appropriately called the Panorama, because of the stunning Mediterranean view from my sixth-floor balcony. It was opposite the main mosque and I thought nothing of that until the mullah began the Friday sermon. It was relayed all over the city by loudspeaker and I had never heard such a hysterical outpouring. The mullah screamed and roared and howled into his microphone. Could it be my mad mullah from the bus depot? Was he whipping the worshippers into an anti-Christian, anti-Western frenzy? I watched anxiously as the congregation emerged. They were mostly elderly men in suits, who paused for a quiet chat in the mosque garden, shook hands and went decorously on their way. When Arabs have a normal conversation, their language is so guttural and they shout so loudly that it sounds like a violent row. So I suppose when preachers preach, they rave like prophets on the Day of Judgment, but are probably just delivering gentle homilies about being kind to your neighbours, or not beating your donkeys.

Again, I missed the ships on the move. All through the day I watched them assembling, and by nightfall there were rows of twinkling lights off-shore, like swags of Christmas decorations. The next morning, they had all disappeared. I pedalled as fast as I could go to Palestine Street, which borders the canal, but the ships had already passed on their journey south and the waterway was empty. I paused to admire the murals of Ismael Pasha and the top-hatted dignitaries at the Grand Opening Ceremony, then went off to Thomas Cook's to book my flight home.

I stayed an extra day in Port Said, because I needed to send some emails urgently. I had not made contact with my friends for two weeks, since my emails from Antakya. The Lebanon had internet cafés, but I was there within a few days of leaving Turkey and there seemed to be no point in emailing again so soon. I decided to wait, but that turned out to be a mistake. Hafez al-Assad had banned the internet in Syria, so it was impossible to send emails from Damascus. There were no internet cafés in Aqaba, none that I saw in Suez and none in Ismaelia. By the time I reached Port Said, I was getting desperate. The last message I had sent my friends was, 'I am crossing tomorrow into Syria.' For the traveller, Syria is a safe and welcoming country, but the people back home were not to know that. They only knew Syria's doubtful political reputation. I guessed that they would have serious concerns about my safety. In Port Said I thought I was in luck when I passed three internet cafés on my way into town. I cycled round them next morning. The first had closed down permanently, the second was closed temporarily, owing to illness, and the third had the repairers in, dealing with a technical problem. 'Sorry. Computers not working. Try tomorrow.' But there was no tomorrow for me. My time in Egypt was running out and I had to move on. In the event, I found no functioning internet café until I reached Alexandria. By this time my friends were so frantic that they had reported my disappearance to the Foreign Office and a red alert had been issued to all our embassies in the Middle East!

It was the first time I had ever used Hotmail on a long ride, and it will be my last. Without Hotmail, everyone knows that I communicate when I get the opportunity. Snail mail, fax and the occasional telephone call all work perfectly well, and if a few weeks go by without a letter, no one worries too much. But once I got a Hotmail address, I created the expectation that I was going to be emailing regularly, and that was just not possible in the Middle East and Egypt. It seemed ironic that what was, by my standards, a relatively safe ride should have caused more anxiety than any of my dangerous ones. No one turned a hair when I was weeks out of touch in the wilds of the Taklamakan Desert and the fiefdoms of the Shining Path guerrillas in the Andes. But when I was enjoying a most agreeable ride through hospitable countries, within easy reach of British Consuls and airports, my friends were distraught! Never again. For the sake of everyone's nerves, including mine, I shall resist both Hotmail and mobiles.

I liked Port Said, though it was contradictory, uncertain of its character. On the one hand, it was a Free Port, its glitzy shops crammed with duty-free cigarettes, electricals and cosmetics. It was a sophisticated place where wealthy Egyptians came on buying sprees and beach holidays. Yet, on the other hand, it was a devoutly Muslim city. I had a radio *munshid* reciting the Koran all the way through breakfast, even in the roof-top restaurant of my modern hotel. And when I cycled off on my journey to the Nile, I was at the end of the Port Said Corniche before I got out of range of the high-decibel drone of the *munshid* from the main mosque. This split personality was all the more puzzling because ports are, by their very geography and trade, more open to outside influences. They are usually much less traditional than places inland. I had circled the Mediterranean from Venice to Port Said and found more similarities than differences along its coast. Lattakia, for example, was more like Greek Igoumenitsa than its own Syrian capital of Damascus. Yet, despite all the duty-free shops, the beach resorts and the great harbour, which decanted coachloads of foreign tourists from visiting liners, Port Said was not a Mediterranean city. It had the feel of Old Cairo.

I discovered this to my cost when I passed a duty-free shop with ...es full of imported whisky and vodka. I went in for a bottle

... is your passport?'

'In my hotel.'

'No passport. No whisky.'

I jumped on my bike, sprinted off to my hotel and back to the shop, passport in hand.

'Visa 48 hours. No whisky.'

I stared at my incomprehensible visa. Had I been given a 48-hour visa by mistake? If so, I had already exceeded my legal time limit. That was not a happy thought in a Muslim country, post September 11th.

I needed to regularise my status with the police immediately.

The Police Foreigners Department had moved since my guidebook was printed and no one seemed to know where it had gone. After an hour or two of frantic searching, I managed to track it down, way out of town beyond the football stadium. The Department Chief himself entertained me most charmingly to tea and sweets, and assured me that my visa was valid for four weeks. Back I went in triumph to the duty-free shop and seized my prize from the whisky shelf. I produced my passport with a flourish at the cash desk and told them the Chief of Police himself had validated my visa.

'Whisky not allowed.'

What they had been trying to tell me before, in their broken English, was that foreign liquor had to be purchased within 48 hours of arrival in Egypt! So, after all that trouble, I still had no whisky. I marched out of the shop fuming. 'Keep your bloody whisky then!' I shouted. It did no good, but it made me feel better.

Alcohol is an excellent killer of intestinal bugs and I'm sure that the main reason my stomach copes so well on my travels is because I disinfect it with a daily dose. My favourite tipple is wine with my dinner, or a glass of beer in wineless lands. But in Middle Eastern holy cities or resorts where tourists are scarce, the restaurants often serve nothing more enticing than Fanta. So I like to keep some whisky handy, and take a relaxing, medicinal snifter before I go out to dinner. In Egypt I ran out and was liquorless until I found a little shop in a back alley in Alexandria, which sold 'Scotch Whisky. Made in Egypt'. It was an aromatic brew, and I felt it would be unwise to drink more than one glass at a time, but it was better than nothing.

* * *

Once I was clear of the refineries and pipe-laying activities which always surround ports, the ride to Damietta was a dream. I raced along with the wind behind me. The road ran along two narrow spits of land, one from Port Said, the other from Damietta, which together enclosed Lake Manzala. The beach to my right was strewn with millions of tiny shells, all perfectly white and perfectly shell-shaped, while the vast lagoon to my left looked like a scene from an Ancient Egyptian tomb painting. There were waterfowl and fishermen poling shallow craft in and out of the reed beds. As I watched, a great cloud darkened the sky and descended on an island, covering it with what looked like snow, but in fact was the wings of herons. Lake Manzala in winter is a resting place for migrating birds and my guidebook promised me pelicans, spoon-bills and flamingos. But the jinx on my ride to Egypt extended even to my birdwatching. I saw nothing remotely exotic – just herons, two wagtails, one hoopoe and a dozen sparrows.

The coastline was idyllic, a feast for the eyes, but it was not a happy place to live. In the middle of so much marshland, water seeped everywhere. The village centres were fetid lakes, which spread to form pools round the houses. The villagers had to take off their shoes and paddle barefoot to their front doors. Horses and donkeys stood patiently in their traces, up to their fetlocks in water. The houses were squat, sound but ugly cubes of brick and concrete. One or two had balconies and were altogether grander, but even they were standing in lakes of stinking water. There was no such thing as garbage collection. The village streets and the neighbouring dunes were dumps of foul-smelling litter. In one village, a coach pulled up and the passengers poured out for refreshments at a roadside stall. Coke bottles, biscuit wrappers, chewing gum, orange peel, cigarette packets and tissues were all tossed blithely to the ground, until the travellers stood, uncon-cerned, in a lake of rubbish. As for the plastic bags! They blew along the sands, floated on the lake, clogged the drains and fluttered from the reeds. Whoever invented them should be shot – or rest unquietly in his grave if he's already there.

Near the villages, fishermen stood by the roadside with baskets of fresh fish, neatly arranged for sale on beds of greenery. One of them shouted 'kalimera' as I cycled by, reminding me of the strong Greek influence along this coast. Then I saw a bunch of brilliant lycra shirts in the distance, speeding along the top of the reeds. I thought it was a mirage, until two red shirts peeled off and sped in my direction. They were worn by two boys of about seventeen on racing bicycles, the first bicycles of that quality I had seen since Italy. They slowed down to inspect Condor and ask me all those awkward questions I can never answer, like 'What is your gear ratio?' and 'Do you ever have problems with cracked hub flanges?' I puffed and panted to keep up with them. Then one of them gave me an apple, and they raced off down a side lane to catch up with the rest of their group.

Egypt is either desert or market garden. There is nothing in between. One moment I was surrounded by white sand and marshes. The next, without any sort of gradation, I suddenly found myself cycling through luxuriant lettuce and cabbage patches. I had reached the area of irrigation around Damietta. Ten months after leaving the Thames Embankment, I was about to catch my first glimpse of the Nile.

16. THE NILE

It flows through old hushed Egypt and its sands,
Like some grave mighty thought threading a dream.

Leigh Hunt, 'A Thought of the Nile'

Until the opening of the Suez Canal, Damietta was one of Egypt's main ports. Prospering on Mediterranean trade and its control of a navigable branch of the Nile up to Cairo and beyond, it was so wealthy in mediaeval times that it attracted the plundering intentions of the Crusaders, despite its Christian credentials. The Virgin Mary is said to have rested there on the flight to Egypt and her chapel on the spot was revered by both Coptic Christians and Muslims. That did not prevent the marauding knights from bombarding the citadel. It was later razed to the ground by the Mamelukes.

Modern Damietta gives no hint of its past glories. The port is still active, but not internationally. It trades only with Port Said, just along the coast. Its mainstay now is furniture-making. I cycled into town past furniture workshops and furniture showrooms, shrines to the gods of middle-class aspiration. When I reached the Corniche along the Nile, the shrines blossomed into palaces, some of Pharaonic size and splendour, Karnak temples of marble, glass and chrome, crammed with beds in the shape of ancient boats, overstuffed armchairs, smoked-glass tables resting on swans' necks and vast wardrobes carved with scrolls and swags. Traffic was buzzing in the general air of prosperity. There was even a brand new hospital, so impressively smart that I took it for a Sheraton or Hilton and went inside to ask the price of rooms! Only the Nile was a disappointment. It was one huge bloated plastic bag and the side streets leading from it were ankle-deep in mud.

In the 1950s, when the Aswan Dam was built by the Nasser Government as a monument to Egypt's independence, the waters of the world's longest river were harnessed and diverted to bring hundreds of acres of marginal land under cultivation. The resulting increase in foodstuffs has helped to feed Egypt's exploding population, but the price has been high. The flow of the Nile has shrunk to a paltry one-tenth of its former volume and is now too weak to hold the Mediterranean at bay. The sea sweeps inland, washing more of the delta away each year and destroying its fishing industry. The Nile is too feeble even to scour its banks and cleanse its ancient bed. Damietta's disgusting plastic bags are just one symptom of the river's sickness. Others are the rise in schistosomiasis (river blindness) and dysentery along its turgid backwaters, and illnesses caused by the heavy use of chemical fertilisers, necessary now that the Nile's rich silt is trapped by the dam. And there is stealthy, unseen damage too. Diversion of water from the cities has forced them to draw down the freshwater aquifers, so that underground salts are rising. Paintings which have survived in their freshness for three millennia are crumbling off the walls and salt is creeping up to erode the foundations of ancient buildings. Even the pyramids are beginning to suffer.

'Hello, my sister! Welcome to Egypt!' Hands were stretched out to be shaken and there were smiles all round as I dodged the tooting cars, bikes and donkey-carts through the grime of the town centre. I missed the one and only hotel on my first transit and arrived back on the Nile Corniche. A passer-by pointed out the top of a startling scarlet skyscraper, labelled Suleman Inn Hotel, which towered, like Jack's beanstalk, over all the other buildings in town. It was as narrow as a ladder climbing the heavens. I cycled back into the main bazaar and realised then why I had missed it. The ground floor was a tiny pastry shop, just big enough to take a counter, two little tables and four chairs. The first floor was a coffee shop and the second floor a restaurant. The lift to the bedroom levels shot up like a rocket into the stratosphere. There was just room on each floor for four identical boxes. I squeezed past the bed and television set to my upright chair. These were the only items of furniture in my bedroom, but they were beautifully crafted, as one would expect in Damietta. Reception was a pocket handkerchief behind the pastry shop, and I wondered where they would find room for Condor, when the basement storeroom was no bigger than a mouse-hole. They solved the problem by leaning him against the plate-glass window, halfway down the basement stairs, where everyone passing by could admire his orange gleam.

Cakes in Egypt are the eastern Mediterranean variety, on sale in every country from Greece to Arabia – baklava and all the other shapes of filo pastry, stuffed with nuts and swimming in honey.

Delicious as they are, a little goes a long way and they ooze so much honey that they have to be eaten on the spot with a knife and fork. They were too light and sugary to eat for breakfast in my room and too squidgy to carry as cycle sustenance. I had breakfasted and snacked for so many weeks on horrendously sweet Middle Eastern biscuits that the very sight of their jazzy packets was enough to set my teeth on edge. I was longing for something, anything, less sickly. In Damietta, I found it. The ground-floor pastry shop sold solid slabs of walnut pound cake. I bought enough to see me through the rest of Egypt. The assistant knew quite well that I was staying in the hotel and had only to carry the cake up to my room in the lift but, despite all my protests, he insisted on putting it into a box, wrapping the box in printed paper, decorating it with a nylon ribbon, then putting the whole parcel into a plastic bag. I reached my room and immediately deposited all the wrapping in my wastepaper basket. Damietta looked as bad at refuse collection as the rest of Egypt and I guessed it would all go straight into the Nile, adding yet another plastic bag to the surface bloating. But it was good cake. I ate a thick slice of it and a couple of mandarins for lunch, meditating on the notice in my bedroom: 'My Dear Guest: the room is your own; so keep your Eye on.'

Cycling up the Nile was quite complicated. There were small towns, where the traffic flow forced me away from the river bank. But with irrigation canals all round me, I was never away from the edge of water. I had water above and below me too. It had rained in the night and I found that stretches of country road outside Damietta were a quagmire. Then it started to rain again. England, France, Switzerland, Italy, Turkey, Cyprus and now Egypt. Rain, rain, rain! The wind was against me too. In Egypt, the prevailing wind is northerly, which is why the Nile has been navigable in both directions from ancient times. Feluccas can drift north, downstream on the current. When they turn south, the north wind fills their lateen sails. I was travelling south west and should have had that reliable wind behind me, helping me on towards Cairo. Instead, the rain was carried on a stiff wind from the west. The traffic covered me in mud and the gale hurled rain in my face. Sometimes I took a wrong turn, as the road signs in the delta villages were all in Arabic. But I had one stroke of luck that morning. I passed a bilingual advertisement for a kitchenware shop in El Mansura, where I was heading, and memorised the look of the place name.

The land was wonderfully fertile, rich black soil positively bursting with giant cabbages. The rain stopped, the sun came out, the market gardens smiled and it should have been a beautiful ride. But there was nothing to lift the spirit. The village houses were drab, monotonous concrete cubes, the fetid pools were broader and deeper after the rain, and the garbage had gone soggy. I seemed to cycle down one endless corridor of putrid rubbish. In a few places, they were trying to burn it, but it was too wet and it smouldered, shrouding the road in an evil miasma. Refuse is the scourge of the Middle East and Egypt. India has even more, but there are scavengers. What the rag-pickers don't collect for recycling is pounced on by dogs, cats, pigs, sacred cows, rats, crows and vultures. In Egypt, there are few of those useful creatures around and the garbage lies on the roadside until it rots. The Crusaders fell sick in El Mansura, through eating contaminated fish. I am blessed with an iron stomach, but by the time I reached the city, even I was feeling slightly nauseous. I treated myself to the best hotel, the Marshal El Gezirah, where I was sure of hygienic surroundings – and furniture in Damietta's most opulently gilded baroque.

I had a wonderful view from my balcony of the full moon over the Nile and settled down to watch a wedding reception which was being held in the formal gardens along the Corniche. It was the perfect romantic setting. The bride, in a flouncy white extravaganza, all frills and puff sleeves, processed arm-in-arm with her business-suited groom down a flight of stone steps while flash bulbs popped. The women started up their high-pitched ululation, fluttering their tongues in the traditional Egyptian manner. The guests clapped rhythmically and drums took up the beat. The celebrations continued far into the night and looked magical under the lamps. Luckily, the rain had stopped and pools of darkness hid the garbage strewn in the gardens and floating on the Nile.

Damietta to El Mansura was my last full day's cycling. Cleopatra's capital, Alexandria, lay on the edge of the western desert, beyond the Rosetta branch of the Nile. There was no road beside the sea through the marshy delta and I had run so short of time that cycling the Damietta branch of the Nile almost up to

Cairo then backtracking down the Rosetta branch to the coast again was out of the question. I should have to swallow my principles, abandon purism and hop on a bus to Alexandria.

It was a long ride through endless cotton fields and small towns swarming with donkey-carts, where buffalo wallowed in the canals. Most traces of ancient Lower Egypt have been swept away over the centuries by the Nile floods, so there were no sights to be seen, no tourists and no hotels. Only a person with a passion for agriculture could find the delta interesting. My own boredom was held at bay by a student in her final year of Engineering at the University of Alexandria. She was one of the Coptic minority, who are emigrating in large numbers, uncertain of their futures in an increasingly Islamic culture.

'I'm a Christian, so I'm working on the refurbishment of a church as my practical assignment. Engineering and architecture are popular degree courses for girls here, and we get good jobs. But I should like to work in America. I have two uncles living in New York and an aunt in California. They could help me get started. If I can't find an engineering job, I shall just travel around for a year or so, paying my way by working in McDonald's or KFC. I don't mind what sort of work I do.'

'I can't tell you how pleased I am to have someone to talk to,' I said. 'I've just travelled through the Middle East and I haven't spoken to a single local person, apart from waiters and hotel receptionists, since I left Turkey. The men don't talk to strange women and the women speak nothing but Arabic. Unless I happen to bump into another foreign traveller like myself, I go for days without conversation.'

'It's not like that here. We're not Arabs,' she said firmly. 'We're Egyptians. Egyptian society is quite different. Men and women mix socially.'

'Would a man start up a conversation with you, if he were sitting next to you in a bus?'

'Of course he would. If we were on a journey together, we'd talk. We wouldn't just sit there like two dummies.'

The Alexandria coach arrived in Sidi Gaber, about 12 miles east of the city centre. I cycled along the Grand Corniche, through the string of suburban beach resorts where Egyptian holidaymakers stay, and found a hotel just beyond the main square, Midan Sa'ad Zaghloul. I felt tired and edgy. It had been a complicated journey.

There were no signposts in El Mansura and I had no city plan, so I had started the day by going round and round in circles looking for the coach station on the outskirts. Then I had had to elbow my way to the ticket counter, persuade the driver to take my bicycle, struggle through Alexandria's honking traffic to the Grand Corniche and search for a clean, respectable hotel that I could afford. At the end of it all, I was utterly limp. Journeys by bicycle are so much simpler. I just get on my bike when I'm ready and stop when I'm tired. No timetables, no hassle, no *baksheesh*.

Alexandria! The very name is evocative. From long association, we see the coast of Normandy through the eyes of the Impressionists. In Alexandria, the associations are literary. It is difficult to stroll along the Corniche without seeing the melancholy figure of Constantine Cavafy, Alexandria's poet, out for his morning constitutional; take tea in the Hotel Cecil without catching a glimpse of E.M. Forster on the next table; wander down a side street without meeting a family straight from the pages of Mahfouz; or walk down Sharia Nabi Danial without seeing Darley and Pombal, who shared a flat there in Lawrence Durrell's *Alexandria Quartet*. Alexandria is a city of literary imaginings, most of them expatriate, a modern myth woven around an ancient capital. For Durrell, it is 'the Capital of Memory'.

The city's cosmopolitan era began with Mohammed Ali, whose bronze turbanned figure still rides its high-stepping charger above the traffic of the Midan Tahrir. His Alexandrian statue shows him in a dignified, statesmanlike pose, unlike his statue in his native Kavalla, where he brandishes his scimitar on a prancing steed. After his installation as Pasha, he set about modernising Egypt on European lines. He built railways, opened factories and schools and introduced the cultivation of cotton from the Sudan. This soon became Egypt's chief cash crop and the source of great wealth during the American Civil War, when local production was neglected. All this trade required a modern port and Mohammed Ali redeveloped the ancient cosmopolis of Alexandria, connecting the port once again to the River Nile by digging the Mahmudiya Canal and opening its docks to foreign trade.

Merchants from around the Mediterranean flocked to take advantage of the new opportunities in Alexandria and the city soon held a fascinating mix of peoples, with Greeks and Levantine Jews perhaps forming the largest expatriate communities. They prospered there, despite World War II and the fall of Mohammed Ali's last successor, King Farouk, in 1952. But disaster struck in 1956. The Suez invasion led to the expulsion of all British and French nationals from Egypt and foreign businesses were nationalised. Then the discovery of an Israeli sabotage unit in the port led to the expulsion of non-Egyptian Jews. Altogether, 100,000 foreigners fled the city, leaving only a handful of Alexandrian Greeks and Jews, many of them too old and frail to uproot themselves.

Modern Alexandria has expanded as Egypt's population has multiplied, and its five million or so citizens are now almost exclusively Egyptian. But Alexandria still has a faded elegance and a Mediterranean feel about it, more akin to the ports of Italy or Spain than to its own Islamic hinterland. Its trams rattle along the Corniche past cream stucco consulates that could have dropped there straight from Nice or Genoa. On my first night in the city, I made a pilgrimage to one of its most famous restaurants, the Greek-owned Élite on Sharia Safiya Zaghloul, an arty place, decorated with posters of Chagall and Picasso. Madame Christina is said to enjoy reminiscing about painters she knew in Alexandria's heady days, but she was nowhere to be seen when I was ordering my moussaka and that rare treat in Egypt, a glass of beer. In fact, the restaurant was a sad place, virtually empty. Middle-class Egyptians prefer the strip lights of McDonald's and Pizza Hut.

My other Alexandrian haunt, The Trianon, was more cheerful. One of the oldest and most fashionable of the city's famous patisseries, its extravagant spendours have been regilded and air-conditioned, to conform with the Egyptian idea of luxury. It was obviously the place where young men brought their girlfriends, to woo them over ice-cream sundaes, baklava and astonishing confections of honey, chocolate and cream. After weeks in Arab cities, where women were never seen in public places, let alone treated to an evening out, the sight of all those smiling girls in Egyptian cafés gave a real lift to the spirits. They were elegantly dressed and looked Greek or Italian, except for the headscarves. The Turks and Egyptians constitute a pair of outward-looking brackets at either end of the Arab Middle East. They will both tell you quite firmly that they may be Muslim, but they are Turkish or Egyptian, *not* Arab.

But I was not in Alexandria for a breath of nostalgia or a taste of international cuisine. I was there because it was once Cleopatra's magnificent capital. When Alexander the Great conquered Egypt in 332 BC, he marched his troops overland through Turkey and Syria, but he obviously needed a port in Egypt to shorten his supply lines. He was also in pursuit of a dream. The first non-racist in history, he wanted to build an empire where the different races mingled freely, with no dividing line between conquering Greeks and conquered 'barbarians'. He wanted his city to lead the world in tolerance and culture as well as power. He selected a fishing village on the Mediterranean coast, which had a good natural harbour, and instructed the architect Dimocrates to draw up plans for a splendid city, to be called Alexandria. In all the excitement of construction, no one guessed that only nine years later his body would be brought there for burial. He died in Babylon at the age of 33.

When his empire was divided between his generals, Egypt was assigned to Ptolemy. He proclaimed himself Pharaoh and was the first in a line of fourteen Greek-speaking Macedonian Ptolemies. Each of them embellished their capital of Alexandria, until it became the most opulent city in the world after Rome, and the undisputed intellectual capital, with its library of 532,000 books. The geographer Strabo, who studied there for five years around 25 BC, waxed lyrical about the city's broad colonnaded streets. And as late as AD 641, at the time of the Arab conquest, it was still described as a city of 4,000 palaces.

Cleopatra VII was the last of the Ptolemies. The Greek rulers followed Pharaonic tradition, so she was married to her younger brother, Ptolemy XIII, and shared the throne with him. He was an ambitious boy, who plotted against her and drove her out of Egypt. In desperation, so the story goes, she gained an audience with Julius Caesar, then the undisputed ruler of the Roman world, by wrapping herself in a carpet and being delivered to his quarters, where she popped out, to his great surprise. She so charmed him that he returned to Egypt with her and deposed Ptolemy XIII. Marrying her even younger brother, Ptolemy XIV (who died in mysterious circumstances shortly afterwards), Cleopatra became in effect sole Pharaoh of Egypt. It was a position she was determined to keep.

As long as Julius Caesar, her protector and the father of her son, was in power, she had nothing to fear from Rome. But after Caesar's assassination on the Ides of March, 44 BC, Cleopatra felt vulnerable in the face of Rome's inexorable progress eastwards. She waited three years to see which way the power struggle in Rome between Octavian and Mark Antony would go, then decided to gamble on Mark Antony. As was seen earlier, she went to Tarsus and succeeded in captivating him too.

What was the secret of the spells Cleopatra cast over these two great Romans? Was she bewitchingly beautiful? The cinema would have us believe so. Claudette Colbert, Vivien Leigh and Elizabeth Taylor have all been cast in the role. The Greek historian Plutarch, writing almost a century after her death, is our chief source of information. 'Her beauty,' he says, 'was not incomparable, nor did it strike those who saw her. But conversation with her had an irresistible charm. Her presence, combined with the persuasiveness of her discourse . . . had something stimulating about it. There was a sweetness too in the tones of her voice; and her tongue, like an instrument of many strings, she could readily turn to whatever language she pleased, so that in her interviews with barbarians, whether they were Ethiopians, Troglodytes, Hebrews, Arabians, Syrians, Medes or Parthians, she seldom had need of an inter-preter.' She was the first of the Macedonian Ptolemies who took the trouble to learn the language of her Egyptian subjects, and they loved her for it.

So the legend of Cleopatra's beauty is not supported by the evidence. She was no film star. Her power lay in her intelligence, her political acumen and her understanding of men. She knew how to play her cards. She won Antony's admiration by sailing up the River Cnidus dressed as Aphrodite, in her golden barge with purple sails. This was a brilliant conceit, designed to charm Antony the man. But she knew that Antony the general needed money for his intended war against Parthia, so her elaborate show was also a signal of her wealth. For all the embroidery around their love affair, they were both cool-headed politicians. Their liaison, at least in the beginning, was an affair of mutual advantage rather than passion. Once she had lured him to Alexandria, Cleopatra 'distributing her flattery and always contributing some fresh delight to Antony's hours of seriousness and mirth, kept him in constant thrall and released him neither day nor night.' They feasted, played dice together, hunted together and enjoyed roaming the streets of Alexandria at night, disguised as servants.

Plutarch is less kind about Antony. He concedes that Antony was handsome, but makes much of his 'ill-timed drunkenness, heavy expenditure, debauches with women, wandering about with a crazed and aching head.' Julius Caesar, possibly the most successful general in Roman history, considered Antony to be the ablest of his commanders, but Plutarch dismisses him as 'simple in his nature and slow of perception'. Summing up, he holds that 'his crowning evil, his love for Cleopatra, roused and drove to frenzy many of the passions that were hidden and quiescent in him, and destroyed whatever good and saving qualities still offered resistance.' Strabo joins in the chorus of disapproval, writing of Egypt being 'ruled with drunken violence'.

Of course, the views of these writers need to be put into context. Octavian won the battle for power in the Roman world, but first he had to win over the Roman Senate and people, among whom Antony had many supporters. So he ran a virulent smear campaign. Strabo, a contemporary, was a great admirer of the Roman system of government and a natural supporter of Octavian against what he perceived as Eastern decadence. Plutarch was writing long after Augustus's death, but mud sticks. Scandalous tales can easily become history, when there is no one to dispute them. Cleopatra was portrayed as a licentious, scheming harlot, but there is no evidence that she took lovers other than her two Romans, to whom she appears to have remained faithful.

Plutarch details the run-up to the final contest. While Octavian was busy spinning in Rome, Antony was doing little to help his own cause. He incensed the Romans with what became known as the Donations of Alexandria. Seated with Cleopatra on two golden thrones, he declared Cleopatra Queen of Egypt, Cyprus, Libya and Syria. Caesarion, her son by Julius Caesar, was to be joint ruler with her. At the same time, Antony declared his own sons by Cleopatra to be Kings of Kings. To Alexander he allocated Armenia, Media and Parthia (when he had conquered it) and to Ptolemy he gave Phoenicia, Mesopotamia and Cilicia. 'Alexander was arrayed in Median garb which included a tiara, Ptolemy in a broad-brimmed hat surmounted by a diadem.' To the Romans, with their hatred of kingship, the idea of Antony's sons being Kings of Kings and wearing crowns was an outrage. But far more serious was the fact that Antony was giving away Roman provinces. Two years later, Antony officially divorced his Roman wife, Octavia, and wrote in his will that his body was to be buried in Alexandria with Cleopatra. The tide in Rome finally turned against him. In 31 BC Octavian was elected Consul and 'a vote was passed to wage war against Cleopatra and to take away from Antony the authority which he had surrendered to a woman. Antony had been drugged and was not even master of himself.'

The two lovers were defeated at the Battle of Actium. Antony committed suicide and Octavian invaded Egypt. Cleopatra began to experiment with poisons, as she had decided to kill herself rather than be put on show in Rome as the prize exhibit in Octavian's victory parade. But she still enjoyed playing with power. She built a tomb near the Temple of Isis and shut herself inside it with as many of her treasures as it would hold, together with quantities of firewood and tow. When he heard this, Octavian was a very worried man. He needed her riches to pay off his army and was terrified that she would incinerate them as well as herself. He kept sending 'vague hopes of kindly treatment at the same time as he advanced with his army against the city'. Cleopatra, as we know, died from the bite of an asp, and she left her treasures for Octavian's taking. But I like to think of her playing cat and mouse, toying with her enemy and dangling him on a string to the very day of her death.

'Octavian, though vexed at the death of the woman, admired her lofty spirit and gave orders that her body should be buried with that of Antony in splendid and regal fashion.' She was 39 at the time of her death and had been Queen of Egypt for 22 years. Octavian completed the conquest of Egypt and proclaimed himself Pharaoh of the land whose independence Cleopatra had schemed so hard to maintain.

At first sight, there is not much left of Cleopatra's Alexandria. There are no significant ruins and it has the look of a gracious nineteenth-century city, marred by a jumble of ugly modern apartment blocks. Yet it is still the same city. Its stones have been used and reused over the centuries, layer upon layer of new building, always covering the same areas. Empires and religions have come and gone, but the sites which were significant or holy have remained so. The groundplan laid out by Dimocrates is the groundplan of modern Alexandria. Cleopatra could walk through the city today and know exactly where she was going.

The two broad avenues, lined with marble colonnades, which so excited the admiration of ancient writers, are still there. They may be lined now with shoe shops and pharmacies, but they still form the city's axes. The Sharia Nabi Danial runs due south from the eastern harbour to Lake Mariout behind the city. It is exactly on the line of the Street of the Soma. The Canopic Way ran from west to east, terminating in the Gate of the Sun, where visitors entered the city. West of the intersection with Sharia Nabi Danial, this avenue is now Sharia Fouad, while its eastern arm is Sharia Horriya.

Dodging the traffic at the busy, nondescript intersection of these two roads, it is difficult to visualise the junction in the days when it was the centre of the great city. Here, at this very crossroads, stood the Soma, the tomb of Alexander the Great. (*Soma* is the Greek word for a body.) It was probably a pyramid, with a temple complex around it. Inside, his mummified body is said to have sat on a throne in a glass coffin, decked in his royal regalia. The last recorded person to pay his respects to Alexander inside his tomb was the Roman Emperor Caracalla in AD 215. After that, there is silence. No one knows what became of the tomb or its exalted occupant. There are a number of theories. It could simply have been destroyed in later conflicts. The pagan priesthood might have removed the body for safe-keeping, when the city became Christian. Or, most tantalising of all the theories, Alexander the Great may still be lying under the Soma. The site is now occupied by the mosque and tomb of Nabi Danial, popularly believed to be the Prophet Daniel, but in fact a less important Danial, just a mediaeval sheik. It remains a sacred spot, even after two changes of religion.

Cleopatra's palace seemed to have disappeared completely, swallowed up by earthquakes and tidal waves. But in 1996, a French marine archaeologist, Franck Goddio, discovered a huge area of ruins on the seabed less than a kilometre offshore. They were ruins of amazing richness – statues, sphinxes, red granite columns, marble pavements and elegant ceramics. It was undoubtedly Cleopatra's long-lost palace. And jumbled among those ruins were chunks of masonry believed to be the remnants of the Pharos, Alexandria's lighthouse, which was one of the Seven Wonders of the World. All these marvels remain on the seabed, because the ambitious plan is to build the world's first underwater museum, where visitors can walk through plexiglass tunnels to view the objects *in situ*. Modern Alexandria likes to think big. In Cleopatra's time, its library was the greatest in the world. Today, a new library is under construction which will be its equal in modern terms. Financed by UNESCO and the Egyptian Government, with help from their wealthy Arab neighbours, it will be an international centre of learning, with a reputed 8 million books in every language and dialect in the world.

Failing a sight of Cleopatra's Palace and Alexander's tomb, the place in Alexandria which interested me most was the Midan Sa'ad Zaghloul. Here, at the north end of Sharia Nabi Danial, or the Street of the Soma, Cleopatra began to build a temple in honour of Antony. When Octavian became the Emperor Augustus, he completed it and dedicated it to himself. It was a magnificent temple, full of fine statues and paintings. And to add the finishing touch, Augustus had two obelisks of Thutmose III transported from On and raised at its portals. Being granite columns, they outlasted by many centuries the Caesareum which they were brought to embellish. When Napoleon's expedition stumbled upon them, hieroglyphics had not yet been deciphered, so his savants had no idea whose obelisks they were. They called them 'Cleopatra's Needles', and that name has stuck. They survived in Alexandria until they were given, one each, to the British and the Americans.

Very appropriately, I spent my last afternoon in Alexandria in the company of a literary expatriate American. He told me he was writing a three-volume book and was about to call his agent in New York. He was worried about the size of his advance on royalties. As far as I could gather, the book was an autobiography, and if some of the tall tales he told me were true, I failed to understand why he was so worried about his finances. He told me, for instance, that he had recently found eight original Salvador Dalis in a dustbin in New York.

'I have total recall,' he said. 'A friend of mine had a house in Camden Square and was living with an artist. When London property prices rocketed, she sold her house and gave half the proceeds to the artist, so that he would feel independent. "Thank you," said the artist. "I'm in love with someone else, so I'm leaving now. Goodbye." She's decided to move to St Ives to get away from everyone. I asked for her address. "You are one of the very people I'm trying to escape," she said. Now wasn't that charming?'

His wild blue eyes were shaded by a dark-blue nautical cap and he wore gold Santiago pilgrim shells in his ears. Perhaps literary Alexandria is still alive and flourishing.

In Port Said, the bright girl in Thomas Cook had found me a bargain flight to London on Olympic Airlines and suggested I stay in Heliopolis, rather than central Cairo. Heliopolis was a pleasant suburb, where life was less frenetic and less expensive, and it was near to the international airport. She recommended the Hotel Beirut, where she had once stayed herself for a conference.

It was an inspired suggestion. Heliopolis was within easy cycling distance of ancient On, my final destination. And it was north of Cairo and its manic traffic. A seamless journey by Jet bus and taxi saw me comfortably installed in the Hotel Beirut, where I looked out over the green lawns and rose-beds of suburbia.

I had two days left before my flight home. On the first day, I took the ramshackle tram from Heliopolis to Ramses Square. When the Belgian entrepreneur Baron Empain designed the garden suburb of Heliopolis, he laid down tramlines to speed the Cairo escapees from their work in the city centre to their Andalusian-style villas and apartment blocks. Those tramlines, and the very same trams, are still in operation. For less than 10p return, I took a trip back to the 1890s. I rattled along past handsome arcades of shops, Moorish fantasies and some later art deco. The turmoil of downtown Cairo came as a great shock after all that faded elegance.

The best way to get to know a city is to explore it on foot, taking short cuts through the back alleys, looking in the houses and shops, and getting an insight into people's lives. So, guidebook in hand, I set off to walk to Mohammed Ali's mosque and palace in the Citadel. Ramses Square is Cairo's northern traffic hub, the nexus of arterial roads, flyovers and walkways, where a disintegrating colossus of Ramses II looks out in disbelief over the chaos. There are no pedestrian crossings – and if there were any, the drivers would be too frantic to bother about them – so pedestrians dart like demented chickens across to the stations and minibus stands. I latched on to groups for safety and we all darted together in terrified clumps. By the time I reached the other side of the square, my nerves were so shattered that I fell into the first taxi. Given the traffic conditions, I was amazed at the driver's cheerfulness. He laughed and joked all the way to the Citadel, while I cowered in the back seat, giving us less than a fifty-fifty chance of survival. I blessed the girl in Thomas Cook. If I had stayed in downtown Cairo, however would I have managed on my bicycle? Cycling in Cairo would be suicide, or at least a provisional booking with the undertaker.

Cairo Citadel dates back to Saladin, but it is Mohammed Ali who has left the greatest mark on it. It was there, in his Al-Gawhara Palace, that he feasted and slew the 470 unfortunate Mamelukes. Perhaps as an act of contrition, he went on to build the tin-domed Mohammed Ali Mosque, modelled on the great mosques of Sinan in Istanbul and Edirne. Its Turkish silhouette dominates the Cairo skyline, but its fancy French clock, the exchange gift for the Luxor obelisk in the Place de la Concorde, still doesn't work. Its tower was under scaffolding when I visited the Citadel. I paid my respects inside the mosque at the marble tomb of Egypt's first great moderniser, then crossed the courtyard to the palace. That too was being refurbished. The furniture I glimpsed through the Stygian gloom looked like Damietta's best – all gilt *à la française*, with frivolous legs and ornate mirrors. The portrait of Mohammed Ali, which I particularly wanted to see, was unlit. It was my usual traveller's luck. Objects of special interest are invariably under scaffolding, under repair or closed for the day!

My Cairo mission accomplished, I made a dash for the tram station and Heliopolis, pleased to break free of the city's chaos. I arrived back in Heliopolis as night was falling, just in time to catch the start of another society wedding, this time in the big Catholic church. It was obviously the wedding season. I was drawn there by the charming sight of two rows of candles lighting up the church steps. The guests trod between them, their shoes gleaming and their eager faces lit from below. It reminded me of Diwali, when all Hindus light paths of candles outside their houses to guide their god Rama home from his wanderings and invite the goddess Laxshmi in, to bring prosperity to the family. I climbed the candlelit steps and crept into the back of the church. The nave was ablaze with candles too and I soon realised that the lack of elecricity had a purpose. When the service began, an enormous screen was revealed, just a little to the left of the high altar. On it flashed the faces of the bride and groom, whose every glance and fleeting expression throughout the service was shown in giant close-up for the benefit of the congregation. What an embarrassing ordeal for the hapless couple! I slipped out to the internet café and sent a few emails on a super-fast computer with a flat-screen monitor. Then I had a Pizza Hut dinner, which made a nice change from kebabs and octogenarian chicken, and strolled down the unthreatening Egyptian streets, buzzing with window-shopping, ice-cream-licking families. The atmosphere was relaxed and Mediterranean, almost like being in Italy.

The next day, my journey ended where the world began, at ancient On. The Greeks called the city Heliopolis, City of the Sun, because it was sacred to Ra, the Egyptian sun god, and that is the name which is now more commonly used. When the capital of Egypt was Memphis, about 14 miles (22 km) south of modern Cairo, the Pharaoh would travel to Heliopolis or On to worship his father, the sun.

The Ancient Egyptians had many creation myths, but the one which gradually assumed paramount importance was the Heliopolitan Creation Myth of the Divine Ennead, or nine gods. According to this myth, the world was watery chaos (Nun). Out of this the sun god (Atum), later identified with Ra, emerged on a mound. Atum created air (Shu) and moisture (Tefnut), who in turn produced the earth god (Geb) and the sky goddess (Nut). These last two divinities then produced Osiris, Isis, Seth and Nephthys, completing the nine gods of the Ennead. From this arose the commonly accepted view of the universe, depicted in many of the tomb paintings: the god Geb forms the base, while the deep-blue goddess Nut, spangled with stars and much elongated, forms an arch over him, supported by the column of the air god, Shu.

On's extreme holiness arose from the fact that it held the *benben,* the sacred stone which was worshipped as that first primeval mound on which the god Atum rose to create the world. Another view is that the *benben* was Atum's petrified semen. The *benben* was said to be the first object illuminated each morning by the rays of the rising sun. Its cult dates back to the First Dynasty (3100–2890 BC), and the first known sun temple, dedicated to Ra-Horakhty (Ra in his manifestation as Horus) was built near the *benben* around 2600 BC. Gradually, all the important gods, such as Atum and Osiris, were subsumed into the cult of the sun god, until the religion verged on monotheism, with Ra the all-powerful ruler of the universe and the Pharaoh as his son, his deputy on Earth. The Pharaoh was so divine that, during his reign, all statues of the gods were given his features, as were the sphinxes.

The sacred *benben* was the prototype of the obelisk and possibly also of the pyramid. This assumption is based on the fact that obelisks and pyramids were all crowned with a gilded capstone to catch the rays of the sun. It was pyramidal in shape and known as the *benbenet*. The role of obelisks as solar symbols was emphasised by the baboons, which were often carved at their base: baboons in the wild always chatter in excitement when the sun rises. Obelisks were raised in On, growing taller and more magnificent as the technical skills of the Egyptians developed. The most popular stone was red granite, which was quarried in the south of the country, at Aswan. There the obelisks were excavated and shaped, then transported down the Nile to On or Luxor, where they were polished, engraved and erected. The obelisks given to Britain, France and America by Mohammed Ali Pasha remained in Egypt for some time afterwards, because the logistics of transporting and raising them were almost beyond the skills of nineteenth-century Westerners. Yet the Ancient Egyptians accomplished these feats regularly, with simple tools and without the benefit of hydraulic equipment.

The raising of obelisks was a royal prerogative. They were important gifts to the gods, often marking royal jubilees or victories. They became so popular that their use spread from On to other Egyptian religious centres, and even abroad. The Canaanites of Byblos copied them; and the Assyrian King Ashur-banipal is said to have removed two bronze-clad examples from Thebes, when he invaded Egypt in 669 BC. They usually stood in pairs before the temple pylons, but no pair of obelisks is still *in situ* today. The last surviving pair, raised by Ramses II (1300–1225 BC) at Luxor, was the pair split by Mohammed Ali in 1819, to make a presentation to the French. They removed it in 1835 and raised it up the next year in the Place de la Concorde, where its gilded pyramidion gleams in the sunshine. The other one of the pair still stands in forlorn isolation before Ramses's massive pylons. Interestingly, in Napoleon's *Description de l'Egypte* there is an engraving of the entrance to the Luxor temple, which shows both magnificent obelisks in their rightful place.

Of the many obelisks which must have stood in On, only one remains, half of a pair raised by Senusret I (1965–1920 BC). Augustus and his successors were the chief culprits. They developed a passion for obelisks and, unfortunately for the Egyptians, the Romans had the engineering skills to satisfy it. Once Cleopatra was defeated and Egypt had become a Roman province, specially designed craft started skimming over the Mediterranean, transporting these huge granite monoliths to Rome. Pliny tells us that the boat which brought the first obelisk excited such great admiration that it was sanctified by Augustus and put on display in the docks at Puteoli. That first obelisk now stands in the Piazza del Popolo, but it was raised first in the Circus Maximus as the gnomon, or marker, of an enormous sundial and dedicated by Augustus to Apollo, the sun god: *Soli donum dedit*. The Romans were unable to read Egyptian hieroglyphics and had no idea what the obelisks were for. Pliny comes up with the vaguest of catch-all suggestions that they 'interpret the operations of Nature according to the philosophy of the Egyptians'. So Augustus's decision to dedicate the obelisk to the sun god was an amazing piece of serendipity. An obelisk to the Egyptian Ra became an obelisk to his Roman equivalent.

As Rome fell into decay, so did its Egyptian obelisks. Many of them smashed as they toppled over and were lost in the general dereliction of the city. Despite this, thirteen still stand, the largest number in the world today, erected on their present sites at different dates. Seven of them have Pharaonic inscriptions, two have inscriptions by Roman Emperors, one has pseudo-Egyptian writing and the rest are unengraved. The most photographed example must be the one which stands in the centre of Bernini's Piazza San Pietro, towering over the crowds who flock to see the Pope. The tallest one still in existence, at a height of 105 feet 6 inches (32.18 m) without its modern base, is the obelisk outside St John Lateran, the Cathedral of the Pope as Bishop of Rome.

Cleopatra's Needle is a puny 68 feet 6 inches (20.88 m), a midget by comparison. But the obelisk which dwarfs them all still lies in Aswan. Designed to be an amazing 137 feet (41.75 m) and weighing 1,168 tons (1,186.7 tonnes), this red granite monster developed a flaw in the quarrying process and was left unfinished, incidentally providing valuable information on Ancient Egyptian quarrying techniques.

My visit to On was the climax of my ride. It was the end to which I had struggled through wind, rain, hail, bad knees and robbery. My hotel was in Heliopolis but, confusingly, modern Heliopolis is not the same as Greek Heliopolis, ancient On. Ancient On lies beneath another suburb of Cairo, Matariyya, and to reach it I needed my bicycle.

A bicycle in Arabic is an *agal*, and 'my bicycle' is *agalti*. After weeks of practice, the phrase came trippingly off my tongue: *agalti, min fadlik* – 'My bicycle, please!' The reception clerk smiled indulgently at my Arabic, while a liveried porter rushed to the storeroom and emerged wheeling Condor proudly across the marble vestibule, to the amazement of the lounging, tea-drinking Egyptians. It was carried down the steps for me and held steady while I mounted.

I cycled along beside Baron Empain's tramline, then lost my way. I was pointed in the right direction by the chemist in a shop bulging with artificial legs, hernia trusses, back braces and other forbidding appliances, whose uses I could only guess at. A dual carriageway, a few street markets and a bus station later, I came at last to the sacred city of the Old and Middle Kingdoms, On.

It might have witnessed the creation of the world at the beginning of time, but the On I found was small and undistinguished, a ramshackle one-donkey town, like so many others in Egypt. Its colour was brown, a cross between the brown of its donkey and the beige of its sand. Brown mud walls, brown *galabiyyas*, brown trees and brown feet treading the brown dust of the streets in brown sandals. The buildings were all squat, tumbledown affairs, overcrowded low-rent houses with flat roofs, so I was surprised not to be able to see Matariyya's one remaining obelisk towering above the skyline. I followed my usual practice, for the second time that morning: I asked a chemist. Chemists' shops are easy to find in any country and chemists themselves, as educated people, generally speak a little of something other than their own language.

The chemist and his two sons were eager to help, but they looked blank when I asked for the obelisk. So I took out my notebook and biro and tried to draw it. 'Radio tower?' they asked, hopefully. 'Water tower? Minaret?' They conferred together in Arabic and I overheard the hesitant word 'stele'. Jackpot! 'Stele' was the term I should have used. One of the boys was deputed to take me to a small park beside the Nile. There, amid pollarded trees, on a pocket handkerchief of sparse dusty grass, the 72-foot (22 m) pink granite obelisk of Senusret I stood in solitary pride. It was one of a pair raised in 1941 BC as thank offerings by the Pharaoh at his jubilee, and it stood outside the long-gone temple to Ra, built by Senusret's father, Amenemhat I, the founder of the XII Dynasty.

Ancient Egypt has become so familiar to us that we read such dates as if they were quite normal. But that monument was quarried in Aswan, floated down the Nile and raised in On almost four millennia ago. Four millennia on that spot! And the people who erected it were literate, with a complex civilisation, great wealth, an empire, a high degree of technical skill and a sense of history. We in the West are no more than infants by comparison. Even Thutmose III, who set up the twin 'Cleopatra's Needles' at On, was a mere stripling – a XVIII Dynasty Pharaoh, who succeeded his wife, Hatshepsut, five hundred years later. And just as Thutmose, in a fit of spite, erased his wife's name from all her monuments, so Ramses II tried to erase all traces of Thutmose from his. It is Ramses' royal names and bombastic epithets that Cleopatra's Needle blazons forth across the Thames. They are deeply engraved on either side of Thutmose's scratched-out hieroglyphics.

I got one of the locals to take my photograph, posing with Condor in front of Senusret's obelisk, then I crossed the park to the Spring of the Sun. An ancient well, with the inevitable Egyptian garbage floating on its water, stood in a walled enclosure. It was here that the sun god came to wash on the first morning of the world. Beside it stood a twisted sycamore fig, the Tree of Life, said to be descended through a series of cuttings from the world's very first tree. As so often happens, a site which is sacred in one religion remains sacred, even when its gods have perished. Its significance is simply transferred. When Heliopolis was part of the Christian Byzantine Empire, the tree became the Virgin's Tree, under which the Holy Family sheltered on their flight to Egypt; and Mary is said to have washed Jesus's baby clothes in the Spring of the Sun. The Coptic Church of the Virgin nearby is simply the last in a succession of holy places built on the same site over four millennia. Religions come and go, but the aura of sanctity remains.

As I cycled back to my hotel in modern Heliopolis, I had one remaining preoccupation. My bicycle had carried me through so much foul weather that it was caked in mud. I was afraid that Olympic Airlines might refuse to accept such a filthy object for their cargo hold. I was wondering if I could wheedle a bucket and brush out of the hotel staff, or persuade one of them to do the job for me, when I passed a garage and saw a man cleaning a car with a high-pressure hose. Would he clean my bicycle that way? Of course he would. Everyone working in the garage came out to watch, as their colleague directed his powerful jet of water into every nook and cranny. They were all highly amused, laughing and joking as the mud of the Nile delta rolled away, even from awkward places like the interstices between the spokes. Condor gleamed, as bright an orange as the day he left the paint shop. I asked the price for the job and the man refused to take anything. In retrospect, I should have insisted. In the general joking and bonhomie, I forgot one of the basic rules of Middle Eastern courtesy, that it is impolite to accept a gift or a tip the first time it is offered. The barefoot man who cleaned my bicycle needed that money, and I should have pressed it on him three or four times, until he felt he could accept it without dishonour. Despite all my years of travel and the best intentions, I still make shabby mistakes.

When the whole ride from London to Egypt had been as tricky as any ride I have undertaken, I might have known that the flight at the end of it would be terrible. Post September 11th, security at Cairo Airport was tighter than ever. It took them about three hours to carry out all the checks and load us on to the plane. Then the fog came down. It was too dense for us to take off safely; and when it had taken such hours to get us all on board, no one was prepared to let us off again and have to repeat the checks when the fog lifted. So we sat on the tarmac for six and a half hours. The plane grew stuffier and stuffier. The children grizzled and the adults' tempers frayed. We were so late leaving Cairo that we missed our connection in Athens and had another long wait there. And when I finally got to Heathrow, I found that the valve on my rear inner tube had snapped off in transit. I had deflated my tyres for the flight, so I had no choice but to push the bicycle all the way home from Paddington. I suppose I should be grateful that neither plane crashed or got hijacked. In line with the rest of the trip, the return journey was uncomfortable, but stopped just short of disaster.

It was a luckless journey. Yet memory is selective. Looking back on it, I see lock-keepers' cottages ablaze with red geraniums, the pure green Rhône, light shimmering on the Venetian Lagoon, racing clouds, Impressionist paintings, snow-capped Alps, the blue Mediterranean, Crac des Chevaliers, the souks of Damascus and Alexandria's Grand Corniche – all wonderful places and wonderful experiences. I passed through Muslim countries, where the people were desperately worried about their future, puzzled and powerless in the face of escalating conflict; and Western countries where they were worried about floods, economic recession and the prospect of war. But East and West, they all made time for me and my bicycle. Through the rosy lenses of memory, it was the best, most beautiful of rides.

THE OTHER CLEOPATRA'S NEEDLE

It would be absurd for the people of any great city to hope to be happy without an Egyptian obelisk.

The *New York Herald*, 1881

In the autumn after my ride, I flew to New Jersey to give a series of lectures. In my free time between talks, I took the train into New York and walked up Fifth Avenue from Pennsylvania Station to Central Park. There, behind the Metropolitan Museum of Art, stood Cleopatra's Needle, the pair to our own Cleopatra's Needle on the Thames Embankment.

Presented to the City of New York by the Egyptian Government in 1879, the obelisk sailed the ocean in the hold of the *Dessoug*. The London Needle was able to sail up the Thames to the spot where it was raised. In New York, the operation was far more difficult, as their Needle had to be transported from Manhattan

Docks to Central Park. It was only a short journey, but it lasted 112 days. It took six days and nights for the obelisk to turn the first corner! It was sucessfully raised in January 1881. The time capsule buried under its pedestal contains a copy of the Declaration of Independence, the complete works of Shakespeare, a guide to Egypt and medals from the American armed forces.

THE SOLUTION TO THE MYSTERY

In my Introduction, I set a detective problem. I wrote that 'everything is not *quite* as it seems' and challenged you to discover the reason.

Here is the solution. Shortly after I arrived in France, at the beginning of May, I damaged my left knee. I mentioned it in Chapter 2. What I did not mention was that the patella was so seriously displaced that I had to come home from Dieppe for treatment. When the knee was straight again, I went back to Europe. I had arranged to meet friends in various parts of the Mediterranean that summer, so I picked up my route in Dijon, where I would have been, had I continued the ride from Dieppe according to my original schedule. That left a gap still to be cycled between Dieppe and Dijon. I filled it in October, in the period between leaving Antalya and returning to Istanbul at the beginning of December. So the ride, which I described as one seamless whole, was nothing of the sort. Dieppe to Dijon was cycled in the autumn, not the early summer, and I dropped a few hints along the way – cannonades of acorns, trees in Normandy weighed down with apples, morning mists, a cold, clammy fog in Dijon, and 'Non à la Busherie', 'Non à la guerre', which clearly refer to American foreign policy after September 11th.

I wonder if any readers worked it out?

APPENDIX A
BICYCLE SPECIFICATIONS

My old faithful Condor, built by Monty Young and his team for my first ride round the world, had a make-over before I set out for Egypt. It started its life with randonneur handlebars, which were later changed to straight ones. Both had their disadvantages. This time, we decided to give butterfly bars a try and I have found them perfect. With new handlebars, a new chain set, new pedals and a brilliant orange respray, my well-travelled Condor rose like a phoenix from the ashes. Its startling new colour has simplified my life. I just have to say, 'It's the orange one,' and it's found immediately in airports and garages. And I feel more secure, because robbers would surely hesitate before riding off on such an eye-catching machine.

Frame	Reynolds 631 Mixte, butted tubes
Transmission	Shimano Deore. Front 28-38-48. Rear 13-15-17-20-23-26-30
Wheels	Deore LX hubs
	Mavic TS19 rims
	DT stainless steel spokes
Tyres	Continental Top Touring 2000
Handlebars	Humpert Pro Bars
Pedals	Shimano M324 SPD
Saddle	Brooks B17 STD
Mudguards	SKS
Pannier rack	Blackburn Ex1
Rear panniers	Karrimore Iberia

APPENDIX B
CLEOPATRA

69 BC	Birth of Cleopatra
51 BC	Joint ruler of Egypt with her brother, Ptolemy XIII
48 BC	Driven out of Egypt by Ptolemy
47 BC	Reinstated by Julius Caesar. Joint ruler with younger brother, Ptolemy XIV
46 BC	Birth of Caesarion, Caesar's son
44 BC	Assassination of Julius Caesar
41 BC	Cleopatra sails to Tarsus to meet Mark Antony, who returns to Alexandria to spend the winter with her
40 BC	Birth of Antony's twins, Alexander Helios and Cleopatra Selene
37 BC	Form of marriage to Antony at Daphne, near Antioch
36 BC	Birth of Ptolemy
35 BC	Antony sends his Roman wife Octavia back to her brother Octavian
34 BC	'The Donations of Alexandria'
32 BC	Antony formally divorces Octavia
	Octavian elected Consul. Declaration of war on Cleopatra
31 BC	Cleopatra and Antony defeated at Battle of Actium
30 BC	Suicide of Cleopatra and Antony
	Egypt becomes Roman province

APPENDIX C
FRENCH FISH

Amande	Clam	Eglefin	Haddock
Anchois	Anchovy	Flétan	Halibut
Anguille	Eel	Gambas	King prawns
Araignée de mer	Spider crab	Grondin	Gurnet
Bar	Bass	Hareng	Herring
Barbue	Brill	Homard	Lobster
Baudroie	Monkfish	Huîtres	Oysters
Bigorneaux	Winkles	Julienne	Ling
Brème	Bream	Langoustes	Crawfish
Bouquet	Prawn	Langoustines	Norway lobsters
Bulots	Whelks	Lieu jaune	Pollock
Cabillaud	Cod	Lieu noir	Coalfish
Calamar	Squid	Limande	Lemon sole
Carrelet	Plaice	Lingue	Ling
Colin	Hake	Lompe	Lumpfish
Congre	Conger eel	Lotte de mer	Monkfish
Coques	Cockles	Loup de mer	Sea bass
Coquilles St Jaques	Scallops	Maquereau	Mackerel
		Merlan	Whiting
Crabe	Crab	Morue	Cod
Crevettes grises	Shrimps	Moules	Mussels
Crevettes roses	Prawns	Palourdes	Clams
Daurade	Sea bream	Praires	Small clams
Ecrevisse	Freshwater crayfish	Raie	Skate
		Rouget	Red mullet

INDEX